D1165702

"Doug Silsbee has written a useful book for anybody facilitating the growth and development of individuals and groups. His approach reaches deeply into human consciousness and experience, where meaningful change and growth occur."

—Harrison Owen, author, *Open Space Technology*

"Doug has a wonderful way of 'unpacking' what coaches do, spotlighting critical elements of this challenging work and shining an even brighter light on the *being* of coaching. I urge you to jump into this rich, thoughtful book!"

—Ann F. Fisher, managing director, Integral Coaching International, Shanghai

"*The Mindful Coach* captures the very essence of what coaching can be. Silsbee marries the art and science of human dialogue, of compassionate listening and advice giving without creating dependency. He guides the reader gently through the seven distinct roles of a true helping relationship. This is a process to be internalized at a deep level and lived every day."

—Rod Napier, Ph.D., professor, consultant, author, *The Courage to Act* and ten other books

"This is *the* guide for leaders committed to helping others learn. The seven roles will help any leader facilitate more meaningful development conversations. This new edition engaged me instantly, with immediate applications in key relationships."

—Darelyn "DJ" Mitsch, MCC, president, Pyramid Resource Group, former president, International Coach Federation

"Coaching is a profession for some and a necessity for many. All of us who lead, manage, or teach are often in the role of the coach, whether we think about it that way or not. *The Mindful Coach* provides a framework that works for the professional coach as well as the everyday manager. Silsbee has created *the* holistic guide to coaching."

—Bill Coleman, senior vice president of compensation, Salary.com

"The tools of coaching that Silsbee outlines, with an emphasis on mindfulness and service, provide the fundamental basis for holistic and integrative physicians to work with patients."

—Patrick Hanaway, M.D., president, American Board of Integrative Holistic Medicine

"*The Mindful Coach* takes the meaning of *coaching* well beyond popular models into a deeply integrated practice of intentionality and professionalism at their highest levels. This book is bound to improve the quality and effectiveness of coaching for all who apply the wisdom contained in these pages."

—James Michael Burke, Ph.D., director, Performance Management Group, Virginia Commonwealth University

"*The Mindful Coach* is warm, sensitive, and intuitive, while at the same time clearly written by a scientific mind. The book provides a simple and cohesive model for the development process, coupled with practical strategies on how to become a more conscious practitioner. Thank you."

—**Alejandro Bolaños, consultant, Central America**

"The development of people is a key competency for business leadership. *The Mindful Coach* provides an inspiring and practical road map for developing masterful coaching skills on the job. This refreshing work showcases coaching in a new light."

—**Karen Wunderlin, consultant, former executive in marketing, GE Appliances**

"Silsbee's analysis of the coaching process is clear and intuitive. Its simplicity allows it to be easily used, yet it's rich in detail, making it a powerful analytical tool for the professional. Wrapped in a holistic framework that accounts for the coach, the client, and the process of coaching, it will enrich the insight and practice of every interested reader."

—**Christopher C. Dennen, Ph.D., president, Innovative Healing Inc.**

"*The Mindful Coach* goes far beyond coaching steps and models, offering a path for coaches to work more deeply and authentically to guide their clients to significant new results."

—**Marcia Reynolds, Psy.D., author, *Outsmart Your Brain: How to Make Success Feel Easy*, past president, International Coach Federation**

"Silsbee's seven voices are an invaluable tool in my multiple roles as an executive, educator, and coach. The rigorous practice of focusing attention on what my associates, students, and executive clients need—in the moment—helps me deliver for them while growing myself at the same time."

—**Kelly Bean, assistant dean, UCLA Anderson Executive Education**

"A clear and integrated model to assist people in understanding and applying the important skills in mindfulness and coaching. Executives from diverse backgrounds will find *The Mindful Coach* an insightful and practical guide."

—**Hannah S. Wilder, Ph.D., MCC, executive director, Advantara Global Executive Learning and Coach Education Institute**

"In his hands-on new book, replete with artful and challenging exercises, Silsbee models the mindfulness depth from which he springs in order to impart a valuable new coaching model based on professionalism, integrity, and dedication to service."

—**Maggie Lichtenberg, MCC, professional coach**

"In serving others, we can get overly focused on specific strategies or tactics and lose perspective of the larger, broader dynamic. *The Mindful Coach* delivers by clarifying, organizing, and contextualizing what it really means to be involved in a coaching relationship."

—**Joe Jotkowitz, president, Essessnet**

THE
MINDFUL
COACH

Seven Roles for Facilitating Leader Development

NEW AND REVISED EDITION

DOUG SILSBEE

Foreword by Marshall Goldsmith

JOSSEY-BASS
A Wiley Imprint
www.josseybass.com

Published by Jossey-Bass
A Wiley Imprint
989 Market Street, San Francisco, CA 94103-1741—www.josseybass.com

This book is printed with vegetable-based inks. The text paper was manufactured using a high yield ther-momechanical pulp that utilizes as much as 80 percent of the harvested tree and is brightened using an elemental chlorine free bleaching process. Our use of lighter weight paper reduces the amount of paper (and trees) required to produce this book.

The poems "Orioling" and "The Ten Thousand Things" are from *Orioling*, by Ann Silsbee. Copyright © 2003 by Ann Silsbee. Published by Red Hen Press, and used by permission of the author.

Readers should be aware that Internet Web sites offered as citations and/or sources for further informatic may have changed or disappeared between the time this was written and when it is read.

Limit of Liability/Disclaimer of Warranty: While the publisher and author have used their best efforts ir preparing this book, they make no representations or warranties with respect to the accuracy or complet ness of the contents of this book and specifically disclaim any implied warranties of merchantability or fitness for a particular purpose. No warranty may be created or extended by sales representatives or writ-ten sales materials. The advice and strategies contained herein may not be suitable for your situation. You should consult with a professional where appropriate. Neither the publisher nor author shall be liable for any loss of profit or any other commercial damages, including but not limited to special, incidental, cons quential, or other damages.

Jossey-Bass books and products are available through most bookstores. To contact Jossey-Bass directly c our Customer Care Department within the U.S. at 800-956-7739, outside the U.S. at 317-572-3986, or fax 317-572-4002. Jossey-Bass also publishes its books in a variety of electronic formats. Some content t appears in print may not be available in electronic books.

Library of Congress Cataloging-in-Publication Data
Silsbee, Douglas K.
     The mindful coach: seven roles for facilitating leader development/ Douglas Silsbee; foreword Marshall Goldsmith. —New and rev. ed.
          p.   cm.
     Includes bibliographical references and index.
     ISBN 978-0-470-54866-0 (cloth)
          1. Executive coaching.   2. Personal coaching.   3. Counseling.   4. Spiritual exercises.   5. Self-actualization (Psychology)—Religious aspects—Buddhism.   I. Title.
     HD30.4.S56 2010
     658.4'07124—dc22

                                                                                2009047(

Printed in the United States of America
NEW AND REVISED EDITION
HB Printing   10 9 8 7 6 5 4 3 2 1

Contents

Exercises, Practices, Exhibits, and Figures   ix

Foreword   xiii

Preface to the New and Revised Edition   xv

Introduction: What Is Coaching?   1

A Working Definition of Coaching   4

Distinguishing Coaching from Other Aspects of Professional Relationships   6

Contexts for Coaching: Four Dynamics   9

Introduction Summary   14

1 The Being of Coaching: Mindful Service   17

Placing Oneself in Service   18

Mindfulness and Self-Awareness   19

Mindfulness and the Three Levels of Experience   23

Attachments and Aversions   25

Conditioning and Habits That Block Mindfulness   30

Coaching Habits   33

Chapter Summary   41

2 Cultivating Mindfulness   43

Self-Observation   44

Practices for Cultivating Mindfulness   48

Coach as Learner   54
Accountability in Service   55
Chapter Summary   56

3 The Seven Voices of the Coach   57
Learning the Voices   58
The Individual Roles or Voices   60
The Voices and Their Aspects   64
Placing the Voices in Context   64
Chapter Summary   72

4 The Master   73
Maintaining Self-Awareness   76
Listening with Focus and Presence   78
Modeling Learning and Growth   79
Embracing the Client with Compassion and Respect   82
Choosing Which of the Operational Voices to
Use at a Given Time   84
The Mindful Master   86
Chapter Summary   89

5 The Partner   91
Establishing and Honoring an Explicit Structure for
the Coaching Relationship   93
Advocating Shared Commitment to Competency-Based
Coaching Outcomes   98
Offering Choice Points and Making Joint Decisions
About the Coaching Process   103
The Mindful Partner   107
Chapter Summary   110

6 The Investigator   113
Asking Questions That Shift the Client's
Understanding of the Situation   116
Helping the Client to Articulate Desired Outcomes   120
Asking the Client to Generate Courses of Action   122
The Mindful Investigator   126
Chapter Summary   130

7 The Reflector   131
Providing Direct and Honest Feedback   133

Directing the Client's Attention Toward His
or Her Capabilities and Potential   137

Encouraging Self-Observation and Reflection   141

The Mindful Reflector   143

Chapter Summary   147

8 The Teacher 149

Providing New Distinctions, Information,
and Knowledge   151

Challenging and Stimulating the
Client's Thinking Process   154

Explaining the Coaching Process, Theory,
and Models Being Used   159

The Mindful Teacher   162

Chapter Summary   165

9 The Guide 167

Encouraging the Client to Take Some Action of
the Client's Choosing   170

Offering Options for Action   172

Recommending Specific Courses of Action   175

The Mindful Guide   178

Chapter Summary   181

10 The Contractor 183

Establishing Clear Agreements About Actions   186

Exploring and Resolving Client Doubts and Hesitations   190

Following Up with the Client About Agreed-On Actions   193

The Mindful Contractor   196

Chapter Summary   199

11 Self-Development Strategies for the Coach 201

Self-Assessment Tools   202

Self-Observation as a Coach   205

Navigating the Model   210

Learning from Your Reflection   216

Reviewing Audio Recordings   217

Obtaining and Listening to Client Feedback   218

Planning Your Own Development   221

Chapter Summary   223

Epilogue: Coaching as a Journey Toward Mastery   225
  About Fluidity and Intuition   227
  Practice as Path   229

Selected Reading   235
Notes   239
Acknowledgments   245
The Author   249
Index   251

Exercises, Practices, Exhibits, and Figures

Exercises

I.1 Defining Coaching for Yourself   9

1.1 Mindful Eating   21

1.2 Building Somatic and Emotional Awareness   26

1.3 The Bell Exercise   40

2.1 Self-Observation of a Habit   48

4.1 Cultivating the Master   88

4.2 Mastering Self-Observation   89

5.1 Self-Coaching as Partner:
Making a Commitment   109

5.2 Partner Areas for Attention   110

5.3 Partner Self-Observation   110

6.1 Self-Coaching as Investigator:
Three Lines of Questioning   128

6.2 Investigator Areas for Attention   129

6.3 Investigator Self-Observation   129

7.1 Self-Coaching as Reflector:
Providing Feedback   145

7.2 Reflector Areas for Attention   146

7.3 Reflector Self-Observation   146

8.1 Self-Coaching as Teacher:
Making Pedagogy Visible   164

8.2 Teacher Areas for Attention   164

8.3   Teacher Self-Observation   164

9.1   Self-Coaching as Guide: Providing
      Impetus and/or Direction   180

9.2   Guide Areas for Attention   180

9.3   Guide Self-Observation   181

10.1 Self-Coaching as Contractor:
      Structuring Actions and Testing for
      Fit and Commitment   198

10.2 Contractor Areas for Attention   199

10.3 Contractor Self-Observation   199

11.1 A Brief Coaching Self-Assessment   203

11.2 Self-Observation on a Specific Voice or Aspect   206

11.3 Bringing Awareness into Using Stronger Voices   208

11.4 Increasing the Use of an Aspect   209

11.5 Questioning and Telling   210

11.6 Building Creative Tension   211

11.7 Focusing on Questioning   212

11.8 Observing Your Coaching Flow   213

11.9 Observing the Impetus Behind Your Coaching Flow   215

11.10 Recognizing Your Projections   217

11.11 Audio Review   218

Practices

2.1   Sitting   50

2.2   Centering   51

Exhibits

I.1   Coaching and Noncoaching Activities in Three Fields   7

3.1   The Voices and Their Aspects   65

6.1   Sample Situation Questions   118

6.2   Sample Outcome Questions   121

6.3   Sample Action Questions   123

9.1   Sample Fieldwork Actions   174

10.1 Sample Individual Development Plan   189

11.1 The Operational Voices   204

Figures

3.1   Septet Coaching Model   67

3.2   The Coaching Space   68

3.3   The Investigator and Creative Tension   69

11.1 The Operational Voices   214

ORIOLING

You love their singing—the thrush, the orioles—
    though they don't perform for you. Theirs is a clan
song: *My bugs, my bough, my mate*, and:
    See how bright the orange and black of my feathers.
Nor do they sing for blighted love the hard
    blues of loss we would, or for joy,
but because they can't help it, because song
    blossoms from the stem of their being bird.
Human, you can't help trying to understand
    what stalk you flower from, what undertow
rises in the flutist to quicken with breath
    the arcs and dips of prior minds, or mind
itself, playing with fugue, with $E = MC^2$
    inventing wheel, organ, flute, B Minor Mass—
Buddha—the bomb. The song you bear buds
    under your mind's tongue like a first word.

                    —*Ann Silsbee*

Foreword

IMAGINE CEOs OF THE WORLD'S LARGEST COMPANIES SPEAKING openly to their coworkers about their efforts to develop themselves as leaders. In the past it would have been difficult, if not impossible, to conceive of such individuals sharing their 360-degree feedback with colleagues, much less asking colleagues for help in the areas they are trying to improve. Today many of the world's most respected chief executives are setting a positive example by candidly discussing feedback and their personal development plans.

In my coaching experience, one of the best ways executives can get their leaders to improve is to lead by example and work on improving themselves. There are two obvious benefits of being such a role model. First, by discussing personal challenges and practicing self-development, executives make it difficult for anyone else in the company to pretend he has nothing to work on. Second, having dialogues with the CEO about business challenges and development needs makes it easier for employees throughout the organization to discuss their own business challenges and developmental needs. This executive candor fosters change and can help turn around even a troubled company.

Unfortunately, CEOs who are arrogant and just tell others what they need to improve, rather than working on themselves, are also models of behavior for the rest of the company. Their behavior is inevitably copied at every level, with people at each level telling their followers how they need to improve. The result is that no one gets better. The principle of leadership by personal example doesn't apply just to those at the top. It applies to every level of management. It applies in both the positive and the negative. And, significantly for us, it applies to coaches too!

As a coach, I've realized that my success with clients isn't about me. It's about being honest with myself about the people I choose to coach. It's about being mindful of my role in this trusted position that we call "executive coach." I don't hold myself up as a "coach expert." There's an ancient proverb that says, "The best leader is the one the people do not notice. When the best leader's work is done, the people say, 'We did it ourselves.'" I believe this to be true for the coach. My success as a coach is dependent on letting go of my ego and realizing that most of what my clients learn about themselves comes not from me, but from their friends, their coworkers and peers, and their families. I just try to provide help when it's needed and assist them in recognizing when they are straying from the changes they are trying to make.

I cannot make the people I work with change. I don't try. I can be mindful in my work with leaders, and that's where *The Mindful Coach*, this wonderful book by Doug Silsbee, is so helpful to me as a coach. *The Mindful Coach* provides both thought leadership and pragmatic guidance for coaches in order that we might bring mindfulness into our work with leaders, learn the territory of working with our own habits, have a set of distinctions for observing ourselves in action, and skillfully navigate the coaching conversation to open real opportunities for substantive change with our clients. Capturing the essence of what coaching can be in *The Mindful Coach*, Doug Silsbee has given us an incredibly valuable and integrated framework that will have significant impact on our field for years to come.

Marshall Goldsmith
Author of *What Got You Here Won't Get You There* and *Succession: Are You Ready?*

Preface to the New and Revised Edition

We work on ourselves in order to help others; and also we help others
in order to work on ourselves.

Pema Chödrön

THIS BOOK IS WRITTEN FOR YOU—IN YOUR ROLE AS AN EXECUTIVE, manager, social worker, therapist, educator, or consultant whose work provides you the wonderful privilege of supporting the growth and development of others. You will discover how to orient yourself within the coaching process, be a more powerful development partner in serving others, and explore a rigorous path of self-discovery.

People who are committed to self-development and who write books have a unique dilemma. Our writing is inherently autobiographical; we cannot help but write from the perspective of who we are at the time we are writing. However, because we are constantly evolving, a book can never be a complete or accurate reflection of us. At some point, we have to say, "Perfect enough!" and put it out into the world as an offering. Then, of course, the book is fixed in the public's mind, and, by extension, *we* become fixed in the public's mind.

When I wrote the original *The Mindful Coach*, it was my statement at the time of what I believed to be most important in coaching. Since then, my own learning, and how I've integrated it into my coaching and my teaching, has increasingly included work through the body and heart. When my son asked me a couple of years ago if I thought I'd write another book, I told him I thought I'd gotten it out of my system. Six months later, I was well into writing *Presence-Based Coaching*. It called me, just as this one had years earlier, and insisted to me that it be written. Who was I to say no?

That second book, reflecting a core principle also true in our own development, transcends and includes this one. By *transcending*, I mean that *Presence-Based Coaching* goes deeper, includes more about the notion of practices, includes body and heart practices as well as self-observation and attention training exercises, and focuses on the presence of the client as well as on the coach. By *including*, I mean that everything in *The Mindful Coach* is consistent with and foundational to the second book. It provides a powerful platform for the work of self-observation and mindfulness in coaching, and it is complete in itself as a body of work that illuminates a particular approach to bringing mindfulness into coaching. Together they provide an integrated language that will carry committed practitioners far in their journey toward mastery.

This new and revised edition has been reorganized in order to further this integration. The new edition refines the Septet Model and offers it more crisply and logically than the original edition. While many of the descriptions of the Voices and the specific illustrative dialogues remain the same, the development of the material is more precise and logical.

For this edition, I:

- Incorporated some fundamental premises about the nature of leadership in order to contextualize the coaching process.

- Integrated the conversation about mindfulness and service as a single theme.

- Revised the Voice descriptions to distinguish several new aspects that I have come to see as important.

- Separated out and refined the material on cultivating mindfulness.

- Integrated distinctions that derive from Buddhism with those from other lineages to offer a more inclusive language for mindfulness and attention.

- Focused the coach self-development chapter on self-observation and the coaching Voices.

- Revised the table of Voices and the overall Septet Model graphic.

- More fully developed the theme of mindfulness in each of the Voice chapters.

- Incorporated additional exercises throughout the book.

- Included a self-coaching theme in the exercises, inviting readers to use each of the Voices to focus and deepen their relationship with the material as they work with it in real time.

The astute reader may ask, "What is the difference between mindfulness and presence? Aren't they the same thing?" The short answer is that mindfulness, as I'm presenting it here, is a rigorous attention to observing ourselves in action, such that we become fluid, intuitive, aware, and exquisitely responsive to what is being brought forward in the conversation. This requires the cultivation of the observer mind, a part of ourselves that is set aside, watching what we do as we do it. When we self-observe as a coach, we are better able to catch ourselves in the act of our habits in order to be more available in service to our clients.

This split attention is a fundamental practice, and central to both books. Mindfulness is what results.

Presence is the underlying state that we access through mindfulness and is also available to the client in the coaching conversation. Presence is the state that allows us to be the most resourceful, resilient, and self-generative person we can be, and that this is, in fact, part of the promise of coaching. *The Mindful Coach* focuses on how we mindfully navigate the coaching conversation in order to be the greatest possible resource for our clients. *Presence-Based Coaching* deepens this conversation to include the state of presence in the client as a fundamental part of the coaching process and how we can both cultivate our own access to presence and then extend it to our clients.

THE SEPTET MODEL

In choosing to serve as teachers, counselors, and coaches, we set ourselves the challenge of recognizing and, where appropriate, setting aside our own agendas and needs in order to better discern and provide what the other person truly needs. In order to consciously serve others, we must continually consider the following questions:

- How do we discern what the other person really needs from us, as distinct from what we believe he or she needs?
- How do we learn to recognize, and manage, our own habits of mind in order to be fully present in every interaction rather than relying on received formulas?
- How do we integrate our own efforts to become more mindful into the development work we do with others?

The Septet Model presented in this book provides a line of inquiry based on my own experience with executives, coach trainees, and others in the helping professions. It is a structure that has proven helpful in enabling us to be more mindful as we support others. The time-honored advice to count to ten before responding when we're angry works because in the simple act of remembering to count, we are exercising the muscle of self-awareness and making a decision about how to respond. Similarly, to be truly in service to those we are working with, we need to study our own minds, befriend and master our own thought processes, and learn to free ourselves from unhelpful habits of mind.

The organization of this approach into seven Voices reveals a central structure for observing ourselves. Each of the Voices represents a role that we play for our clients in the coaching process. For each role, I've outlined a specific and concrete set of skills and behaviors that can be practiced and learned; I refer to them as Aspects. By identifying our patterns of strengths and weaknesses, and the habits of mind that lie behind them, we can develop ourselves systematically to be better at each of these critical roles.

LANGUAGE

Although I've chosen to use the language of the emerging field of coaching, including the terms *coach* and *client,* this book is meant for practitioners of many professions. Most of you, my intended readers, will be full-time professional coaches, business leaders, or organizational development and training specialists. A few of you will be therapists, social workers, or clergy. Some will act as coaches in several capacities in your lives.

A common denominator for you, my readers, is that you are involved in facilitating the development of *leaders*. These might be leaders in a formal role, such as CEOs or vice presidents of a company or executive directors in a nonprofit. However, it is my intention to broaden our understanding of leaders to include all of us. Whether or not we actively lead others in an organization, we are all leaders of our own lives and are ultimately and solely responsible for what we do with them. Coaching points us consistently and urgently toward this salient fact. If we conceive of a leader as anyone who is moving toward a commitment of some sort, then coaching is the process that supports another leader in fulfilling on her commitment and thereby creating a more intentional, effective, and fulfilling life.

These scenarios provide examples of what I define as coaching relationships:

- An executive coach helps a senior leader formulate her own ideas on how she can build support for her latest proposal.

- A manager provides a subordinate with feedback on an in-house presentation.

- A parent asks questions that reveal the consequences of her teenager's actions.

- A therapist asks questions that help a client see how he contributes to the problems in his marriage.

- A high school principal explores with a teacher how to make a history class more engaging.

- A pastor questions a parishioner, inviting her to be curious in her spirituality.

You may not label yourself as a coach and others may not call you such, but you will recognize yourself in these pages because you have accepted responsibility for developing the capabilities of others and supporting them in fulfilling on their commitments as leaders in their own right. Whatever the nature of your work, this book is written for you. We'll explore the definition of the term *coach* more fully in the Introduction, but for now, discard any preconceptions about that term and consider it as applying to yourself in any relationship where you are interacting with another person in service to his or her learning, growth, and change.

Also, consider the term *client* as applying to the recipient of that coaching, whether it's a manager you're supporting, a counseling or social work client, a direct report, a paying private client, your child, or a member of your congregation. The examples in this book are drawn from many arenas.

To avoid committing to any of the awkward and cumbersome options available—"he or she" followed by syntactic tangles of "his or her" and "him or her," "they" when the syntax calls for the singular, or "s/he" (Ugh!)—I've most often used the gender pronouns "he" and "she" alternately at roughly the same frequency, keeping a consistency regarding who's who within a passage or a chapter.

The term *Master* is used to describe one of the Septet's Voices. I recognize that, even uncapitalized, this word comes with baggage for some people, who will hear connotations of patriarchy, dominion over, a male controller, or all of these. (Wait! Stop! Look inside. What reactions are you noticing within yourself, right now, to the word? This looking-within is central to both knowing yourself and deriving greatest value from the book. The simple act of recognizing your patterns of thought, and attachments to particular interpretations, is essential to opening yourself to new ones and is in itself a step toward our goal.)

Meaning is made; it can be dissolved, shifted, or created anew as well. *Master* is the word that means most closely what I intend: a gender-neutral term for a person with great skill, with self-mastery, an artist; it links closely to the word *mastery,* which I use extensively. A master has looked inward to cultivate a high level of self-awareness and to recognize and rise above habitual judgments, impulses, and reactions. A master has the capacity to make skillful choices about what to become and how to interact with others. The Master Voice is central to coaching.

Most of the dialogues are based on real conversations with real clients. Names and particulars have been changed, and the dialogues have been heavily edited in order to illustrate a particular point.

Where both a first and last name are provided, these are the real names of people who have been a gift in my life and without whom this book would likely not have been written.

STRUCTURE OF THE BOOK

After an Introduction that serves as an orientation to coaching, the first two chapters explore the nature of habits and mindfulness, invite you to consider mindfulness as integral to serving others in a coaching capacity, and offer specific means for cultivating your own mindfulness.

Chapters Three through Ten present and explore the seven distinct Voices through which coaches do their work. One chapter is devoted to each Voice and elaborates the aspects that comprise that Voice, providing extensive sample dialogues that bring these distinctions to life. Chapters Five through Ten also include an exercise each that invite you to use your learning with the book as a self-coaching practice in itself. Think of this as a mini-curriculum within the structure of the book. Other exercises invite you into further self-assessment and self-observation around that Voice.

Chapter Eleven provides a range of approaches to deepen your work with the Septet Model. These are based on the principle of self-observation and include self-assessments and a range of pragmatic awareness tools that you can integrate into a comprehensive self-development strategy. The brief epilogue invites you to enter into this as a lifelong journey of practice for the sake of serving others consciously as you develop yourself.

I encourage you to take nothing in this book on faith. I want the book to be an experience for you, not just a collection of ideas. The more you experiment, test the ideas and exercises, and try them on for size, the more you will benefit. In particular, I provide exercises in Chapters Five through Ten in which you can apply the coaching Voices to your own learning process; engaging yourself in your own relationship with the material will reveal a great deal.

The Mindful Coach extends an invitation to discover for yourself how to make your coaching relationships deeper and more fulfilling for both parties in the conversation. There are no prescriptions here.

Some of what's presented won't suit your needs; other ideas or practices may be transformative. Discerning which is which is *your* discovery work.

Consider the material as a series of testable hypotheses. Be a scientist. Open yourself to these ideas, try them out as rigorous experiments, and observe the results closely. Through observation, you will quickly learn which practices enhance learning for you and your clients. You are responsible for the choices you make about using what proves itself. Let go of the rest.

Finally, both the original writing and the revisions of this book have been quite a learning process for me. Many others have shared their wisdom and ideas with me along the way. I've learned more from writing it, from discussing these ideas with friends and colleagues, and from watching myself in the process than I ever could have imagined.

May your own discovery process be as rewarding!

Introduction:
What Is Coaching?

You cannot teach humans anything. You can only help them discover it within themselves.

Galileo

Only people who die very young learn all they really need to know in kindergarten.

Wendy Kaminer

OUR LIVES DEVELOP MEANING THROUGH THE PURSUIT of worthwhile commitments. Leading, either in the context of an organizational role or in our own lives, implies a direction. We establish this direction through making commitments to certain business results, effective relationships, completing projects, or making some contribution important to us. The direction and nature of our leadership is shaped and revealed through these commitments. We can therefore see coaching as a means to build the competencies required to fulfill on our commitments.

While this is true, the reverse is also true, and perhaps more salient for this book. Specifically, we make commitments as leaders *because* making a commitment places us in motion, impelling us into

1

learning and development. Our commitments make life interesting and worthwhile.

When we make any strong commitment, we are virtually assured that we will stumble at times. We will face unanticipated challenges from the world, which will not necessarily cooperate with our agenda. Our habits, blind spots, and shortcomings will most certainly be revealed.

Making a clear commitment to anything worthwhile therefore requires a corollary commitment to the curriculum of developing ourselves so that we can deliver. The bolder and more radical our leadership commitments, the more rigorous our own curriculum of self-work must be. And, our self-work allows us to make stronger commitments in the world.

It is self-evident that making a commitment to coaching others is a means to support the self-work of our clients. A commitment to coaching others also requires the corollary commitment to engage fully and rigorously with our own curriculum of self-development.

In working with many thousands of people over decades of teaching workshops and coaching leaders, I've come to believe that what it takes to become better at anything is fundamentally pretty simple. All it requires is paying attention. More specifically, it requires bringing rigorous attention to the habits of mind, beliefs, assumptions, and embodied behaviors that shape who we are in the world, suspending them, and committing ourselves to new possibilities that we were previously unable to see or act on. At bottom, that's really all that's required.

Yet we all know, from countless New Year's resolutions and attempts to give up bad habits and replace them with good ones, that "simple" doesn't equate to "easy." The practiced habits of our personalities, and the very strengths that have helped us to be successful in the past, at some point become limiting and occasionally suffocating. The essential offer of coaching is to liberate us from these learned constrictions into new possibilities for leadership in our own lives and organizations, greater effectiveness in moving our commitments forward, and greater contributions to a world that is in dire need of what we each can offer.

With roots in the human potential movement, organizational development, psychotherapy, and learning theory, coaching has become a well-established field. Corporate culture has broadly accepted coaching as an essential leadership competency; many organizations have launched internal training programs to teach coaching skills to their managers. The whole field of professional and personal coaching for individuals has been expanding exponentially.

As in any other growth industry, professional coaching has seen a rapid development of new concepts, approaches, and adaptations. At the same time, questions have arisen about what qualifications, training, and certification processes distinguish professionals who are likely to provide useful service to their clients from people who just declare themselves to be coaches and hang out a shingle.

It can be difficult to separate the substance from the fluff—frankly, there's a lot of the latter—but this book attempts to return to the heart of what makes coaching powerful. The essence of coaching is a nuanced, one-on-one relationship that aims at accelerated individual development. It is about the universal skills and ways of being that enable powerful learning conversations to take place and their application in diverse contexts.

While the body of work on group and team coaching is growing, in this book I explore coaching as a one-on-one process. I do so because understanding group and team coaching begins with understanding individual coaching. I aim to illuminate how coaches shape themselves to be development partners for others. From there it is relatively easy to extrapolate to group and organizational coaching contexts.

The offer of this book—a pragmatic coaching model of seven Voices—is one approach to meeting the requirements of any coaching situation. We begin our conversation with a fuller working definition of coaching in general, followed by some underlying hallmarks of successful coaching, regardless of the venue in which it takes place.

A commitment to the cultivation of self is essential to earning the right to support others in their own journeys. Those of you who are after a quick set of techniques to add to your coaching toolkit or a logical how-to-coach manual will be disappointed. Rather, think of this book as a doorway into your own self-work, a pragmatic approach to the corollary commitment of bringing yourself fully to the essential process of serving your clients. Familiarity and competence with your inner world is both a consequence of and a prerequisite for mindful coaching as described here.

A WORKING DEFINITION OF COACHING

Much has been written by others about what coaching is and what it isn't. For our purposes here, we'll define it quite broadly as *that part of a relationship in which one person is primarily dedicated to serving the long-term development of effectiveness and self-generation in the other.*[1] Let's take a look at the elements of that definition.

"that part of a relationship . . ."

Some relationships that involve coaching—for example, between a coach and a paying client—are exclusively built around the learning, growth, and change of the client. In exchange for the coach's expertise, the client pays the coach money. In many other situations, however, coaching represents part of a more complex relationship.

Consider a department head with ten managers reporting to her. She has supervisory responsibility for the entire unit and is held accountable for its collective performance. A significant portion of her job involves organizing—making scheduling and budgeting decisions, delegating tasks, and monitoring the work of the whole department. That portion is not coaching. Coaching comes in when she works one-on-one with her direct reports to provide feedback, support them in problem solving, and discuss new challenges and opportunities for their own professional development. Thus, coaching is a critical part of the manager's relationship with each of her direct reports, but it is not the entire relationship.

Similarly, parents often coach their children in the context of a larger relationship. Whereas basic parental interactions—duties and pleasures such as providing food and shelter, establishing rules and enforcing discipline, or enjoying a game of catch for its own sake—are not considered coaching, others certainly are, such as helping an eighth grader learn algebra and teaching a teenager how to drive, and these activities would fit our definition. (Although generally, as children move into their teenage years, they are less and less willing to be coached by their parents, even then, and sometimes especially then, opportunities arise for parents to coach them.)

". . . primarily dedicated to serving . . ."

This part of our definition means that the learning and growth of the client are the overriding consideration in a coaching relationship.

However, they are not the sole consideration. "Solely dedicated" would imply that whatever the client wants goes. But in addition to commitments to clients, coaches always have a responsibility to take care of themselves. "Primarily dedicated" means that there's room in the relationship to articulate and address the legitimate needs of the coach as well. And in fact, coaches can significantly learn and develop through the relationship too; reciprocal learning is inherent in the process. I will offer practices for making this reciprocity and coach learning systematic, while always orienting the conversation toward the client's developmental needs.

The coaching relationship is often a professional one, in which the coach is paid by the client or a third party such as a company, an agency, or a congregation, but it is a personal one as well. Therefore, it requires setting up an explicit framework at the beginning that will work for both parties. That framework needs to spell out the nature of each person's responsibilities, including keeping appointments, being respectful, and remaining truly engaged, and these should be made explicit at the beginning. Establishing guidelines and mutual expectations for the coaching process is central to enabling the coach's dedication to serving the client.

"... long-term development ..."

It is absolutely appropriate at times to provide quick answers to a client's direct questions or immediate needs for help. But it is also important to remain aware that this is not the only approach to supporting the client. If we always give in to the temptation to go for the quick fix, we will most likely be undermining initiative and fostering dependence. Helping clients build long-term capabilities means helping them develop their own problem-solving skills. This long-term view needs to be kept in mind and made explicit.

Development encompasses a number of meanings. According to *Webster's New Universal Unabridged Dictionary,* to develop is "to become fuller, larger, better, etc.; to expand . . .; to strengthen . . .; to unfold gradually, as a bud." Development implies that the raw materials are already there, that nothing is being created from scratch. In coaching, the client's development means that she is growing into her potential, becoming increasingly intentional and proactive about what she wants to achieve and who she wants to be.

". . . effectiveness and self-generation in the other."

The long-term goals of coaching are both effectiveness and self-generation. *Effectiveness* means that the client becomes more competent and successful, according to her own defined standards and goals, at delivering on commitments in the content area of the coaching: building a business, learning a better tennis serve, getting or changing a job, or any other endeavor she and the coach have agreed to focus on.

The second desired outcome of coaching is self-generation. In his book *Coaching: Evoking Excellence in Others,* James Flaherty notes that well-coached people understand that there is always more to learn, and a self-generative person is a lifelong learner.[2] *Self-generation* means taking personal responsibility for developing one's own capabilities, and ultimately it implies an independence from the coach.

There are many formats for coaching. In my own practice, I have coached in hour-long phone conversations, half-day sessions in an executive's office, day-long conversations beside a mountain creek, and Skype or e-mail exchanges with someone on a different continent.

It's not the schedule or the setting that determines whether coaching is happening, but the nature of the work, specifically the dedication of the relationship, in whole or in part, to the development of effectiveness and self-generation in another. Beyond that dedication, the practical details are dictated by what best serves the learning process given the requirements of the individuals and circumstances.

DISTINGUISHING COACHING FROM OTHER ASPECTS OF PROFESSIONAL RELATIONSHIPS

If, like the department head above, coaching is only one portion of your work, you will be helped by clarifying which parts of your overall professional activity are or are not coaching.

Exhibit I.1 illustrates examples of coaching and noncoaching activities in three professional venues. Even if your own profession is not one of the three, the table should help you consider how various activities do or don't fit the definition of coaching as we've framed it. (Note that I've used *subordinate, student,* and *patient* in the table, as seeming more natural in the context of the professional realms

EXHIBIT I.1.

Coaching and Noncoaching Activities in Three Fields

Professional Realm	Coaching Activities	Noncoaching Activities
Managers and executives	• Holding career development conversations • Eliciting and discussing options for how to accomplish work • Providing feedback about a subordinate's behaviors • Asking a subordinate for alternative options	• Delegating authority or tasks • Invoking authority as leverage or to get something done • Making annual review assessments and compensation decisions • Outlining a strategy for others to follow
Teachers	• Asking questions that encourage a student to think differently • Working with an individual student on test-taking strategies • Processing experiential learning activities with an individual • Tutoring one-on-one	• Grading tests and homework • Lecturing and group discussions • Disciplining students • Interacting with an individual student when authority is the leverage for behavior change
Health care workers	• Asking the patient to observe symptoms more closely • Helping the patient to see and understand his body as a whole system • Making suggestions for patient self-responsibility in treatment • Working with staff on bedside manner	• Making an expert diagnosis • Prescribing medication, tests, or treatment • Viewing patients as a complex mechanical system with a breakdown • Managing the medical practice

represented. However, throughout the book, the word *client* is used in general discussions in order to reinforce the point that the coaching process is essentially the same across disciplines.).

Looking for exceptions to the generalizations in the table will help you hone your own understanding of the distinctions between coaching and other activities in relation to your own unique circumstances.

Everything in this book is intended to invite you to do your own mindful discernment, not to constrain you with imposed definitions. The ultimate goal is learning to know in your gut when you are in service to a client's needs and when you are serving a different agenda.

With the examples from Exhibit I.1 in mind, we can make some further distinctions about what coaching is and isn't. For example, a person is not coaching when she:

- Uses authority or positional power to motivate the "client" by stating organizational expectations or implying consequences for noncompliance
- Makes unilateral decisions that directly affect the client
- Diagnoses the client using an "expert" system (although this is an important function in many fields, it often serves a different primary agenda than the client's learning and development)
- Makes decisions based on the needs of the larger system over the needs of the individual
- Communicates out of an emotional need, implicitly placing that need higher than the learning needs of the other

These activities may be necessary, legitimate, and valuable parts of a professional relationship, and they may result in client learning. But they are not coaching.

Obviously, the distinction between coaching and noncoaching activities sometimes blurs. I encourage you to draw on the guidelines above to define the boundaries of coaching in your particular arena. Clear distinctions about the professional activities you perform that are and aren't coaching will provide the basis for ongoing discernment and lay the groundwork for everything that follows as you expand your expertise as a coach. Exercise I.1 will help you get started.

The purpose here is for you to try out this book's definition of coaching and get you thinking about when you're coaching and when you're engaged in some other legitimate aspect of your professional relationship with a client, whoever that client might be in your particular context. As you integrate coaching into your work, based on the results of your observations and your own process of learning as

---

EXERCISE I.1.
Defining Coaching for Yourself

1. Write a brief summary of your job responsibilities. Include those that entail coaching, and describe the objectives of coaching as you do it in your context.
2. Consider again the definition of coaching I've presented: *that part of a relationship in which one person is primarily dedicated to serving the long-term development of effectiveness and self-generation in the other.* Think about it in relation to
   your job and the people whose skills you feel responsible for developing.
3. Get specific. Make a two-column table like Exhibit I.1 and fill it out with some specific examples of what you do in your interactions with the people you coach. In
   the left-hand column, put examples of interactions that fit the definition of coaching that I have provided. In the right-hand column, put examples that are excluded
   by the definition.

---

you work with the ideas in this book, you are certainly free to modify
my definition or create your own.

CONTEXTS FOR COACHING:
FOUR DYNAMICS

At this point, it is important to distinguish between developmental and performance coaching, the former being the focus of this
book. In developmental coaching, the learning and development of
the person being coached is the primary driver of the coaching. In
performance coaching, the primary drivers are organizational goals,
and the coaching aims to make the client a more effective contribu-
tor to those goals. Performance coaching is often informed by some
form of gap analysis, 360-degree feedback, or another assessment of
competencies that the organization considers important.

While everything in this book is also relevant to performance
coaching, it is written with developmental coaching in mind. This is
in part because I personally orient toward the latter, but also because
a discussion of developmental coaching includes methods and subject matter that might be excluded by the more narrowly focused
performance coaching agenda. Be assured that both the principles

of human development and the learning dialogues I describe will be relevant and important in any form of coaching. At the same time, while performance coaching often requires assessments and competency models not discussed here, their use is entirely consistent.

In the early days of coaching's inclusion in corporate training and development repertoires, it was often seen as a last-ditch investment for saving managers who were derailing, but coaching simply imposed from above is unlikely to be a wise investment.[3] Although coaching can occasionally work when it is strongly recommended or prescribed for someone, the client must be genuinely open for coaching and have a real desire to learn and develop. No one can be successfully coached if he doesn't want to be coached. It is incumbent on the coach to discern, in conversation with the client, if this opening exists before committing to an engagement, or risk being set up for failure from the outset.

Developmental coaching is focused on the development of competencies and capacity, as distinct from reaching performance goals. The establishment of competency-based versus goal-based outcomes supports this thrust. It is reasonable, of course, to expect that greater competency will lead to results. Yet orienting the process toward results over competencies can lead to pressures that actually impede the learning process. A better focus is on building the skills and capacities that will allow the client to perform effectively for the rest of her life in any circumstance than to narrow the focus to next quarter's results, only to deliver success that isn't replicable because there is no foundation under it.

Let's look at how the context of the coaching situation can support or undermine a viable relationship between coach and client. Understanding how to set up and maintain a healthy win-win situation is critical.

Client-Initiated Coaching

Executives, managers, entrepreneurs, and people in the midst of significant transitions often hire private coaches to help them pursue their dreams and aspirations or to support them in addressing the problems they face. Many areas of specialization (executive coaching, small business coaching, creativity coaching, life coaching, and so forth) could be identified here. Usually the client finds the coach by word of mouth or other form of referral; sometimes the coach finds the client. Either way, the client is eager to enter into the coaching relationship.

The important thing about this kind of situation is that it is a one-on-one contractual relationship, for an exchange of fees, between two people free of organizational constraints. Sometimes the client is paying the bill directly; other times the client is paying out of an employer's funds but has authority to do so, or can get the necessary signature, without any involvement by a third party. Since the person paying the bill is the one who is being served, the dynamic is pretty much self-regulating: if the client is getting what she believes she wants and is paying for, the relationship is successful. If it is not, she will renegotiate or terminate the contract.

Third-Party Involvement and Consequences

A more complex situation arises if a third party has a vested interest in the outcome of the coaching. Consider the following situations:

- An executive wants a high-potential direct report to be coached in order to take on additional responsibility.

- A higher-up in a social service agency has his own agenda for the outcome in a particular case or cases.

- A manager is in trouble, and coaching is an effort to remediate the situation. The client's job may be at stake, for instance, and the coach may be required to make progress or outcome reports to a third party who has the power to hire and fire, promote or demote within the organization.

- In health care, social work, or counseling settings, a third-party payer may place constraints on the coaching process or may condition continued support on demonstrable results or actions taken.

- Coaching is being provided to managers by human resource specialists or other line managers who are not in a supervisory relationship to the person being coached. Here the coach represents organizational interests as well as the client's interests.

In all of these third-party situations, it may be a challenge to ensure that the coaching is truly dedicated to the long-term development of the client. The key, of course, is to put the various agendas on the table from the beginning and construct a coaching process that explicitly addresses them all. If there is to be communication about progress or outcomes to a third party, being explicit about confidentiality in advance is especially critical.

The third party's goals must be respected. So, for example, if I'm coaching a manager in an organizational setting, I always ask the authorizing person, as a litmus test, whether it will be a good use of the organization's investment if the client leaves the organization as a result of my coaching. If the answer is yes, then I feel more certain that I can really serve the client's needs without being caught between those needs and the organization's goals. Whatever the situation, it will be important to ensure that the client's goals aren't in conflict with those of any third party involved.

Sometimes there are foreseeable consequences to the client for not achieving the coaching outcomes expected by the third party. The bad news is that the client may well be resistant or resentful about being coached in the first place. He may or may not recognize the problems that the third party sees. In that case, coaching may need to begin with determining if there is compatibility between the client's goals and those of the third party. The bottom line here is that if the client is unwilling or unable to engage in the coaching process in service to some motivation of his own—even if it's to jump through someone else's hoops in order to keep a job—the coaching cannot succeed. The good news is that the leverage provided by the dynamic with the third party can sometimes be helpful in getting results.

Transitioned Relationships and Issues of Inequality

Another special dynamic results when a noncoaching prior relationship of some sort (with a colleague, friend, former supervisor, or business partner, for example) becomes a coaching relationship. Generally in any relationship with meaningful engagement, elements of coaching (mutual learning, exchange of ideas) will be present. The difference is that now, some portion of the relationship is explicitly dedicated to the learning and development of one of the parties.

When this transition takes place, a new kind of relationship is formalized—one in which it is now understood that one person will be learning with the support of the other. This can be awkward, especially in collegial or peer relationships, because it can imply a new inequality within the relationship.

This means having an open exchange of mutual expectations, and a frank discussion about how other aspects of the relationship will be affected. It is important to bring these issues to the surface and address them. Doing so may build comfort initially, place boundaries around the content of coaching, and allow coach and client to agree not to discuss the coaching content outside the portion of the relationship dedicated to coaching.

Supervisory Relationships and Differing Interests

The last type of coaching situation we'll consider here arises when the coach is the client's direct supervisor in an agency, business, or other organization. Here the coaching element is inevitably influenced by the power differential resulting from the authority of the coach or boss over the client and by the potential for the interests of the supervisor to differ from those of the individual.

Coaching in a supervisory relationship often occurs in order to increase the subordinate's skill in meeting organizational objectives. This is generally referred to as performance coaching. Performance coaching can be very helpful to the subordinate, at least when both feel comfortable that the subordinate's goals are consistent with those of the employer. Performance coaching becomes more delicate when the subordinate has other career interests or sees his performance more favorably than does his boss.

In order for coaching to be successful in a supervisory relationship, four conditions must be met:

- The goals of the boss must not be in conflict with the personal and professional goals of the subordinate, or the boss must be able to place other considerations temporarily in the background in order to coach in good faith, in the best interests of the subordinate.

- The subordinate must feel motivated and committed to learning and development for reasons of his own.
- Both parties must be able and willing to draw distinctions between the coaching aspect and other aspects of their relationship. They must learn to separate the development process from power issues and supervisory consequences.
- The boss and subordinate must trust each other that the first three conditions are present.

If all these conditions are met, the two parties can sometimes build a coaching relationship dedicated to the client's growth. If any condition is absent, supervisory coaching will be difficult, and there may be more appropriate means of supporting and developing the subordinate.

I recommend to my clients who are coaching direct reports that they set aside a special time and circumstance for the coaching in which the supervisor's authority and other aspects of the relationship can be placed in the background, so the time is dedicated to the service of the subordinate's development. I also recommend they be explicit about when the coaching is over.

The nuances of coaching within a reporting relationship are challenging, and it is generally better for coaching to be provided by someone outside the client's lines of authority. Someone in a different reporting line in the organization can often provide mentoring or coaching with organization-specific knowledge, but with fewer power issues. And for coaching that is more development than performance oriented, someone completely outside the organization is generally best suited to support the client's developmental needs without compromise.

INTRODUCTION SUMMARY

In this book, we are exploring coaching as a broad-based one-to-one development relationship. Although coaching also has many other applications, I am defining it here as *that part of a relationship in which one person is primarily dedicated to serving the long-term development of effectiveness and self-generation in the other.* The book is written to support anyone, regardless of profession, who is supporting the development and leadership of others, whether as a coach, a manager, a consultant, a physician, or a counselor.

In any of the relationships described here, coaching can take place in informal interactions—say, meeting by the water cooler for a brief exchange. The descriptions of coaching in this book, however, will be based on the assumption that most high-level coaching takes place in conversations that are dedicated to that purpose. The book, then, presents a model of coaching that will guide any professional in structuring conversations dedicated to the development of others.

As coaches, we must remain aware of our commitment to the learning and growth of the client. The client is in charge; we are in service to the development of the client. To the extent that we allow ourselves or a third party—or, more precisely, our own needs and goals or those of an organization—to drive the agenda, we risk undermining this primary mission.

The most challenging of the specific situations discussed in this chapter is coaching within a supervisory relationship, where both parties must be able to place the authority differences in the background in order to maintain a clear focus on the goals and needs of the client.

1

The Being of Coaching: Mindful Service

Service is the rent we pay to be living. It is the very purpose of life and not something you do in your spare time.

Marian Wright Edelman

If one is estranged from oneself, then one is estranged from others too. If one is out of touch with oneself, then one cannot touch others.

Anne Morrow Lindbergh

SERVICE IS IMPLICIT IN OUR DEFINITION OF COACHING: whether you do it as a professional coach with an executive client, a manager with an employee, a teacher with a student, or a health care worker with a patient, coaching means placing yourself in service to another. In turn, placing oneself in service requires a broad quality called mindfulness.

This chapter begins with an exploration of service and its implications for our mindfulness. In developing the notion of mindfulness, we'll touch on the levels of experience that are available to us in every moment, the nature of the habits that cloud our mindfulness, and approaches for cultivating mindfulness in ourselves and, by extension, in our clients. As you will see more and more in later chapters, coaching can be considered in large part as a process of cultivating greater mindfulness, and thereby resourcefulness and choice. By the end of the chapter, we will be ready to delve into the seven roles, or Voices, through which effective coaching is expressed.

PLACING ONESELF IN SERVICE

Leadership is often done in the name of service; an entire field of "servant leadership" has sprung up to describe and deepen this leadership ethic. Unfortunately, some of what is done is not so helpful; leadership can often be self-service or arrogance disguised as help for others. True service means discerning and providing what is needed. This requires a high level of commitment and care. Ethical service is done consciously, with self-awareness, and for the benefit of the client.

The coach represents, and stands for, the client's highest potential. As coaches, we can sometimes see the possibilities for a client's success more clearly than he can. It is true service to believe in someone's potential and encourage him to realize it, to help him set goals and develop strategies for achieving them. It is also true service to help a client acknowledge his limitations, help him work to overcome them, and accept him fully even when he can't bring himself to take the plunge into change.

To place oneself in service is noble. It does not mean being subservient or putting oneself in a "lesser than" position in relation to the other. It is, rather, a dedication—a clear commitment to attend primarily to the client's needs for the time being.

Service is what allows coaching to happen. It is enabled by an agreement that works for both parties about the parameters of their relationship, including logistical arrangements, mutual responsibilities, fees, third-party agendas, and other concerns. Above all, the coach must be able to respect and support the outcomes that the client seeks. The partnership between coach and client must be structured as a win-win so that both parties sense that their underlying needs are being met. This frees the coach up from her own separate concerns, making it easier to truly serve.

Being of service does not mean that we avoid giving tough feedback or dance around difficult issues. As coaches, we must sometimes participate in emotionally challenging conversations or tell our clients things that are hard for them to hear. Service depends on our ability to participate honestly for the learning of the client and not for needs of our own that we ourselves may not even recognize. To serve, we first must understand what's going on within. Only then can we speak and coach directly, clearly, and compassionately.

If we feel irritated and impatient in a coaching conversation, for instance, we need to ask ourselves what part of that impatience comes from our own agenda and what part has to do with the client. Letting these emotions go unexamined may be easier for us, but it won't serve the client. It might be useful to the client for us to describe how his behavior affects us—for instance, to say that we notice our impatience rising and to suggest a connection between what we notice in ourselves and the client's behavior. If we do so, however, it must be by choice and in recognition that in this particular instance, it may be helpful for the client to recognize how his behavior may affect others.

So our own impatience can express itself in several ways. We can simply let it be acted out according to our own habits and agendas, but, if we are committed to service, we must find a way to use our impatience as a starting point for providing difficult needed feedback in a compassionate way. The difference depends largely on our own degree of self-awareness, enabled by mindfulness.

MINDFULNESS AND SELF-AWARENESS

Placing ourselves in service is a powerful way to catalyze our own self-awareness. As soon as we place some of our needs and agendas off-limits, they'll show up full force. If you don't believe this, try going on a sugar-free diet for a week. Or giving up coffee. Or stopping just about anything that is habitual for you. All of a sudden, you *really* want that thing—whatever it is.

Mindfulness is the inner state in which we can observe ourselves in action. It enables the self-awareness, for example, that in this moment, I am irritated, or happy, or craving that cup of coffee, or I am just about to say something to my client that might be better not said. Awareness, in turn, allows us to consciously choose whether to say, or withhold, that thought.

The importance of mindfulness in serving cannot be overstated. The mindful coach knows, from her awareness of her own feelings and thoughts, when she is serving the client and when not. She knows if her personal agendas and judgments are in the way, and what to do with them if they are. She is able to be mindfully present with the client and to listen and respond clearly, with acceptance, and without judgment.

Committing to service requires the corollary commitment to a self-development curriculum in mindfulness. Self-awareness—noticing and suspending one's own habits and agendas—is a primary requirement for being an effective coach. But ultimately the coach himself benefits too. The client benefits from being served well, and the coach benefits from learning to be of service, from learning the discipline of true mindfulness.

A commitment to cultivating mindfulness will provide you with a lifetime of learning opportunities. It will also greatly deepen your experience of coaching and your ability to be present and effective as a coach.

As a concept, mindfulness is central in a mushrooming volume of professional and business literature.[1] The term comes from Western translations of the formulations of Buddhist teachers. Some of the other terms I will use (*attachments* and *aversions*) come from the same tradition. I have chosen to organize this book around these particular terms and distinctions in part because they are informed by my own personal work and lineage of teachers, and in part because they, more than any other language I've run across, point directly to the granular nature of experience that seems to be central in being mindful and aware. This language is pragmatic, relevant, contemporary, and consistent with current scientific understanding. We can use it to understand more precisely what goes on inside us. Still, I acknowledge that other vocabularies and conceptual frameworks could also serve as platforms from which to develop the ideas presented here. For example, Daniel Goleman's domains of emotional intelligence (self-awareness, self-management, social awareness, and relationship management) come to mind.[2]

The cultivation of mindfulness is a lifelong process. As you read this book, give yourself lots of permission to be a beginner and to experiment. Because you are probably a well-educated, successful, intelligent, quick learner, you may expect that you will be "good at" mindfulness. Watch out! This internal standard will spectacularly interfere with your learning in this particular realm because the very orientation toward achievement and performance makes it particularly challenging to simply look squarely at what *is* and accept it fully.

I invite you to engage this material not as a reader seeking to efficiently assimilate a new body of knowledge into the way you do your work. Rather, approach it with genuine curiosity, seeking what you might discover about yourself and how the experiences contained within this book might challenge what you think you know. Instead of fitting this material into the existing frameworks of your understanding, be open to how it might expand those frameworks and enable entirely new ways of experiencing yourself and engaging in relationships.

Exercise 1.1 provides a beginning experience of mindfulness.

EXERCISE 1.1.
Mindful Eating

This exercise is a variation on a traditional eating meditation.[3] It's an excellent experiment for directing your attention and noticing your own habits of mind at play. (It's hard to read the directions and perform the experiment at the same time. You could read the whole thing through and then turn your attention to the exercise, make a recording to listen to, or ask a friend to read it out loud as you do the exercise.)

Begin by selecting something that you enjoy eating, and procure three small bites. Fresh raspberries, small pieces of dark chocolate, or pieces of dried fruit work well. (You could, of course, later extend this practice to an entire meal.) I'll describe the practice with berries.

Cup your three berries in one hand. Settle yourself in a chair. Be comfortable. Let go of other activities and distractions, and let your body relax.

Now, take one berry and look at it as if you'd never seen a berry before. You could imagine that you just arrived here from Mars, and someone handed you this berry, and you are exquisitely curious about what it is. Sense its color, texture, patterns. Smell it. Bring it to your lips, but without touching them. Experience it fully, using all your senses, being exquisitely curious.

Notice any response in your body. What happens in your mouth in anticipation? Are you salivating? Is there any sense of craving in your chest? Any emotions? Memories of other times eating berries? Notice everything that arises in you in relation to this little berry.

Now, slowly place the berry in your mouth—not chewing, but letting the flavor slowly emerge. Sense the flavor spreading in your mouth and how the flavor is subtly different in different parts of your mouth and tongue. Sense every nuance of flavor and texture. Feel the place where your teeth and your tongue meet the skin of the berry.

Very slowly and mindfully, chew the berry. If you notice your thoughts wandering or your attention elsewhere than on the experience of eating, bring it back to the sensation of the berry in your mouth. This is a practice in one-pointed attention, an opportunity to "mono-task" all too rare in our busy modern lives. Make the most of it.

Notice the urge to swallow, and sense the urge itself. Let the berry linger; chew slowly and bring your attention back to the berry over and over until there is nothing left in your mouth but berry juice. Then swallow, and sense the berry juice flowing down your throat. Let yourself experience the absence of berry in your mouth. What is it like to have the berry gone?

Now take the second berry, and bring the same fresh curiosity to this berry. You've never actually looked at this berry before! How is it similar to the first? How is it different? Look. Feel. Touch. Smell. Sense not just the berry, but every sensation in your body at the same time. Place the berry in your mouth, and notice your mouth's response to it.

Consider momentarily that millions of years of evolution went into the perfection of this berry. A farmer grew this berry; someone picked and packed it; a truck transported it; someone placed it on the shelf in the store for you to buy—a miraculous chain of events, each of which was required to give you this precise experience. Notice the feeling of gratitude in you. Be present with the unique experience of eating *this* berry. It's the only opportunity you'll ever have for this particular experience, this particular moment.

Again, let the berry linger, become juice, and be swallowed, becoming part of you. Take your time. Enjoy. Be present and mindful.

Now take the third berry and experience it fully. Notice again and again that your mind goes off somewhere. Practice bringing it back. Over and over. That's all there is to do. You are practicing focusing your attention—noticing everything that is available to notice, and bringing your attention back, over and over, to your own experience.

Exercise 1.1 provides the opportunity to notice what arises as we try to maintain mindfulness on one simple task. We may experience desire or dislike. If we pay close attention, we may notice a subtle impulse to eat the berries fast. We may experience new sensations, our distractibility, or boredom, or sheer pleasure, or impatience with this silly exercise, or a desire to keep reading. The range of possible responses to such a simple practice is astounding.

This of course is the point. When we focus on something so elemental, the nuances of our experience are illuminated. All that experience is there all the time anyway; it's just that we rarely see it so clearly. Learning to be conscious and appreciative of how our own minds work is essential to becoming effective and authentic as coaches. When we coach, our client and our coaching become the objects of our total focus and attention.

MINDFULNESS AND THE THREE LEVELS OF EXPERIENCE

Contained within every moment of our lives are three levels or domains of experience. We can actually distinguish many more nuanced levels, but for our purposes, three will suffice: sensation, emotions, and thoughts. Generally, each of these three levels correlates with a particular part of our nervous systems.

Sensation is the first level, and the one that operates the most quickly in us. The smells of my daughter fixing sautéed eggplant sandwiches downstairs for lunch, the sound of the rain falling outside my window as I write, the sensation of a warm dog belly on my toes, the feeling of my weight pressing down in my chair, the pulsing of my heartbeat in my throat. When I am mindful, I am aware of all of these sensations.[4]

Emotion is the second level. At their root, emotions also have a component of sensation. When we look deeply, we can find the locus of emotion in our body. Yet emotions have a life, an energy, and a power all their own. Emotions can be very strong forces, taking over our awareness and driving behaviors that often are counterproductive. They can bias us and restrict our range of possible responses. Because my wife was irritated earlier when I left my dirty shoes in the front hall, I feel some anxiety as she walks into my office even though it may well be that she's coming to tell me how much she's enjoying the sound of the rain on the roof. I notice that I'm ready to react and defend myself against her irritation. Again, there's nothing "real" about my anxiety; it's an experience that will pass.

Thoughts are level three. The major components of most people's daily experience are thoughts, images, and self-talk or mental chatter. Our mental pictures of the future, plans, memories, and threads of conversations that constantly run through our brains take most of our available mental bandwidth. Because of how the brain is organized, this mental chatter or busyness often crowds out our awareness of our emotional and sensational selves. When we are mindful and present, we are aware of all three levels operating within us. Being mindful allows us access to the full range of each of these levels of experience. However, modern life seems to expect high levels of mental activity and thinking. While this is normal, an unintended and unfortunate consequence is that we often cut ourselves off from and diminish our access to our emotions and sensations. Mindfulness, then, means opening ourselves back up to all the levels of experience that the precious, miraculous human body makes available to us.

It is important to see that these experiences of thoughts, emotions, and sensations are fleeting. There is no real substance to the experiences themselves. The taste of the raspberry, the experience of gratitude, the memory of a previous berry experience: all arise in our awareness, and then fade away.

This is inherent in the nature of consciousness. When we are mindful, we become aware that everything is fleeting and transient. Every moment of experience is simply a temporary configuration of our nervous systems that will pass. Seeing this, we can become less attached to the experiences, stories, and emotions that we previously thought were real and substantive. Less attached, we become freer to let the difficult experiences go, responding to what the next new moment requires of us. Becoming attuned to ourselves means that we are able to take notice as feelings, sensations, and thoughts arise. This enables us to choose whether to put more energy into them or simply let them go as being unhelpful.

Cultivating nonattachment is pragmatic. When we are aware of our full experience, we are freer in how we may respond to what happens. For example, if someone challenges us in a meeting, a coaching client has an emotional reaction that affects us, or if we notice that we are about to make a strong statement rather than ask an artful question, we can observe our reaction, know that it is fleeting, and let it go, coming back to the present moment and our best creativity and resourcefulness about how best to respond. This nonattachment, which will be discussed at length later, is central to mindful coaching.

Here's a description of an experience that lasted perhaps half a minute but shows more about the interrelationship of the three levels of awareness.

As I'm coaching my client on the phone, I am mindful as I listen after I ask a challenging question. I notice my heartbeat, the pressure of my feet on the floor (sensation). Also in the realm of sensation,

I notice silence on the line. In response to that silence, I notice anxiety (emotion) and tension (sensation) arising within me, immediately followed by an interpretation (thought) that I have pushed her too hard and an impulse (sensation) to jump in and rescue her by saying more. Being mindful, I'm also aware of my own tension and self-judgment, and so I make an intentional decision (thought) to sit quietly for a minute until the client can process the question.

This little drama transpires in seconds, yet when I slow down and pay attention I can begin to notice how the process works and consider its elements before I decide on a course of action. In this instance, when I pay attention, I also notice that the anxiety (emotion) and tension (sensation) subside and are replaced by calm (sensation). When I hear my client respond to the question with a new insight, I feel energized (sensation) and decide that the question was helpful (thought).

All the levels are linked, and they are constantly shifting and moving through us. Such is the flow of life—fleeting. As experience, none of it is permanent. All experiences are temporary phenomena that arise and dissipate. Normally when I'm busy, I don't notice all the subtleties. When I am paying attention, the subtleties arise, are observed, and then easily pass. Nothing I can do can make them permanent.

Though they form the basis of what we think we know, the seemingly fixed patterns of experience are always shifting and changing. To see this is to begin to become mindful. This is what it means to pay attention: expanding our experience to study and appreciate the intricate components of which it is constructed.

Exercise 1.2 provides an opportunity to begin to notice the subtle emotional and somatic experiences that are available during any experience, even when not eating fresh raspberries!

ATTACHMENTS AND AVERSIONS

Along with levels of experience, a second set of experiential distinctions is critical to the work of a coach: attachments and aversions, the directional urges within us that drive our interpretations and, ultimately, behaviors. When we pay close attention to the granular nature of our own experience, attachments and aversions turn out to

EXERCISE 1.2.
Building Somatic and Emotional Awareness

Under the surface content of any experience is a wealth of subtle emotional and somatic (felt, sensation-based) experience to which we can increase our sensitivity and awareness over time. Awareness of what is going on with us below the surface is key to building our mindfulness. Being able to bring this awareness into our conversational space is central to the proposition of mindful coaching.

Have a series of conversations. These could be coaching conversations or simply exchanges with a spouse or a friend. The conversations should be about something meaningful and engaging to both of you. Following each conversation, take about ten minutes in a quiet space to jot some notes about what you noticed within yourself, independent of the content of the conversation:

- What pleasant emotional states did you notice?
- How did you experience connection or intimacy with the other?
- How did you experience concern or resistance or defensiveness?
- Where within the boundaries of your own body did you sense the experience of some element of tension, anxiety, or discomfort?
- What sensations did you notice: increasing energy, the feeling of your arms or hands moving, the pressure of your body pressing into the seat or your feet on the floor, warmth, or coolness?

These questions are unusual, and you may find yourself struggling for responses. If you don't have answers to some of them, that's fine. The point is to be curious and to keep looking. Because this is an unfamiliar way to pay attention to our own experience, it will pay to repeat this exercise a number of times. The information is there; most of us are just not accustomed to looking for it. The more you direct your curiosity and attention into yourself, the more you will begin to notice the vast range of emotional nuance and sensation that is constantly present within you.

---

be the very foundations of our unique personality. We can think of them as pairs of opposites that guide our actions and condition our behaviors and choices. One of each pair is something that we desire; we are attached to this. The other of the pair is something that we avoid; we have an aversion to that. Recognizing and letting go of our internal attachments and aversions is the key to being mindful and present and, ultimately, to serving our clients.

A specific attachment or aversion we may develop as individuals is likely to fall into one of four main dichotomies:

- We are drawn toward pleasure and attached to finding it/we avoid pain.
- We seek material gain, trying to get what we want/we try to avoid losing what we have.
- We want to be known and respected/we have an intense dislike for shame, embarrassment, and loss of face.
- We are attached to praise and to being appreciated and even adored/we wish to avoid blame and responsibility for negative things.[5]

These influences are all around us, intensified by our upbringing and our social experiences. Advertisements condition us to crave cold beer, telling us that we will experience pleasure, even attract a mate, by drinking it. Employers and schools, through pay and grades, seek to motivate us by encouraging attachment to rewards and praise. Our parents taught us not to cry, to work hard, to shape ourselves in a particular way in order to earn approval and love. We are taught that it is good to get what we want—a good job, stability, creature comforts, a loving spouse—and to fear the loss of these things.

None of this is bad. It just is. What matters tremendously is that our experience of life is controlled by our attachments and aversions. We are attached to the aspects of each of these pairs that we label as positive; we crave them and pursue them. We are averse to, resist, and avoid the aspects that we label as negative. But as hard as we work to get what we want and to avoid what we don't want, we can never know what any experience is going to bring us. For example, a casual acquaintance of mine won $2 million in the lottery. Talk about fulfilling an attachment to wealth! He quit his job, moved to an upscale neighborhood, stopped seeing old friends, and started a small business, but he didn't put much energy into the new enterprise. It seemed that the challenge and energy had gone out of life. He drank a lot, and he died of a heart attack a few years later. Enormous financial gain did not bring him happiness.

Another friend had breast cancer. She went through months and months of painful treatments and suffered greatly from anxiety about her future. Now, fully recovered, she has an appreciation of all of life's gifts that most of us feel only occasionally. She is clear about what she wants to do and how not to waste her life energy. She is much happier than before. As desperately as she might have wanted to avoid having the experience of cancer, it became a doorway into a more fulfilling life for her. Every day is now a gift.

Why doesn't successfully following what we're attached to, and avoiding what we have aversions to, guarantee us happiness? Because those very attachments and aversions are at the very root of our suffering. As Lama Surya Das writes in *Awakening the Buddha Within*,

> *It's easy to become so enmeshed in our worldly goals that we lose sight of the bigger picture. Without more foresight and perspective, we cannot help but prioritize foolishly. The ups and downs of office politics and interpersonal dynamics, for example, will overly affect the untrained mind. One minute you can feel like a winner, elated and on top of your game; the next you're in a slump, defeated, hopeless, and depressed.*[6]

We interpret outside events through our inner attachments and aversions. For instance, we interpret someone's "You look good today!" as a compliment or as an offensive come-on, depending on our thoughts about the circumstances and our emotional history with that someone. While the comment was simply words directed from one person to another, the attachment or aversion we experience can drive a warm smile and a sense of connection, or a rush of irritation and a hurried rush into the next room.

Try a little thought experiment to get more in touch with how you experience attachments and aversions within yourself. First, imagine something that's particularly inviting to you: the smell of freshly ground coffee or dark chocolate or a childhood memory of your grandmother. Look for a tiny upwelling of desire, a tinge of want that arises as you call this experience to mind. It will be fleeting and subtle, but if you pay close enough attention, you'll likely feel a slight pull of desire being triggered by your imagining. This is attachment.

Now try the reverse. Imagine taking a clean plastic spoon, inserting it into your mouth, filling it with saliva, removing it from your mouth, looking at it, and then sticking it back in your mouth.[7]

Notice the revulsion that arises. That's aversion. For most people, it's pretty strong. We can tell ourselves that the spoon was clean, that the saliva came from our body and returned to the same place. So what's the big deal? But our body's instinctual reaction is a strong aversion. Again, it's subtle, but as you learn to watch your mind at work, you'll notice more and more how a brief thought (pleasant or unpleasant) will trigger fleeting but sometimes strong emotions and sensations.

People committed to a path of mindfulness are working toward noticing and accepting these subtle phenomena. We don't need to get rid of any of our attachments or aversions; it is simply helpful to become aware of them and how they influence our actions. (And it's also important to remember that becoming aware of our habits of mind can lead us quickly to self-judgment and a whole new attachment—to self-improvement.)

For instance, I described a scenario about coaching over the phone. In it I noticed some tension in myself around my client's initial silence in response to a tough question. The noticing is sufficient. I don't have to change anything. It certainly wouldn't be helpful right then to get into a tizzy about my tension, or to fight it, or to analyze where it comes from. None of that would help me be more present for my client in the moment. It was sufficient to simply notice the tension and see it for what it was—a temporary feeling that would pass as soon as I let it go. The whole point is just seeing one's mind at work:

> We might feel that somehow we should try to eradicate these feelings of pleasure and pain, loss and gain, praise and blame, fame and disgrace. A more practical approach would be to get to know them, see how they hook us, see how they color our perception of reality, see how they aren't all that solid. Then [they] become the means for growing wiser as well as kinder and more content.[8]

In my own experience and in training and mentoring hundreds of coaches over the years, I've encountered certain attachments and aversions that are relevant to the helping professions, coaching in particular. Consider for yourself which ones have been or are likely to be helpful as you work with clients:

- We want to be seen as competent by the client/we want to avoid being seen as ineffective or unhelpful.

- We value a personal connection with the client/we try to avoid tension or conflict in the relationship.

- We look for a sensation of aliveness and creativity/we are impatient with rote conversation.

- We like the security of coaching according to a specific template or model/we try to avoid being seen as uncertain.

- We want to earn additional fees or appreciation/we fear being fired or taken for granted.

To the degree that our actions and behaviors are shaped by our own attachments and aversions, we are responding to our own desires to attain pleasure and avoid suffering rather than to the client's needs. By cultivating mindfulness, we become better able to make wise choices about how we can best serve our clients.

CONDITIONING AND HABITS THAT BLOCK MINDFULNESS

As we grow up, become socialized, and learn to function in society, we learn certain patterns of thought and interpretation that seem to work for us. The aggregate process of acquiring and internalizing these habits, of shaping ourselves to get what we want in our lives, we can call conditioning.

Over time our patterns become embedded as habits: automatic ways of processing information, interpreting what we see and hear, and making decisions about how to respond to life's events. Like fingerprints, our individual patterns of habits are unique. They are as varied as the world's cultures, families, and individuals; the aggregate of these patterns we call personality.

Habits, or conditioned patterns of behavior, are default responses to life's complexities. We learned them well, presumably because they worked for us earlier in life. And given who we are now and our current life circumstances, we may begin to discover that these habits limit our creativity, render us ineffective, or cause us to suffer. Our attachments and aversions hold these habits in place; we can think of them as the internal guidance that steers our behavior over and over into our habits or defaults.

Mindfulness does not require figuring out the origin of a habit. Rather, we learn to observe the habit as it arises, in all its nuances and subtleties, with its accompanying and precursory attachments and aversions. We can literally sense the attachments and aversions arising within us, as we sensed our attachment to chocolate and aversion to saliva. With this self-awareness (really, an expanded sense of our own truth in a given moment), we find ourselves with a choice about whether to act out the conditioned habit or choose a new response that may be more useful.

Habits have five elements: a trigger, three levels of conditioned responses that arise rapidly and sequentially[9] through the three levels of experience, and a resulting behavior.

Trigger: Something happens around us that we sense and that evokes a response.

Somatic response: Our body automatically responds to this sensory input. This is the biological organism responding, and it is observable as sensation (energy, tension, tightness, warmth, numbness, and so forth). Generally this is the first element of a constellation of linked responses.

Emotional response: Feelings arise based on our deep history; they are observable as emotions (anger, anxiety, joy, excitement).

Mental response: Mental formations provide meaning for our experience and rationale for our response. These are observable as language (stories, interpretation, justification). Because this is the highest order of response, it generally follows the first two, although the entire constellation can arise in less than a second.

Resulting behavior: Behavior flows out of the constellation of phenomena that arises. Observable as acts (movement, speech acts, and so on).

Some of our habits serve us well. They help us respond effectively to life's invitations and challenges. We even come to think of them as good traits of character. I grew up in a family of scientists. In part because of my early experiences, I have a boundless curiosity that impels me into learning and has led me to seek out opportunities for personal exploration and reflection that have made a fascinating journey and have helped me succeed in my professional life.

However, some habits of mind that have served us in the past may at some point become limiting, even detrimental. Because they are habits, our mental energies continue to follow these established pathways in our minds, like a stream following a worn groove over bare rock. Meanwhile, like seeds stranded on the bank above, new ideas, new ways of thinking, and new possibilities for our lives fail to sprout for lack of water. These worn grooves, while a metaphor, have a literal corollary in the default patterns of neurons that fire in our brains and form the elemental basis for our habits and personalities. Our habits are physiologically encoded in our bodies.

For example, in my very intellectual family of origin, we communicated about ideas but not about feelings. Much went unsaid, and strong expressions of emotion were discouraged. As an adult, I married a woman who is much freer with her feelings, whatever they might be and however rawly they might emerge. My conditioned response, instilled over years of living in an emotionally unexpressive family, had always been to either shut down or flee in the face of someone else's expression of intense emotion, especially anger.

In my marriage, this didn't work so well, and I have had to negotiate with my own habits. When my wife is angry about something, I still have to work hard to stay present and resist the urge to shut her out. She, in turn, works hard to address the source of her anger without overreacting. It requires mindfulness on both our parts to be aware of and then abandon unhelpful habits and cultivate new behaviors in their place. In all realms of life, becoming aware of the opportunity to choose new behaviors over old ones is the essential challenge of growth.

This is not what we label psychotherapy, as valuable as that endeavor might be for many people. We don't need to understand all the details of where our conditioned patterns came from, or revisit the early experiences that imprinted unhelpful habits in our minds. We can, in any moment, step beyond our patterned responses by simply becoming aware of them and seeing instead the multitude of alternatives that is available to us. It is a simple shift in perspective, an expanded view. This, in short, is what we seek to help clients do through coaching.

A helpful view is to be curious about your habits and to "make friends" with them. Your habits (presumably including some of the ones described in the previous section) are there because the organism that is you has learned well how to get along in the world. Your habits have served their purpose. Now you are becoming curious about their subtleties and bringing awareness to the entire constellation of what arises with this habit. This is different from working at changing the behavior. Rather, you're expanding and deepening your awareness of something that is in fact quite complex and miraculous.

The secondary effect of this awareness is that down the road, you'll become able to sense the first arising of the pattern and choose whether to go the rest of the way with it or replace it with something new. The journey starts with your self-observation.

COACHING HABITS

We all have habits of perception and response that impede our ability to be mindful as coaches, and in my experience many fall into the discrete categories that I discuss below. (Marshall Goldsmith also helpfully describes twenty-one habits of successful people, at least some of which will apply to each of us.[10]) Naming our habits allows us to first observe, and then interrupt, our habits. I offer these in the same spirit.

The purpose here is not to overwhelm you with a litany of obstacles to mindfulness but to develop a language for talking about habits. The simple act of recognizing how any one of these habits influences you, and accepting it without judgment or self-flagellation, is a moment of awakening.

Each of these habits will be accompanied by somatic, emotional, and cognitive experience. Familiarity with your particular favorite habits requires attending to the granular phenomena that together

---

SOME COACHING HABITS OF MIND

- Self-judgment
- Social identity
- Projections
- Philosophical positions
- Emotional triggers
- Routines
- Distractions
- Expert mind

make them up. Read, inquire into the nature of your own experience, and smile with recognition whenever you see yourself reflected here.

Self-Judgment

Let's begin by looking at what we sometimes do when we become aware that we're behaving in a less than perfect way. For example, I might notice that I'm feeling easily distracted as I listen to my client talk about an emotional experience that he's had. I notice my attention wandering; my gaze drifts out the window. By noticing my distraction, I have immediately become more self-aware; this brings me back to the present and provides an opportunity to listen more carefully.

Once I notice my distraction, however, I tend to scold myself. Little tapes go off in my mind: "A sensitive coach and mindfulness author isn't supposed to be distracted," "I'm being selfish," "I'm a lousy listener," and so on. This sort of self-judgment is, of course, rooted in my well-intentioned desire to measure up to some artificial standard of attentiveness I am attached to and measure myself against. The tendency toward self-judgment is just another habit of mind, another groove my thoughts follow. The truth is, I was distracted for a moment. That's all. No big deal.

If I launch into self-judgment, I allow my attention to shift once again. Instead of ignoring my client because of the view from the window, I'm ignoring him because I'm wrapped up in my own inadequacy as a listener. Either way, I'm not listening.

The trick, then, is simply to notice your self-judgment as it arises. Awareness and acceptance take the energy out of these habits. They lose their grip on us and, with it, their capacity to make us suffer. Any additional energy that we put into fighting them, trying to get rid of them, or analyzing them takes us away from the present just as surely as any other distraction would do.

Social Identity

Our habits of mind are often rooted in social identities that we seek to preserve or strengthen. James Flaherty explains social identity in terms of two images that interact with and reinforce each other.[11] One is the image that people have of us, which shapes how they interact with us. Clients come to us, whether we are a manager in an organization or a paid coach, with certain expectations that we can help them. Knowing this, we are more likely to respond in a way that fulfills those expectations. The other is the image we have of ourselves—the story we ourselves believe about who we are. Since this story gives our lives meaning and our ego an identity, we become attached to the story and seek evidence to support and reinforce it.

For example, I can be attached to maintaining a social identity as a knowledgeable person with good ideas and information to share. This identity is reinforced by clients who pay me for those good ideas. And I have an aversion to appearing stupid or lacking in knowledge. This isn't a bad thing, but it does present traps of which I need to be aware. If my energy is going into protecting or reinforcing a social identity, I am no longer fully available to my clients.

Any role can serve as a social identity. As Flaherty puts it, to the extent that our "relationship with others . . . has become hardened through a repetition of behavior and bound by the inflexibility of expectation," we become trapped in that role.[12] It quite literally becomes a worn groove in our consciousness. To change such a habit requires mindfulness and discipline. While the client's own habits often reinforce habitual, unconscious behavior on the part of the coach, the responsibility falls on us to do our own work in recognizing the social identity we are attached to.

Projections

Above my desk I have a picture drawn by my daughter many years ago, when she was about seven. It's one of those elementary school drawings where you trace the outline of your hand, then decorate it to turn it into a Thanksgiving turkey. Megan, however, took the assignment in a slightly different direction and drew a lovely chicken. It's done on black paper, and the sky is filled with little white stars and chicken footprints. The head of the chicken is looking up at the sky, and the title at the bottom says "Chickens like star gazing!!!!" I think this drawing is both hilarious and profound.

Just as we do, Megan's chicken sees herself in the universe. Where we might see a heroic Orion—a human being—with bow drawn, the chicken sees her own footprints in the stars. We look at the world through the filters of our experiences and then interpret what is going on out there in a way that affirms our own identity. This feels both gratifying and reassuring. But such projections are just a mental game we play.

We project on our clients in the same way, finding ourselves reflected in them. Those aspects that we judge and resist in others are likely to reflect traits that we also have difficulty accepting in ourselves. This is both a source of compassion and a source of trouble. Nancy Spence puts it this way:

> *At the heart of understanding projection is accepting the awareness that we are experiencing the perceptions we have about people, events and situations. What we are seeing out there is what we are doing inside.* Accepting this awareness means accepting responsibility for how we react to others. *Sometimes it is not easy to acknowledge that the difficulty we have with others is only a reflection of the difficulty we have with some aspect of ourselves. Sometimes it is not easy or pleasant to recognize we are always looking into a mirror.*[13]

I might be talking to a client about how overwhelmed she feels by her inability to focus on important planning issues in the face of three hundred e-mails a day in her inbox. I can empathize with her because in the face of countless demands, I find it difficult to find time to write. But I can also feel irritated and frustrated because of her apparent inability to prioritize in order to get things done. Not so coincidentally, those emotions are simply my projection onto my client of my own frustration with my challenges in prioritizing important work; the emotions have nothing to do with my client and everything to do with me.

For sure, if I can understand the frustration my client feels, this may help me to see possible ways for her to manage the challenges she faces. But projections are also trouble. Both the sense of comforting intimacy and the feelings of irritation that we experience when we see ourselves in our clients impede our clear view of the client. They can easily trigger our own attachments and aversions, unconsciously steering our coaching to seek the former and avoid the latter.

Projection also makes it all too easy to assume that what works for us will work for them—which may or may not be true. Further inquiry might uncover major differences between my situation and that of the client—differences that would point to different solutions. If I'm caught in my projection, the likelihood is that I'll quickly assume that I understand and so fall into a coaching approach that is based more on my own history and needs than on those of the client.

When we're projecting, we're not seeing things as they are. We have become attached to an interpretation that reveals something about ourselves. When we confuse ourselves with a client, we cease seeing that person and her situation as fresh and unique and are no longer a mindful resource in service to her learning.

Philosophical Positions

Belief systems and philosophical positions are part of our personality and identity, but they are also arbitrary and conditioned. And just like other aspects of who we are, they shape how we express ourselves and limit our understanding.

Let's say that I believe that the answers to all of life's questions reside within the individual. There are ways in which this belief may serve the coaching process. It might, for instance, lead me to ask probing questions that will in fact help the client discover her own resourcefulness. At the same time, that belief, if rigidly adhered to as a philosophical position, may also prevent me from playing one of a coach's key roles—that of a teacher. I'm far less likely to share my own experience or suggest specific alternatives if I believe that the answers to a client's questions must always be found within her own experience.

It behooves us all to become increasingly aware of the philosophical positions that we hold and to be mindful of their implications.

Emotional Triggers

Certain stimuli trigger emotional responses. These are the levels of experience arising and infusing our awareness so that we are no longer mindful and available. As coaches, when we get wrapped up in strong feelings and reactions, we cease to be present with our clients.

I worked with a client whose job was at risk because of some ineffective behaviors. He insisted that he had been "set up" by people around him who had focused on a few minor negatives and ignored the overwhelming positives. His unwillingness to take ownership of any part of the problems he was having in the workplace triggered frustration in me, as well as anxiety about my abilities as a coach. In this case, my emotional reactions made it a significant challenge for me to remain connected and respectful with this client.

Although our emotions may provide information that's useful in the coaching process—in this case, sharing my own reactions to my client's behavior in our conversations led him to see why his colleagues reacted to him as they did—a coach must be able to recognize his or her own feelings and work to keep them from influencing the work that is being done with the client in inappropriate ways.

Routines

We all tend to get numbed by routine. I fly frequently on business. It is an enjoyable drive from my home through the mountains to the airport. One day when I checked in at the counter, the agent politely informed me that I had the wrong ticket. I looked at it closely. Unfortunately, although the date, time, and destination matched, the flight, which I had booked myself, left from an entirely different airport, in the other direction from home and now three hours away. Clearly I hadn't been paying attention when I turned onto the main road. (My wife still laughs at me about that one, a quarter of a century later.)

I take some small comfort in the fact that as Ellen Langer reports in her book on mindfulness, "William James [told] a story of starting to get ready for a dinner party, undressing, washing, and then climbing into bed. Two routines that begin the same way got confused, and he mindlessly followed the more familiar one."[14]

Routines help us get things done, but they may also put us to sleep. Because it's easiest to stay in our worn grooves, we follow a habit without paying sufficient attention to whether it is taking us where we want to go.

As coaches, we tend to follow the same line of questioning, falling into the same pattern of conversation with a client time after time. But when coaching becomes routine, we're at risk of not paying attention. We miss openings that the client gives us—nuances of tone or wording that may represent a breakthrough. Under the influence of an attachment to the illusion of being competent and comfortable, and an aversion to exerting the energy, or taking the risk, of trying something new, we fall asleep at the wheel.

To counter this tendency, ask yourself, How can I disrupt my routines? What can I do to help me see each coaching client and conversation in a fresh way?

Distractions

Most of the professionals I know are exceedingly busy. Interruptions are constant, and the time available to focus on a single task seems to decrease daily. The fragmentation of time and experience that has become a seemingly inescapable part of our lives makes it difficult to focus on important tasks or to feel productive at the end of the day.

But while it appears that this is externally driven and we have no control over the distractions that plague us, closer scrutiny shows otherwise. Yes, there are external demands, but it's an internal urge that leads us to interrupt what we're doing to take that phone call, or get lost in our e-mails, or attend right now to whatever else is pulling at us in the moment. We can heed that voice or not; it's a choice. Neither choice is right nor wrong, but each has consequences.

Internal distractibility is characterized by rapid and often unconnected thoughts, tangents, and ideas, and it results in a lack of focus. Because our minds can process information a lot faster than conversation proceeds, we are at choice about how to use this extra mental capacity. A mindful choice is to focus our full attention on what we're doing rather than be distracted by unrelated matters.

Expert Mind

Just as routine can put us in a metaphorical sleep, so can the overconfidence that comes from expertise. Once we have achieved a certain level of mastery, it's easy to believe that we know how to do something. The most perilous stage for a teenage driver isn't the very beginning, when everything seems new and the driver is careful and attentive. Rather, it comes when she thinks she has it down; she's got her license, the state has anointed her a driver, and she experiences long-awaited freedom. Then the risk is overconfidence; the driver doesn't know what she doesn't know.

As an alternative, Shunryu Suzuki suggests that we cultivate a beginner's mind: the quality of attention that results when we are seeking to learn something new. It's the antithesis of the self-hypnotism that can result when we believe we have mastered something.

In the beginner's mind, there is no thought that "I have attained something." All self-centered thoughts limit our vast mind. When we have no thought of achievement, no thought of self, we are true beginners. Then we can really learn something.[15]

When we become attached to our own identity as knowledgeable—when we assume we have all the answers—we cease to pay attention. This puts us at risk for missing something important about a client or a situation.

In my own practice, I felt quite confident when a client named Ruth asked me to coach her in developing her delegation and management skills—after all, this was one of my areas of expertise. Since coaching by phone had always worked well for me, that's how I set up our relationship. It was only later, when she told me she had auditory processing difficulties, that I realized that this was one reason that we hadn't made any progress after several long-distance conversations. But by then she had made the decision to stop working with me, and I could hardly blame her for my own inattentiveness.

The mindfulness we lose when we are attached to our expertise can be regained when we let go of thinking we know anything. Beginner's mind serves us because we are more able to see what's in front of us with fresh eyes. Try Exercise 1.3 as a way of recognizing your own habits, attachments, and aversions in the context of a conversation.

EXERCISE 1.3.
The Bell Exercise

Find someone willing to sit with you for a few minutes and talk about something of significance. An account of a challenging experience from which they learned something of value will work well.

Engage your partner in a conversation, and simultaneously observe yourself in action. Your role is only to ask questions. No statements are allowed. (A statement is defined as anything that ends in a period: "That must have been difficult," or "Something like that happened to me," or "Oh, no!")

The idea is to catch yourself experiencing an attachment. If you have a small bell, ring it every time you notice any urge to make a statement (or simply raise your hand as a signal).

Also, ring the bell any time you notice your attention anywhere other than on your partner. For example, you notice your habitual urge to reflect back what you're hearing. *Ring.* The phone rings and you notice yourself wondering who's calling. *Ring.* You notice yourself wondering if a particular thought was a question or a statement. *Ring.* You notice yourself worrying about whether the person will be offended if you ring the bell, and realize that you have an attachment to being liked. *Ring.* You get the idea.

Although you may notice that ringing the bell feels rude, it is actually a signal to the other person that you are mindful and that you just brought your attention back to her.

The point of Exercise 1.3 is not that making statements is bad. Rather, we simply declared them off-limits as an exercise in becoming aware of the pervasive urges that drive us all the time.

By doing this, we begin to notice the incessant habits that we live in. We become mindful: part of our attention is in the doing, the conversation, the listening. And part of our attention is observing ourselves in the acting. This split attention is how we practice and build mindfulness.

Being mindful opens the possibility of not being driven by our habits and of living every moment in a way that is maximally creative and resourceful. This is the essence of self-generation. (A chapter from my second book, *Presence-Based Coaching,* can be downloaded at no cost from my Web site and adds significant depth to this exploration of self-generation.[16])

CHAPTER SUMMARY

Coaching begins with a willingness to place ourselves in service. This is a commitment to bring ourselves fully to the coaching relationship and attend to the client's needs. Service requires placing the client at the center of the relationship and attending to how our own needs and agendas might undermine this.

Mindfulness means being aware of our own experience, moment by moment. It is in this mindful state that we become aware of our habits and how they might undermine our service to our clients if we lack rigor.

All human experience comprises three levels: cognitive, emotional, and sensation. When we bring our attention into the granular experience of each of these levels, we become more alive, more sensitive, and better able to identify our habits and unconscious tendencies as they arise.

Our habits are held in place by attachments and aversions. We can sense these within us and learn to intervene with our habits before they lead to behaviors that undermine our commitment to service. We can recognize certain habits that impede our mindfulness as coaches: self-judgment, social identity, projections, emotional triggers, routines, distractions, and expert mind. Learning to recognize these through self-awareness and self-monitoring is essential.

CHAPTER 2

Cultivating Mindfulness

Patience means allowing things to unfold at their own speed rather than jumping in with your habitual response to either pain or pleasure.

Pema Chödrön

The most basic and powerful way to connect to another person is to listen. Just listen. Perhaps the most important thing we ever give each other is our attention. . . . A loving silence often has far more power to heal and to connect than the most well-intentioned words.

Rachel Naomi Remen

IN ANY LEADERSHIP ENTERPRISE, ENTERING INTO A commitment will require us to recognize and deal with limiting habits, behaviors, and patterns of thought. Once we become conscious of these habits of mind, we can embrace them as helpful or let them go so that they no longer limit us. This is one of the keys to change, which is what we support our clients in achieving. But if we are to help others navigate this territory, we must first explore it ourselves.

Over the past decades, mindfulness has become an overused concept in pop psychology, various branches of what's called the human potential movement (including the coaching industry), and the intersecting realms of commerce and merchandising. True mindfulness, however, requires great attention and effort. Being mindful means "to be aware of our bodies, aware of our feelings and emotions, aware of our thoughts, and aware of events, as they occur, moment by moment."[1] The definition for being *conscious* is remarkably similar: "having . . . knowledge of one's sensations, feelings, etc., or external things; aware of oneself as a thinking being; knowing what one is doing and why; . . . an awareness of what one is thinking, feeling, and doing."[2]

We have all experienced moments of mindfulness. Time seems to stop, and we are fully present with whatever is happening at the moment. This can be blissful: taking communion at church, the intimacy of looking into the eyes of a loved one, being moved by the sight of a mountain. Or it can be mundane: noticing a moment of quiet in a frenetic day, a pause in a conversation when you know that something important and new has emerged, the recognition that we aren't upset about something that previously had us anxious. What these moments have in common is simply being present, being deeply conscious of what is happening. This is mindfulness.

In coaching, this mindfulness might show up as a surge of appreciation for our client, an insight about just the right question, or jointly discovering a new way of looking at the challenge she is facing. With this often comes a sense of connectedness and a delight in what is unfolding in the moment. These moments sometimes seem to happen spontaneously, and the heightened awareness they evoke quickly slips away. We can greatly increase the availability of these moments, and the creativity, resourcefulness, and compassion that often accompanies them, through mindfulness practices. As the Zen teacher Baker Roshi said, "Enlightenment is an accident, and practice makes you accident prone."[3]

It sounds simple, but people spend a lifetime trying to learn to become mindful. Cultivating the ability to stay mindful is spiritual practice of the highest order and promises mastery over the tenacious habits of our own minds and emotions.

With the basic understanding of mindfulness and habits from the previous chapter, we will move on to pragmatic approaches to cultivating your own mindfulness in service to your clients and to the coaching enterprise.

SELF-OBSERVATION

A key to building your skills as a coach is to cultivate the ability to observe yourself in action. Our clients will also require the ability to self-observe in order to cultivate new behaviors and options in relation to the challenges they face in their own lives as leaders of organizations and leaders of their own lives. Self-observation is foundational to everything that follows in this book.

While you are fully engaged with your client, a part of your mind stands slightly apart and detached: you are observing yourself and observing the client at the same time.[4] This "observer mind" provides awareness in the moment and the vantage point from which to see many things, among them which Voice you are using and why. You experienced this in the bell exercise in Chapter One.

As we practice self-observation, we become aware of two kinds of conscious experience: an active mind and an observing one. It's as if your consciousness has two parts. The first part is the one that acts, that does whatever you're doing in the world. The second is the observer mind; this is the part that watches. For example, take a moment right now to notice that as you are reading this paragraph, you can also observe yourself in the act of reading.

Throughout the rest of the book, we shall see that our ability to observe ourselves in action and shift between coaching roles depends on our capacity for self-observation; developing that capacity is the point of most of the exercises. We will see self-observation as both an ongoing awareness to be cultivated at all times and a specific structured learning activity that we can engage in or suggest to a client.

Self-Observing Habits

Traditional approaches to changing behavior often rely on good intentions. However, real change requires both being able to observe ourselves doing what isn't working and knowing what an alternative might be. Then we must interrupt our well-rehearsed automatic tendencies and, in the heat of the moment, replace a habitual behavior with an unfamiliar one.

Self-observations are key to this intricate process, and help us:

- Develop the capacity to observe our behavior objectively, almost as an outsider might see us
- Replace the inner critic that makes it more difficult to change with a neutral acceptance
- Eventually be able to stay present during an event and choose a more effective response

Self-observations are simply a structure designed to observe a specific behavior consistently. A self-observation usually defines:

- The behavior to be observed (for example, interrupting others in meetings)
- The structure of the observation process (when you'll observe it, for how long you will do this practice, how often, and what you can embed in your system to remind you to do it)
- Specific questions to be considered about what happened, what your inner experience was, and what the results were

The questions are designed to shed light on the nuances of the behavior as it arises. Often questions address the somatic, emotional, and mental levels of the experience, as well as observing what impact the behavior had on yourself or others.

Using self-observations over time leads to change generally, as follows:

- We use twenty/twenty hindsight to reflect at the end of our day. We remember that we actually did engage in some heinous behavior (for example, interrupting others) earlier in the day. We jot down notes about our experience and become curious. ("Hey! Maybe I really do interrupt!")
- After several days, because we are collecting data, we become more attuned to the behavior, and notice it sooner. ("Oops! I just interrupted Joe!") It is still hindsight, but closer in time.
- Soon the internal observer, which we've been cultivating, begins to notice what we're doing as we do it. ("I'm interrupting Joe right now!") Because the bulk of our awareness is still identified with the seemingly important thing we're interrupting Joe to say, we likely finish saying it anyway. Nevertheless, awareness is dawning.
- We begin to notice our impulse before the behavior. ("I feel my energy increasing and my back straightening. I feel impatient. I know what we should do. I'm about to interrupt Joe. No, this time, I'm going to hear him out instead. Slow down, relax, breathe, listen.") Now we are changing our behavior. But it happened simply, easily, almost by itself.

Self-observations are of tremendous value and can be designed for nearly any behavior, including both behaviors that you would like to use and those that you use excessively or inappropriately.

Self-Observation and Sustainable Change

Self-observation is simply a learning device. It's a means to build structure and accountability around the intangible quality of presence, or awareness in the present moment.

A self-observation can be constructed around any behavior, coaching related or not, that you wish to pay more attention to. Since they are useful for clients as well, it will add greatly to your coaching repertoire to be comfortable creating them and to have experienced how using the structure works for you.

Sometimes our default instincts are the right thing to do. Our habits are there because those behaviors have historically worked for us in getting what we wanted and needed. However, to increase our range of responses to a given situation, and especially to replace an ineffective but frequently practiced behavior with a more effective and novel one, we must be aware in the moment of what we are doing.

Through self-observation, we (and, by extension, our clients) build the capacity to pay full attention to what we are doing at any moment. If we are present, we will notice our habitual behaviors arising before we act them out. The early, often subtle somatic aspects of the habits are the warning bell that we're about to do what we usually do. Significantly, paying attention to what's happening in our bodies is the most direct means into presence anyway. This present moment awareness is what provides us with the moment of choice that Viktor Frankl, Stephen Covey, and countless others have spotlighted for us.

Recent neurological research (see the work of Jeffrey Schwartz and David Rock, for example[5]) is increasingly demonstrating that our brains and extended nervous systems are literally capable of rewiring themselves as we learn new habits. It takes energy, commitment, and attention to do so. And most important, it takes repetition of a new behavior, with full awareness.

Therein lies the key to sustainability. With this level of attention to the granular nature of our habits, we become increasingly able to recognize an old habit arising to make a choice to do something different and more effective. As we make this choice with full attention, our brain is literally building new neural pathways, which, with sufficient practice, will become strong enough that they are the new default.

What we experience as normal will have shifted, and we will have replaced an old, impulsive habit, with a new and consciously chosen way of responding to similar situations. Exercise 2.1 offers an opportunity to experiment with this phenomenon.

EXERCISE 2.1.
Self-Observation of a Habit

Choose some particular interpersonal habit of yours that you are aware of and wish to change. At this stage, choose one that's not too strong and doesn't create major problems for you—say, interrupting people in conversation, saying "um" frequently, or talking about yourself without asking questions of others.

Now, for two weeks, twice a day (say, at lunchtime and again at the end of the day), jot down notes about when you used that habit in the past several hours. No need for extensive notes. Simply write down what happened; what you felt in the realms of sensation, emotion, and thought; and what triggered the habit. You're not trying to change anything but simply to become more aware of what's going on inside you in relation to that habit.

This will be a brief experience in the very essence of change: the ability to choose, moment by moment, what you will experience and the actions you will take.

As you do it consistently over the course of the two weeks, you'll notice that through the practice of writing notes after the fact, you will increasingly become aware of the habit in the moment. You will come to find that over time, this leads to much greater self-awareness and the ability to observe your habits as they arise, and therefore to make choices about whether to follow the habit or do something different.

PRACTICES FOR CULTIVATING MINDFULNESS

Mindfulness is a matter of practice. Like anything else that we aspire to master, we must engage with a consistent set of practices over time. When we want to play the piano, we take lessons and practice. The same with golf. Likewise, mindfulness requires a set of practices that, with repetition over time, builds the muscle of our self-awareness so that our mindful state becomes less of an accidental phenomenon, and increasingly accessible and stable.

I distinguish here the idea of a practice from that of an exercise. An exercise is designed to be done once or a few times, in order to generate information or insight. A practice is designed to be done over an extended period of time. A coach of mine once requested that I begin a tai chi practice, and to do it as if I were going to do it for the rest of my life. I'm a quick study and am accustomed to getting acceptably good at something fast, then moving on to whatever is next. Committing to anything for the rest of my life put me in a very different view and was exactly what was necessary to move me out of a performance frame of mind and into a practice frame of mind.[6]

There are a vast number of specific tools and practices for cultivating mindfulness. Conversations with your friends and colleagues, a quick search on the Internet, or a tour through the self-help and spirituality sections of a good bookstore will turn up any number of resources on the topic. (You can also view or download a specific set of practices designed for mindfulness and presence from my Web site.[7]) You must discern for yourself which writers, teachers, or programs are useful for you. Do some research and try things out, but pursue only what both seems authentic and speaks to you.

At the same time, remember that mindfulness is a pragmatic, not an esoteric, pursuit, and help in attaining it can be found in many contexts, including in everyday activities as well as regular practices. Here are some simple things you can do that will help you become more aware of yourself and your habits of mind while learning to be more focused and attentive to the moment. Cultivating mindfulness in any area of your life will be helpful in others.

SOME MINDFULNESS PRACTICES

- Meditation
- Centering
- Physical activity
- Creativity
- Time outdoors

Meditation

There are many forms of meditation, some secular and some connected with specific religious practices.[8] All are basically attention training.

At its most basic, meditation involves sitting still, focusing on your breathing or a symbolic object, noticing the thoughts, images, and feelings that arise, then letting them go to come back to the object of meditation (Practice 2.1). As Western scientists are documenting in their most recent studies, meditation has physiological as well as psychological benefits.[9] For our purposes, meditation is a fundamental practice that builds the capacity to direct our attention where we choose and to notice the nuances of our experience, moment by moment, as they arise and pass away. When we do this over time, we become much more self-aware and much less attached to a particular thought, emotion, or sensation. We begin to embody the understanding that all our experiences are temporary and fleeting and relatively insignificant.

PRACTICE 2.1.
Sitting

Find a place to sit comfortably, with your back supported. Place your feet flat on the floor. Keep your back straight, but not rigid. Relax your shoulders. Close your eyes.

Take three deep breaths. Then breathe normally. Allow your attention to follow your breath. You might focus your attention on the sensation of coolness at the end of your nose as the air moves in and out, or on the sensation of your chest and abdomen rising and falling. Count each outbreath, up to ten, and then begin again.

When (not if, but when) you notice your mind elsewhere or that you've stopped counting, begin again. Do this over and over. There is no goal to count to ten without missing or to never get distracted. Nor to marvel at the parade of thoughts and emotions and sensations that will insistently march through your awareness as you sit. It's simply a practice in bringing your awareness back, over and over again, to your object of attention—in this case, your breath.

If you've never meditated before, do this for five minutes a day, twice a day. Then work up to ten, fifteen, and twenty minutes. It will change you.

Centering

Centering is a practice of bringing our attention into the body. It reduces the brain's compulsive activity and allows a different sense of self to emerge.

Practice 2.2 is one version of an exceedingly simple practice that can be astonishingly powerful over time. Another of the many versions is available on my Web site.[10]

PRACTICE 2.2.

Centering

Sit in a comfortable chair. Place both feet flat on the floor, and have your back straight.

Read this practice through a couple of times, and then put the book down. Take a couple of deep breaths, and let your attention follow these instructions. After reading each instruction, give yourself ten seconds or so to allow your attention to fully experience what is described in the instruction. Keep your eyes open.

- Sense your *feet* touching the floor, the pressure from the weight of your feet and legs pressing on the soles of your feet (pause to sense).
- Sense the similar pressure of your *sit bones* pressing into the seat of the chair (pause to sense).
- Let your *shoulders* drop, relaxed and heavy.
- Let your *chest* open somewhat, as if your heart had a window opening through the front of your body.
- Bring your *neck* back slightly, so that your head is stacked directly on top of your shoulders.
- Let your *jaw* soften and relax, simply hanging from the hinge.
- Let your *eyes* be soft and your peripheral vision emerge, taking in what's to the left and right of you.
- Have your *gaze* be level—not down at the floor or up, but straight across.
- Let several deep *breaths* flow in and out; notice that your body relaxes a bit more with each outbreath.

Notice how you are different now. How is your attention? What do you notice now that you didn't notice five minutes ago?

With practice, centering becomes a powerful way of reorganizing ourselves in the moment. By bringing our attention into ourselves, we begin to access greater sensation and body awareness. We become more sensitive to the subtle experiences that make up the tapestry of our lives.

Physical Activity

Yoga, jogging, dancing, and walking are great stress relievers; they get the blood circulating and help us get out of our heads and into our bodies. Sports like golf, tennis, and skiing require a balance between a focus on technique and a relaxed, concentrated mind. All sports have a mindfulness aspect that's been called the "inner game."[11] (Basketball coach Phil Jackson of the National Basketball Association knew this when he taught his Chicago Bulls mindfulness techniques on their way to becoming a dynasty in the 1990s, winning seven championships.)

Physical activity provides a complete set of sensations to be aware of. Parking our bodies on the treadmill and exercising while watching TV at the same time can be a good way to build muscle mass, but is not a mindfulness practice. Become conscious of your body: where it needs attention, where it feels good, what it's asking for. Practicing body awareness while being physically active will also help you tune into your own physical reactions as you're coaching, and to your client's body language as well. If you pay attention to them, these cues can alert you to your own emotional reactions or to something that's going on with your client.

Creativity

All people are creative, but in our society, most of us have not been encouraged to explore this aspect of ourselves since we drew paper outlines of our hands to cut out in kindergarten. The process of being expressive in some sort of physical way—music, painting, pottery, metal fabrication—is simply a discovery of another realm of your inherent intelligence. Yes, it comes more easily to some than others, but it's available to all of us. If you already have such an outlet, pursue it and seek to become more aware of your own creative process as you do so. If you don't, find a way to tap into this realm: dance lessons, a poetry or singing class, woodworking, gardening.

Using your breath, your hands, or your body to create something in the physical world exercises parts of the brain that aren't usually activated by knowledge work or the routine tasks that so many of us do for a living.[12] Also, you are nearly certain to get in touch with your own attachments to "being good at it": just more conditioning to let go of on the path to mindfulness.

Time Outdoors

Natural settings put everything into perspective. There is an order in nature that is beyond us. The natural world can be experienced as dangerous and unpredictable, or as bountiful and benign, depending on your relationship to it. However, its vastness and variety—even today, when the influence of human beings is disrupting its rhythms—can be restorative for someone who spends lots of time in an artificial environment, being frazzled and pulled in multiple directions by purely human concerns.

I'm lucky enough to live on sixty-three acres in the mountains of North Carolina. After my morning walk to the river with my dog, Lyra, I'm a different person. Of course, I can fuss and obsess in the woods just as easily as I can in my office, but out there, it's more obvious that it's my mind that's producing that activity rather than the environment. At the same time, the physical activity and the beauty of what I see all around me serve to reduce mental chatter and bring me into the present.

Most of us can find places to walk among trees or along moving water; those who can't might bring stones or plants or other reminders of the natural world into their environment. Finding a place to reconnect with the natural order of things isn't simply a nice thing to build into your vacation; it's a fundamental need of the human spirit, and one of the most powerful places to practice mindfulness.

I strongly recommend that if you want to be in the business of building your own mindfulness and extending this to others in your work, commit to one or more ongoing practices such as those described in this section. There is no shortcut, no other way, than to engage in practice consistently and rigorously over time.

COACH AS LEARNER

Coaching provides a continuous opportunity for us to practice, one in which the mindful coach, as well as the client, learns and grows. As I've already suggested, we study ourselves, constantly and gently seeking to become better at what we do. When we place ourselves in service to our clients' learning, we develop our self-awareness both in order to serve well and to be able to make the claim that we know the territory enough to support our clients in similar self-development.

Although it has it dangers, one of the wonderful things about coaching is what we learn from seeing ourselves in our clients. I recall discussing this with a man I'll call Marty, a highly capable engineering director. Brilliant, tenacious, and likable, Marty grew up in a hardscrabble working-class environment and was the first in his family to go to college. In spite of his obvious competence and the respect he had earned from everyone on his management team, he still suffered from bouts of acute insecurity, usually triggered by stress. When this habit of mind closed in on him, he often interpreted the innocent gestures of others as reflecting a lack of confidence in him. This fostered more stress, which made him still more sensitive. He still functioned well, but he wasn't having much fun.

The experience of coaching Marty shed light on my own internal dynamics. As the son of two Ph.D.s, who grew up in an academic environment, I often felt I wasn't smart enough. When insecure, I can get tense and sensitive to the cues that tell me what others think about my ideas. In other words, it was easy to see myself reflected in Marty, and that illuminated ways in which I sometimes overcompensate or worry too much about what others think.

While we learn as much from our work with clients as they learn from us, we must remember that if we are to serve them well, we need to keep the focus on their needs, not ours. When we stay mindful, our experiences that are similar to our clients' can lead to compassion, insight into possible practices that might lighten their load, and self-awareness about how we ourselves might grow. When we're not mindful, these similarities may cause us to ignore the differences or unconsciously assume that strategies that worked for us will work for him.

This is one of many examples that illuminate that we must be in the learning game ourselves. This earns us the right to work with clients.

I strongly recommend that if you want to coach others, you be coached yourself. There's no substitute for a partnership with a seasoned professional with whom you have good chemistry and who will both challenge and support you in your own development process. Furthermore, the experience of being a client will teach you a great deal about resistance and motivation, give you a gut feel for the dynamics of change, and help you learn how to coach others with sensitivity and integrity.

ACCOUNTABILITY IN SERVICE

I have worked with some of my clients for years, and I know that the coaching has been valuable to them, but there have also been periods when we didn't seem to be accomplishing much. I could reassure myself by saying, "Well, So-and-So seems to be happy, so she must be getting what she needs," but while the absence of client complaints can be comforting, it's not the best indicator that good coaching is taking place. In truth, there have been times when a client and I were, each for our own reasons, just going through the motions.

Because this kind of subtle collusion can sneak into the relationship, true service requires that although we recognize that the process of change can sometimes slow to a crawl, we build a certain rigorous accountability into our agreements with our clients. Accountability means doing the following.

- Together with the client, we define the outcomes of the coaching in observable ways, and we commit ourselves to working together to achieve them.

- We specifically state that the coaching relationship can be renegotiated at any time. We ensure that the client will feel at ease to say, "This isn't working for me," or, "I think I'm done for now."

- We make the coaching process explicit and share as much about how we coach as our clients are ready for. This is part of helping them learn to coach themselves, and it supports them in being an informed client and a full coaching partner, able to make strong requests of us in support of their needs.

- We ask for feedback from our clients about how we are doing as coaches. This can be done informally, as in asking the client what's working and what isn't. It can also be done more formally with an assessment system that allows a coach to elicit specific feedback from his or her clients.[13]

- We state clearly that the end result of our coaching will be that the client no longer needs us. We accept this from the outset and make it explicit with the client.

The coach's responsibility is to weave these principles into the fabric of the coaching relationship. These are key elements of partnership, and the process of addressing them reminds us that we have placed ourselves in service to the client, and sends a strong message to the client about what we stand for and the extent to which we can be trusted.

CHAPTER SUMMARY

Service in coaching is the process of engaging with the fullest possible awareness of the client and his or her developmental opportunities. The resulting quality of being requires recognition of our own needs, agendas, and blind spots and a willingness to set them aside in service to the client.

Mindfulness is the state of being aware of our own sensations, thoughts, feelings, and judgments. As we become more self-aware, we learn to identify and acknowledge our own habits of mind and so prevent ourselves from becoming trapped by them; as we see and accept them, they tend to dissipate, giving us a clearer view of what is around us. Mindful self-awareness is the essential starting point in serving our clients well.

This heightened consciousness provides the best platform from which to coach others. It is unbiased by our own agendas. It allows us to be aware of the nuances of what the client brings. It is open, spacious, and accepting. This is what we cultivate through our own mindfulness practices.

We can cultivate mindfulness through:

- *Self-observation of our habits and tendencies,* becoming intimately familiar with how they arise, and thus able to intervene with ourselves to choose a more effective response. Self-observation is critical in building sustainable change and furthers this through a learning rather than a performance agenda.
- *Other practices* such as meditation, centering, physical and creative activities, or being in the outdoors.
- *Committing to our own learning process,* such that we are in the learning business ourselves. If we want to coach others, it is wise to be coached ourselves.
- *Building accountability with our clients* so that they are informed consumers of our services and rigorous partners able to make informed requests of us.

The Seven Voices of the Coach

We cannot live for ourselves alone. Our lives are connected by a thousand invisible threads, and along these sympathetic fibers, our actions run as causes and return to us as results.

Herman Melville

Jazz is a very democratic musical form. It comes out of a communal experience. We take our respective instruments and collectively create a thing of beauty.

Max Roach

ASEPTET IN MUSIC IS A GROUP OF SEVEN MUSICIANS playing together. The Septet in this book consists of seven integrated roles, or Voices, that we take on as we coach: the Master, the Partner, the Investigator, the Reflector, the Teacher, the Guide, and the Contractor.

In this overview chapter, I'll share the origins and purpose of the Septet framework, present a brief overview of each Voice, and offer some suggestions about what this model might mean for you in whatever venue you serve as a coach. The following seven chapters explore the separate Voices in depth.

This Septet Model is an artificial construct for helping us look at what precisely we do as coaches. Think of it as a general guide to getting from the beginning to the end of a coaching conversation.

Most important, the model represents a pragmatic set of distinctions, or differing roles, particularly relevant to the domain of coaching. Good linguistic distinctions are important because they enable us to differentiate items that are similar in many respects. For example, once we possess the distinction *vase,* we are better able to distinguish a vase from a wine glass, a water glass, or a champagne flute. In the case of coaching, the distinctions of the Voices provide both the basis and means for self-observing ourselves in action, and therefore for placing ourselves in service.

As we coach, self-observation, coupled with mindful awareness of the attachments and aversions that sometimes (often!) drive our choices of Voice, allows us to understand and organize ourselves toward what our clients really need from us. If we are mindful in using the Voices and consciously choose among them as we help others develop their own skills, our coaching will be greatly enhanced. Think of the Septet as a structure to guide your self-awareness and your ongoing inquiry into who you are as you coach.

Each Voice has its own tone and way of expressing itself—in a sense, its own musical timbre and tuning. That notion suggests a need to listen to the client's voice as well. When we're in tune with our clients, when our own conditioned patterns are set aside and we are fully present, we are able to choose the Voice that's most appropriate and most helpful at a particular time. In practice, we often shift quickly and fluidly among Voices, both shaping and responding to a dynamic, ever-changing conversational song.

Like many other forms of music, conversations involve some agreed-on structure—a basic theme or melody line—but the participants also improvise, listening to the conversation as a whole and responding to what is emerging in the moment. At various moments, one or another participant or voice steps forward to take the lead, and the same piece of music or conversation is never "played" twice in quite the same way. Improvisation, spontaneity, and an interplay among the voices in the band ensure that the music is fresh and alive, a reflection of a unique moment in time.

LEARNING THE VOICES

To switch metaphors for a moment, you could consider the Voices— roles you play as a coach—as being like the skills you learn in order to drive a car. In learning to drive, we begin with the mechanics.

We learn the pieces, one skill at a time. We learn how to start the car, how to use the accelerator and the brakes, how much of a turn of the steering wheel produces what result. Then we begin to integrate the skills, accelerating, braking, and steering as we navigate the landscape. We learn the rules of the road and what to expect from other drivers. With practice and attention, we become smoother and smoother as we drive. Soon we don't need to think about the turn signal, the windshield wipers, the transmission; we just know how to use them. It feels smooth and seamless because we've internalized the skills involved.

But driving is an activity that requires full attention, even at high levels of mastery. The best drivers are always alert; although they rarely think about the mechanics of driving, they're fully aware of what they're doing at all times. They're attentive to the performance of the car, to the road, to the changing positions of the cars around them, and they are making countless minor decisions intuitively and easily as they seek the best and safest possible course through the traffic.

Like learning to drive a car, using the Septet Model will likely seem awkward and complicated at first as you focus on one Voice at a time, seeking to understand what it means and how to use this role in your own context. You may feel self-conscious when you try a Voice that's not well practiced for you, and it can certainly feel overwhelming to think of mastering all of them.

Over time, however, you'll become more comfortable and less self-conscious. When we've practiced and done our work around each of the roles, we come to know how and when to be the Investigator, the Reflector, or the Teacher, for instance, and how to notice when we're not doing it mindfully. We learn to shift smoothly and seamlessly among the Voices. We become more fluid and less concerned about the distinctions or the roles as we learn to integrate them, sometimes playing two or three in rapid succession.

At this point, it will be important to avoid becoming overly confident, thinking, "I've mastered this." When we feel on top of our game, the temptation is to forget to be mindful. The moment we become attached to the idea that we know something, we stop learning and paying attention. Our egos are invested in being good at that thing, and we seek to present ourselves to our clients as being good at it. It is only by persisting—noticing our lapses of attention, maintaining the alertness of a beginner, and bringing attention to our areas of not knowing—that we continue to stay present and grow.

We must remember that there is always room to deepen our understanding of our own attachments, aversions, and habits of mind and that learning how to bring our full attention skillfully to our clients is a lifelong process. Continually seeing ourselves as learners is important to being truly mindful coaches.

A note to perfectionists: Learning to use this approach will be much easier if you don't take it too seriously. By this I mean that as you experiment with it, remember that it's only a construct. Be gentle with yourself as you try out new ideas. See what happens; the work here is to discover what enables you to improve your skills and effectiveness. Getting all tangled up in using a complex system perfectly will interfere with your learning process and make it much less fun. Let your curiosity and intelligence guide you, rather than holding yourself to an artificial and perhaps impossible standard for getting it quickly. Cultivate your own beginner's mind.

The Septet Model will have served its purpose when you can look back at a coaching session, see how you moved easily into each Voice as it was needed, know that you offered the fullness of yourself as expressed in all the Voices, and didn't have to think about it.

THE INDIVIDUAL ROLES OR VOICES

The idea for the Voices originated with a client who was exploring the possibility of moving into coaching as a profession. In an effort to define for himself what coaching was all about, he came up with a list of roles that a coach plays, which we spent time discussing together. The roles (and the distinctions among them) have changed considerably as I've explored them over the years. I used to call them the Seven Hats before I appreciated fully their synergistic nature and found more useful language for describing these key distinctions and how they integrate.

Still, we can also think of the Voices or roles almost as archetypes, like puppets in a Punch and Judy show, easily recognized by their hats. As the puppeteer, we select and put them up on stage as called for by the moment, and we express ourselves through the voice of each puppet at the appropriate time. As with puppet characters, we can also begin to recognize the pull or the inner feel of each Voice and its identifiable behaviors.

While the puppeteer more or less follows a script, the coach allows the conversation to be shaped according to her pedagogical expertise and awareness of the emerging needs of the client.

THE SEVEN VOICES OF THE SEPTET

- *Master:* stays self-aware, models growth and learning, remains fully present
- *Partner:* defines, negotiates, and shares responsibility for the coaching relationship with the client
- *Investigator:* finds out what the client's true needs are; gathers information about the client's situation, desired outcomes, and possible actions
- *Reflector:* provides feedback and encourages self-awareness in the client
- *Teacher:* provides distinctions, language, and knowledge new to the client
- *Guide:* provides impetus and ideas for action
- *Contractor:* encourages mutual accountability and monitors client follow-through

---

The Master

The Master is the overarching role that encompasses and supports all the others. The Master is the ground from which the others spring, the puppeteer that inhabits and animates the puppets.

A Master has done the inner work of knowing herself and developing the capacity to use her skills wisely, artfully, and effectively. These meanings of the word are central to the Septet Model of coaching, in which the Master evokes the presence and awareness of the coach—the consciousness, if you will, of the puppeteer. The Master is, more than something to do, a way to be. The Master includes the observant, conscious part of the mind that discerns what the client needs, when to shift roles in order to move with those needs, and how to stay present and as free as possible from the limitations of our own conditioning. Like the conductor of an orchestra, the Master pays attention to the whole and shapes the tempo and feeling of the music being played, even when other Voices are leading.

The Master Voice is the least directive of the six and differentiated from the others because it concerns the way of being of the coach rather than what she is actually doing. We can think of the next six Voices as operational roles that the Master can put to work; they are the "puppets." Each represents a more specific element of coaching and is identifiable by actions, behaviors, and choices of words. At times, two operational roles may be at work simultaneously, and the lines between them can blur. Nonetheless, the distinctions will be helpful in supporting our mindfulness.

The Partner

As the Partner, the coach focuses on building a win-win structure for his relationship with the client and on honoring and maintaining that structure. The Partner Voice involves the client in decisions about the course of the coaching relationship and supports the client in taking increasing responsibility for her own learning. The Partner represents the coach's commitment to the client's outcomes and takes responsibility for the maintenance of mutual trust and respect.

The Partner Voice is responsible for initial contracting; we differentiate this from the Contractor Voice, which follows and focuses on defining action steps to be taken after the coaching conversation.

The Investigator

The role of the Investigator is to ask questions. This is the Voice that many training programs for coaches emphasize, for the good reason that asking good questions is at the core of coaching. The purpose of the Investigator's questions is to support the client's deeper understanding, not to procure answers for the coach or allow the coach to formulate advice. Speaking as the Investigator, the coach challenges the client to look at the situation differently, clarify what he or she wants, and identify what can be done to bring these outcomes closer. In this role, the coach is a learning partner with the client because both learn from the questions asked.

The Reflector

I think of the Reflector and the next two Voices as operational "sharpeners" of the Investigator because each advances the coaching process by clarifying and sharpening the client's answers to the Investigator's questions. I present the three sharpeners here in increasing order of directiveness. We will see in subsequent chapters that our attachments and urges can easily drive our use of those Voices, so it is important to be mindful when we use them.

By taking the role of Reflector, the coach serves the client as a mirror, providing feedback to the client and encouraging the client to seek feedback from others as well. Speaking in this Voice, the coach promotes the client's self-awareness regarding the choices at hand and the consequences of those choices. The Reflector also encourages the client to become more self-observant and helps find ways to do this. The Reflector supports the client in discerning his real potential in a situation, and in paying close attention to the capabilities and resources he brings to the challenges of the moment.

The Teacher

The Teacher Voice is a provider of information, language, and knowledge that the client is not able to readily access himself. The Teacher provides these distinctions in order to help the client see his situation, and options within it, more clearly and expansively. The Teacher provides ways of looking at things, models, and tools for interpretation. The Teacher also challenges the client's thinking process, encouraging the questioning of assumptions and the exploration of the logic of his or her view of the situation at a deeper level. The Teacher is not the traditional role of an expert, in that the coach does not prescribe solutions.

The Guide

The Guide's function is to present alternative pathways forward and encourage the client to take action. The Guide helps a client commit to doing something practical and concrete, to creating change on the ground. At its most directive, the role of the Guide includes recommending specific courses of action.

The Contractor

The Voice of the Contractor is generally heard when the coach is wrapping up a topic or concluding a conversation. The Contractor negotiates clear and specific agreements for the client to act on, stands for accountability to action, and follows up about results in subsequent conversations. In this role, the coach is developing the client's commitment to substantive change by exploring resistance and helping to resolve doubts. The Contractor supports the client in transforming new insights into concrete actions. (Note that the initial contracting and setting up of the coaching relationship is the function of the Partner.)

THE VOICES AND THEIR ASPECTS

Each of these seven Voices, then, represents a role of the coach. In general, the Voices increase in level of directiveness, from the Master (which is really the coach's way of being) through the operational Voices, to the Contractor, which is very specific and concrete. This increasing directiveness also contains the seeds of attachments, and the potential for overuse, as we explore in subsequent chapters.

Each Voice also encompasses several more specific functions that I refer to as Aspects. The Voices and their Aspects are laid out in Exhibit 3.1.

Each of these Aspects could be further elaborated and subdivided, and the taxonomy could become quite intricate. I could list hundreds of coaching behaviors, and nearly as many ways of describing the coaching process as a whole. Think of these Voices and Aspects as a gradient of possible responses within the interaction between the coach and the client. In identifying seven Voices and a few Aspects for each, I've attempted to draw useful distinctions without parsing things so finely that the model becomes entangling.

PLACING THE VOICES IN CONTEXT

As we explore the Voices in the next seven chapters, we'll also discuss how they interact. For now, let's look at the general elements of the coaching process within which the Voices serve the client.

EXHIBIT 3.1.

The Voices and Their Aspects

↓ **Generally Increasing Directiveness** ↓	*Master*
	Maintains self-awareness
	Listens with focus and presence
	Models learning and growth
	Embraces the client with compassion and respect
	Chooses which of the operational Voices to use at a given time
	Partner
	Establishes and honors an explicit structure for the coaching relationship
	Advocates shared commitment to competency-based coaching outcomes
	Offers choice points, and makes joint decisions about the coaching process
	Investigator
	Asks questions that shift the client's understanding of the situation
	Asks the client to articulate desired outcomes
	Asks the client to generate courses of action
	Reflector
	Provides direct and honest feedback
	Directs the client's attention towards his or her capabilities and potential
	Encourages self-observation and reflection
	Teacher
	Provides new distinctions, information, and knowledge
	Challenges and stimulates the client's thinking process
	Explains the coaching process, theory, and models being used
	Guide
	Encourages the client to take some action of the client's choosing
	Offers options for action
	Recommends specific courses of action
	Contractor
	Establishes clear agreements about actions
	Explores and resolves client doubts and hesitations
	Follows up with client about agreed-on actions

Figure 3.1 is an elaboration of the Septet Model, placing the Voices spatially in relation to each other and the coaching dynamic as a whole. Recall that the Voices, and the interrelationships among them, are distinctions that allow us to observe ourselves, our clients, and the coaching process itself differently. Describing the relationships among the Voices before describing them in detail is intentional; these are the relationships that make coaching so powerful. I invite you to consider, in Chapters Four through Ten, each Voice in the larger context of the coaching conversation.

Coach and Client Live in Separate Worlds

Coaching is made possible because coach and client inhabit distinct worlds. Our world is entirely composed of what we uniquely perceive and interpret. This is determined by our particular personality, in which is embedded the cumulative total of the history, perspectives, cultural and gender conditioning, and habits of interpretation that are unique to us.

Conversely, if we were exactly like our clients in every way, we would be unable to provide anything of use. It is precisely because we have coaching expertise, different life experiences, and a view of our client from the outside (they can access only their insides!) that we can offer something of value.

We assume that both coach and client are emerging masters. In other words, each is engaged in a learning journey. Perhaps they are in different places on that journey, but each is fully committed to a path of development in service to specific commitments. This recognition animates the coaching process and encourages an attitude of compassion and mutual learning.

Creating the Coaching Space

When coach and client come together, their worlds temporarily overlap. The overlapping area, then, we can think of as the coaching space, in which coaching can happen. It doesn't mean that these two distinct worlds collapse into one; the coach and client bring their own interpretations, history, and knowledge into the conversation.

Coach and client are committed partners. Both are responsible for the establishment and maintenance of the coaching relationship.

FIGURE 3.1. *Septet Coaching Model*

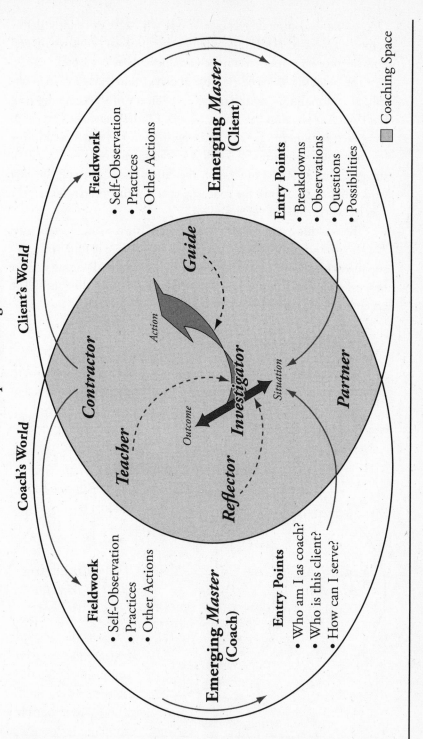

Coach's World   Client's World

Emerging *Master*
(Client)

Fieldwork
- Self-Observation
- Practices
- Other Actions

Entry Points
- Breakdowns
- Observations
- Questions
- Possibilities

Guide

Contractor

Action

Teacher

Investigator

Outcome

Situation

Reflector

Partner

Fieldwork
- Self-Observation
- Practices
- Other Actions

Emerging *Master*
(Coach)

Entry Points
- Who am I as coach?
- Who is this client?
- How can I serve?

Coaching Space

One or more contracting conversations will serve to jointly define competency-based coaching outcomes that both can commit to, and how the process can be structured to achieve these outcomes.

The coaching Voice of the Partner plays a particular role in establishing and maintaining the safety and efficacy of the coaching relationship. As I develop the Septet Model, I'll designate the Partner as the Voice responsible for maintaining it from the coach's end. The Partner both structures and serves as caretaker and a guarantor of the coaching space within which the coach and client can do their work. Figure 3.2 shows the coaching space at the intersection of the coach's world and that of the client.

The coaching space is not simply established through structure. We also extend compassion and positive regard, free of judgment; this supports the client in entering into a sometimes challenging change process with less defensiveness and with a felt sense of the coach's full acceptance and support.[1]

Establishing Creative Tension

Within the Coaching space, a lot can happen. The two people come together from their separate worlds. For an hour or a day, they

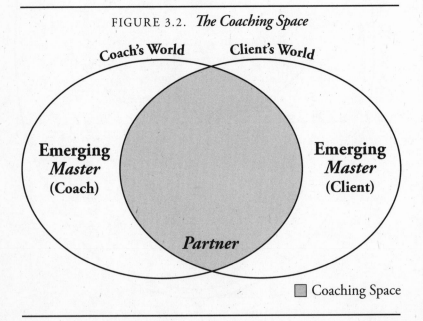

FIGURE 3.2. *The Coaching Space*

Coach's World   Client's World

Emerging *Master* **(Coach)**   **Emerging** *Master* **(Client)**

Partner

⬛ Coaching Space

join together, sharing a learning conversation as partners. This conversation is shaped primarily by the curiosity that each brings to the session and is led by questions.

At the center of the coaching inquiry is the Investigator, typically leading with a series of questions that provide a basic structure for the conversation built around three core inquiries:

- What is the situation? (Situation)
- What do you want? (Outcome)
- What will you do to make this happen? (Action)

These lines of questioning, in this general progression, evoke a new understanding of the client's situation in all its complexity, including a clear view of previously unseen possibilities for action. Given this expanded view, the client then explores what she really wants, defining outcomes in palpable, energizing terms. When a certain tension exists between the current situation and a newly defined future possibility, the client is ready to take new actions that produce learning and move her towards the outcome.

Figure 3.3 shows the central element of creative tension. The Investigator's three lines of questioning build a tension between the current situation and the preferred outcome. This tension provides the energy and motivation toward action. This is the fundamental thrust of coaching: an evocative, question-driven process through which the client newly understands her situation, defines what she wants, and takes action to produce it.

FIGURE 3.3. *The Investigator and Creative Tension*

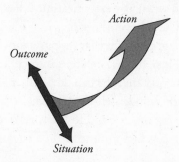

Sharpening the Questioning Process

Within the coaching space and supporting the questioning process of the Investigator, the three sharpener Voices (Reflector, Teacher, Guide) also play their parts. These Voices take "solos" as they interact with the client and with each other to provide the best possible support for the client's development.

These Voices are increasingly directive. The Reflector helps the client see herself clearly and understand both how she contributes to her current situation while discovering new levels of agency within it. The Teacher offers new distinctions and information, including about the coaching process itself, which allows the client to perceive herself and her situation in new ways. The Guide encourages action and sometimes offers concrete suggestions.

Each of the Voices comprises a distinct set of functions within the coaching process; together, they integrate to support the learning process.

Iterative Action Learning Through Fieldwork

Coaching approaches change as an ongoing developmental process. Done well, it addresses both the contextual challenges that the client faces on a daily basis and the internal landscape of the client's awareness, experience, and interpretation. The iterative process of moving from conversation, to real-life experience, to conversation, to experience allows experimentation and skill development over time. The learning venue alternates between session and the rest of life.

Development is put to test in the real world, which often pushes back, sometimes fiercely. The coach provides support, challenge, and accountability through ongoing iterations, supporting the client in substantive change when the system around her often seems to be conspiring to keep her forever the same.

The Contractor is the Voice that supports the client in translating all the energy and insight that emerges into concrete commitments (referred to as fieldwork) that she can do between coaching conversations. This fieldwork includes self-observations, practices, and actions related to the learning process and to the specific commitments that the client is being coached around. (The coach, being committed to her own learning, also engages in similar fieldwork, so that the coaching process fosters mutual learning.)

Entry Points

The client enters each subsequent conversation in a new and different place. Life having encroached on the best laid of plans, the awake learner will inevitably bring new questions, possibilities, observations, and breakdowns. This stimulates curiosity, and in the iterative process described above, the learning agenda for each coaching conversation tends to emerge from the client's experiences preceding the session.

In order to meet the client where he is, the Master is required to let go of her preconceptions and comforting assumptions that the client is a known quantity or even that his relationship with the coaching issues is the same as when they completed the previous conversation. She enters the coaching space holding three questions: Who am I? Who is this client? How can I serve? A genuine openness to these three questions allows us to place ourselves in service to what the client needs at this moment.

Integral and Sustainable Mastery

My clients tend to be successful professionals who are managing huge numbers of requests and demands. Sustainable change requires that coaching activities be designed to be realistically integrated into their busy lives.

The goal is that the client develop lifetime competencies that she can apply anywhere after coaching has ended. Coaching is most sustainable and effective when all levels of the client's development are addressed: cognitive, emotional, somatic (body based), and spiritual. Because who we fundamentally are is expressed through all of these levels of experience and because development in one area always affects the others, engaging the whole person greatly accelerates real and sustainable change.

Engaging the body through awareness, with practice over time, demonstrably produces physiological changes in the default neural patterns that underpin habits and behaviors.[2] Coaching supports the building of a new body that has the flexibility, strength, energy, and capacity to be the person described in the coaching outcomes. The practices and fieldwork put in place with the help of the Guide and Contractor greatly accelerate this.

Each of us is constantly being revealed, moment by moment, as we live our lives, including as we coach. The mindful coaching approach emphasizes that we, as well as our clients, are in a lifelong process of learning and development. As works in progress, we recognize ourselves as emerging Masters-in-the-rough, always paying attention and always becoming more of who we are.

We can think of the overall enterprise of coaching, then, as accelerating the development of mastery in both the coach and the client.

CHAPTER SUMMARY

The Septet Model is an integrated coaching model whose primary elements are the seven coaching Voices. We can think of these as roles that the coach plays at particular times in the coaching process in order to support the client's development. The distinctions among these Voices also provide the basis for coach self-observation and mindfulness.

The seven Voices of the Septet Model are, in generally increasing order of directiveness:

- *Master:* staying self-aware, modeling growth and learning, being fully present
- *Partner:* defining, negotiating, and sharing responsibility for the coaching relationship and outcomes with the client
- *Investigator:* finding out what the client's true needs are; gathering information about the client's situation, desired outcomes, and possible actions
- *Reflector:* providing feedback and encouraging self-awareness in the client
- *Teacher:* providing distinctions, language, and knowledge new to the client
- *Guide:* providing impetus and ideas for action
- *Contractor:* encouraging mutual accountability, monitoring client follow-through

Each of these Voices includes further distinctions, called Aspects; there are twenty-three in the complete model (see Exhibit 3.1).

The Voices function as an integrated whole in which one or another Voice takes the lead at particular times. The Septet Model in Figure 3.1 illustrates spatially how the Voices relate to each other and provides the context for the exploration of the Voices in the next seven chapters.

4

The Master

We can do no great things—only small things with great love. I am a little pencil in the hand of a writing God who is sending a love letter to the world.

Mother Teresa

Experience is not what happens to you; it is what you do with what happens to you.

Aldous Huxley

WE WILL BEGIN (AND WILL END) WITH THE MASTER, because she is, as I said, qualitatively different from the other Voices. This "way of being" encompasses the mindfulness and awareness that we aspire to bring to our lives; it stands behind, coordinates, and animates the other Voices we may choose to use as coaches. The Master is about being; the others, while informed by the mindfulness and presence of the Master, are more about doing. Mastery blends skill and experience with attention in the moment. The quality of being that we recognize in people we name as Masters is the same quality that describes "authentic leaders" or that we recognize in people who are said to have "leadership presence." We have seen the concept of the master glorified in media representations of athletes and artists, pop stars and poets. And, we can find mastery all around us, in mechanics and midwives, cooks and carpenters—in ourselves as well as in others. Perhaps we notice the fluidity and efficiency with which we flip burgers on the grill. Perhaps we deliver a perfect tennis serve or golf shot, or a strike in bowling. Or we prepare a dish in the kitchen, adding touches of this and that, knowing how it will all fit together.

And sometimes, as coaches, we notice that we are listening attentively and fully to our clients as they speak: we are energized and engaged and able to draw on all our skills. These are moments of mastery, and we have all had them. The role of the Master isn't about *what* we're doing; it's about *how* we're doing it. In other words, the Master is present in the moment.

We have all had experiences of being fully present and alive. It happens, for example, when we listen with rapt attention to a speaker who is fascinating and passionate, or to a piece of music that soothes or energizes us. It happens when we are moved by a beautiful sight—a waterfall, a mountain, the way moss grows on a rock—or when an unexpected event jolts us out of our routines.

Of course, we will never experience this presence of mind consistently; it is the human predicament to have conditioned habits of thinking and behavior that get in the way. Our personal work is to recognize these habits, examine them, and let them go if we determine that they are unhelpful. This is simply a matter of making choices. We also support our clients in doing this work for themselves. For both client and coach, the path toward mastery we are examining here is a path of mindfulness. My second book, *Presence-Based Coaching,* provides extensive discussion and practices for building your access to presence.[1]

Ultimately mindfulness results from the simple exercise of the willingness to be here, to be present. It's a choice, available to us all the time, to suspend our habits of mind and mental games and just be there. This is critical if we are to be fully present, creative, and resourceful in our coaching work with our clients.

Sometimes mindfulness comes easily. (Yesterday clearing my desk was a snap, and I was very present with my coaching clients.) Sometimes it feels very hard; our habits of mind grip us tightly and we have to work to overcome one resistance or another. (Monday, the clutter on my desk seemed overwhelming, and I frittered away time in unimportant tasks, feeling scattered and inept. It took real will to mobilize myself for an important client call.) Still, even in challenging moments, it comes down to a simple choice. Sometimes we feel able to easily focus and be attentive, and at other times we don't. The choice, the opportunity for mindfulness, however, is always there, right in front of us. Making that choice over and over in each moment of our lives is the first step on the way to mastery. That's the deal.

To do any kind of work well, we need to set up our surroundings to support this state of consciousness, attending to our physical comfort and reducing distractions. As I write this piece, I'm sitting at my desk in the quiet early morning. My desk is clear of the clutter that sometimes sprawls across it. The large window, facing east, has a view of the knoll opposite the house. The trees on the knoll are silhouetted against a sky that's just beginning to lighten as dawn approaches. The overhead light is off, and a small lamp shines a soft light upward in the corner of the wood-paneled room. I have a candle burning on my desk, a birthday present from my son. It is peaceful and quiet. Such surroundings are conducive to being present and self-aware.

Think again what mindfulness looks like in a coaching conversation. Being fully present means being fully engaged with the client. We are attentive, alert, energized, and relaxed. We don't have expectations for what the client should do or where the session should go, but we are open to new possibilities and new ways of seeing the client and her situation. We are engaged.

We notice when urges arise within us—an urge to convey an idea, for instance, or to make a recommendation, or to make sure that the client gets something that we deem to be important. When these urges arise, we ask ourselves about their origins. Do they arise from our own attachments and habits of mind? Are they helpful responses to the client's needs? Then we either act on these urges or let them go. It's the job of the coach to ask questions, make inferences, and share ideas with the client. The key point is that as we do so, we are not bound up in our own attachments; there's no judgment about whether we did it well or not, just a commitment to remaining constantly aware of the client and of ourselves.

ASPECTS OF THE MASTER

- Maintaining self-awareness
- Listening with focus and presence
- Modeling learning and growth
- Embracing the client with compassion and respect
- Choosing which of the operational Voices to use at a given time

Let's look now at the five specific Aspects of the Master Voice, noticing how mindfulness underlies each one.

MAINTAINING SELF-AWARENESS

Self-awareness means the capacity to observe oneself in action. This aspect operationalizes the self-observation work discussed in Chapter Two. Recall that we can artificially separate our mind into two parts. The first, the active mind, is engaged in the action of the moment—typing, cooking, walking, reading, talking with a client. The second, the observer mind, stands aside: watching, noticing, ever alert. The observer mind is like a scientist: interested, dispassionate, objective. It notices what the rest of the mind is doing, and when we heed its observations, it brings us a new perspective on what we are feeling and doing.

Once attentive to these observations, the active mind decides what to do with them. Generally if what has been observed is an unproductive habit, we will choose to discard it and bring our attention back to what we are doing. But if what has been observed is useful, we can choose to act on it. Having noticed, we are aware of choices that take us beyond our conditioned and habitual responses.

Let's look at a fictional scenario that illustrates the operation of this dual awareness in a coaching situation:

"I really need some help with this speech," the client says to the coach. He's an executive at a large utility company who's scheduled to address an industry convention in a week's time. "I need to be convincing—all the major players will be there—but I don't want to look arrogant. Brilliant but down-to-earth. Can you help me figure out how to do that?"

Yeah, right! the coach is tempted to say, with more than a hint of sarcasm. *Simple as pie.* But then her training as a professional kicks in.

"Of course," she responds, "that's my job." She feels a little flustered by her initial reaction of irritation to the client's request.

"Let's think about the audience," she continues—always a good place to begin. "Who are these major players, and why do they think you have something important to say?"

Whoa! says a voice in the coach's mind. *There was a bit of an edge in that question. And look at his face—he's not too pleased.*

"It's a group of executives," the client says more formally, with a hint of defensiveness in his voice, "getting together to discuss emerging trends in state utility regulation. They invited me, as an expert, to talk about the strategies that have served this company so well under my leadership."

So much for humble! the coach thinks to herself. But then a different inner voice engages her in a dialogue with the one that just spoke up:

A little judgmental there, aren't we, coach? Might want to watch that.

But he IS arrogant.

So?

Arrogant people irritate me.

And how does that help you do your job?

Well, actually, not at all in this case. I guess I need to let it go.

It takes a few more moments, but having made that decision, the coach is able to get herself back on track and help her client focus on the issues of concern to him.

"So tell me," she says, with new interest in the topic. "What's your message? What do *you* think about the new regulations? Let's talk about what you think needs to be done."

In the thoughts or inner voices above, I doubt that you as a reader had any trouble distinguishing the active mind that reacts personally and immediately from the observer mind that stands apart and represents a more objective view.

Being self-aware means being attentive to both, but this puts us in a delicate position. It's all too easy to move to a place of self-judgment as we begin to see how easily and constantly our own opinions and judgments of others arise. "There's no way I can catch all of that stuff," you may well lament. "And, how can I act at all—do my clients any good—if I'm always second-guessing myself?" It can all seem a bit overwhelming.

We need to redefine some terms here. In the realm of self-awareness, success doesn't mean being perfectly attentive or being free of feelings and attachments that arise in the course of coaching (or any other activity, for that matter). It does mean committing ourselves in an ongoing manner to paying attention to what's going on inside ourselves—what we're feeling, our judgments, our attachments and aversions, our distractions. Each time our ability to notice these things increases, we are, by definition, succeeding in becoming more mindful and observant.

We are conditioned beings. Every small moment of self-awareness, of noticing a judgment or an urge or an attachment or an aversion, is a small awakening. The goal, and the only measure of success, is our commitment to doing this work, to paying attention.

LISTENING WITH FOCUS AND PRESENCE

"Listening with focus and presence" means that the coach, whether in person or by phone, or even by e-mail if that's what the circumstances allow, is present in the moment—as fully attentive to the client as he can be, listening carefully to what she has to say, and keeping the conversation open.

Darya Funches describes the requirements of this kind of presence:

> We cannot be present . . . when we are preoccupied with how we are being seen or experienced, or with determining the "right thing to do." We can be present only when we are in touch with our feelings, thoughts, and intuitions in the moment. The gift of presence gives [coaches] access to an area of "creative indifference," enabling them to work with clients without predetermining how things should be and what they should do.[2]

For clients, our engaged focus and presence as listeners—our interest, acceptance, and confidence—is evocative. It creates a context within which a client can find her own footing and move to a new awareness about the specific situation under discussion. It creates a sense of safety and possibility. In *Co-Active Coaching*, Laura Whitworth, Henry Kimsey-House, and Phil Sandhal describe this type of presence in coaching as the promotion of "spaciousness":

> Spaciousness . . . means complete detachment from any particular course of action or any results that the client achieves. The coach continues to care about the client, the client's agenda, the client's health and growth, but not the road the client takes to get there, the speed of travel, or the detours that might take place in the meantime—so long as the client continues to move toward the results the client wants. . . . The spaciousness of the relationship requires that the coach must not be attached to whether clients take suggestions, or, if

they do, whether they do it "right" or "wrong." Either way the client is right. It is a paradox that the coach often expects more of clients than they dare dream for themselves, and yet clients are unconditionally supported whatever they do. That is the breadth of the spaciousness in the relationship.[3]

Presence in this sense is experienced by others as a "deep listening," which James Flaherty describes as "not merely the engagement of the ear and the auditory nerve [but] a full engagement of the attention, thought, and intention of the coach in the conversation."[4]

Whitworth, Kimsey-House, and Sandhal describe in *Co-Active Coaching* three levels of listening, and their framework is relevant to this Aspect of the coach in the role of Master. In Level I listening, they explain, "our attention is on ourselves. We listen to the words of the other person but the focus is on what it means to us." We've already looked about how our own tendencies to be self-centered hinder our ability to serve our clients. In Level II listening, "there is a sharp focus on the other person . . . a great deal of attention on the other person and not much awareness of the outside world." Such an excessive focus on the client's every word and desire on a superficial level is also too narrow, since it impedes our ability to be mindful of other sources of information. Level III listening, however, expands our awareness to include information from all sources.[5] At this highest level, listening includes everything that our senses experience, as well as emotions, thoughts, the environment, and the context in which the coaching is taking place. This is the essence of mindfulness.

This level of openness, of listening coupled with acceptance and support, is what we call presence. Presence is beyond the skill of listening and is what allows real listening to take place.

MODELING LEARNING AND GROWTH

The third Aspect of the Master concerns the way we lead our lives. As coaches, we earn the right to work with our clients by acquiring knowledge of both our specific areas of expertise and the larger territory of learning and change. Our exhortations to our clients to "create the life you want" will sound hollow and hypocritical if we have not sought to do the same. It's not that we must demonstrate mastery in everything that we touch. It's that we must be fully engaged in our own pursuit of mastery. In so doing, we model for our clients a way of living life fully.

Darya Funches describes the cultivation of presence as becoming "the embodiment of your message about learning and change." We experiment on ourselves, using the rich opportunities with which life presents us as a practice field for learning and growth:

> *The gift of presence requires change practitioners to become more "whole" in the work they do. Although they must recognize the appropriate role to fill in relation to the client, they must also integrate themselves as whole beings into that role. If that role is considered substantially different from one's own personal identity and experience, work becomes a form of personal death, as opposed to an experience of growth and vitality.*[6]

This speaks to the essential nature of integrating our entire life experience into the work that we do. Our effectiveness as coaches does not result from an academic understanding of learning and change. It requires knowing what growth and change feel like from the inside—knowing how to be successful in our endeavors *and* being familiar with the ways in which we (and presumably others) undermine ourselves and sell ourselves short.

In the end, it's our own life experience that enables us to:

- Understand, empathize, and offer insight into what our clients are going through
- Help our clients see their challenges and obstacles in a larger, safer, context
- Express confidence in our clients, grounded in our own experience of having faced similar challenges
- Provide a model to our clients as people who have experienced both success and failure and maintain a robust faith in possibility and change

While we will share our own personal experience with clients only with discretion, that experience is always there, in the background. I believe that my own encounters with both success and disappointment—and my willingness to reflect on each—have made me a better coach.

A number of years ago, I decided to finally fulfill my long-deferred desire to become a musician. In a moment of inspiration, I sat with my wife and a close friend, and we each created a plan for something major we wanted to accomplish in our lives, promising to support each other in those endeavors. Mine was to take up the saxophone. As a frequent dabbler, I knew my own tendency was to jump into something new and exciting, feel that it was going to change my life, and then slowly watch my commitment erode as the novelty wore off. I knew that for me, the challenges would be to not get attached to my rate of progress and to stay with it.

All went well for a while. I bought a horn, found a teacher, and started playing. It was fun, and soon I could play the themes of a few old jazz standards. Of course, I had music in my head that my fingers couldn't come close to playing, and it felt frustrating at times, but I could also see progress. I was excited that I was staying with it, and I felt I was stepping into a vision of myself as a more artistic, expressive person.

Then my wife and I bought sixty-three acres of land and a house north of town and decided to open a retreat center. The process of transforming a barn into an inspiring meeting place was tremendously consuming of both time and energy. Soon the saxophone lessons became harder to schedule, and I stopped finding the time to practice. Launching the retreat center had assumed more importance as the central dream in our lives; making music went on the back burner as a latent ambition.

While playing a musical instrument is something I will come back to in the future, I learned much from this whole experience that makes me a better coach. For example, I know what it is to move through long-held blocks and fears to start something new and to experience the huge release of energy that results from making a commitment to something long resisted. I know the struggle to cultivate the discipline of practice. I know both what it's like to set goals and achieve them and what it's like to set goals and watch my own commitment erode in the face of competing priorities.

These dynamics are part of the reality of change. Coaches who blithely say that you can accomplish anything that you set your mind to may be speaking their belief. But that kind of statement doesn't acknowledge the struggle, the fear, and the starts and stops that often accompany significant change. Being able to relate to these struggles and being grounded in our own experiences of success and failure make us more compassionate and more knowledgeable when we coach others through their own experiences. If we wish to provide authentic service, we need to own a working knowledge of the kind of territory they are crossing. This means that we experiment with ourselves—we try new things and are open to change. Our own life is the practice field for what we bring to the coaching relationship. We can support our clients authentically to the extent that we learn how to do this ourselves.

Obviously we don't live our lives this way solely to be more credible as coaches. We do so because experimentation, self-awareness, and a willingness to change are part and parcel of living life fully. In seeking a purposeful, empowered, and meaningful way of living, we come to better understand what it means to be self-generative. And this cannot fail to help our clients.

EMBRACING THE CLIENT WITH COMPASSION AND RESPECT

Compassion and respect for the client are central to the coaching process. Pema Chödrön writes:

> When we talk of compassion, we usually mean working with those less fortunate than ourselves. However, in . . . trying to help others, we might come to realize that compassionate action involves working with ourselves as much as working with others. . . . Only in an open, nonjudgmental space where we're not all caught up in our own version of reality can we see and hear and feel who others really are, which allows us to be with them and communicate with them properly. . . . To the degree that we have compassion for ourselves, we will also have compassion for others. Having compassion starts and ends with having compassion for all those unwanted parts of ourselves, all those imperfections that we don't even want to look at.[7]

Being compassionate, then, is a way of seeing that begins with an acceptance of self, with all our warts and weaknesses. When we cultivate this in ourselves, we are able to extend it to our clients and others with whom we have relationships. To the extent that we judge and think negative thoughts about ourselves, we are likely to fall into the same traps with others. And we must guard against that. But having compassion does not equate to a soft-hearted, mushy, feel-sorry-for-those-less-fortunate-than-ourselves mantra. It's a clear practice, a stance that requires toughness and rigor.

Here's an example from my own experience. Years ago I was involved in a guided group led by Nancy Spence. I was committed to the group, which met for five hours monthly, but it was a busy time for me professionally, with a lot of travel. We would meet to do our work together and Nancy would give us "homework" assignments, usually drawing from a text with which we were working. All too often I would be lax about doing the homework. In part I was resisting the content, and in part I was simply too busy to devote sufficient attention to it. I would come to the class, which I enjoyed and found valuable, with a certain amount of guilt. I sometimes felt as if I hadn't earned the right to be present in the group.

Nancy, however, was not judgmental in the least. She was just as warm and welcoming toward me as she was toward anyone else. Her total acceptance and appreciation made it clear to all of us that any judgments and critiques about our "performance" came from within ourselves. It was, in fact, my own standards and lack of acceptance of where I was that caused me the anxiety about my inadequate preparation. Her neutrality, or creative indifference—her presence as a listener—allowed me to see myself more clearly and to see what I had to work on.

That's the essence of being present as a listener. Our full attention is available for our clients, no matter what they are going through. Our support and acceptance do not waver. In not reacting to their "stuff" and not projecting our own, we ensure that our interactions become a neutral and safe place in which our clients can see, and do, their own work.

As James Flaherty points out, "Many times the limitation on our respect for someone is not so much in what they're doing as it is in the imposition of our values on what they're doing."[8] We must be able to separate two very different things: the workings of our own minds versus what is real and true about the client. This requires sufficient self-awareness to know what our own values and judgments are, notice when they show up, and decide whether they are relevant.

To reach the level of respect we need to have in order to work with someone, it will be helpful to look closely at the choices he has made in the past and the context in which these choices were made. The context includes both the external circumstances within which the client operated and his conditioning and belief systems. Most often, this kind of understanding makes it much easier to find a place of compassion and respect from which to operate.

Maintaining an expanded view enables the coach to be accepting and supportive of a client even in the face of significant difficulties and distress. It also is enormously helpful in assisting that client to move to a more self-accepting, empowered view of her situation.

Treating a client with compassion and respect does not mean that the coach needs to accept or agree with everything that the client says, does, or thinks. That would make for a relationship in which the coach would have nothing to offer and no progress would ever be made. And we shouldn't forget that the client has every right to ask us about our own values and beliefs. Respect is not automatically conveyed; it is developed jointly. The coach and client must have sufficient mutual respect around the content areas in which coaching is occurring to enable them to work together.

However, even when we understand this fuller picture, sometimes it is impossible to respect choices made by the client that seem self-destructive or even unethical. If the client's beliefs or behaviors are such that the coach can't find this place of respect, then the coach should end the coaching relationship, or not enter into it in the first place.

CHOOSING WHICH OF THE OPERATIONAL VOICES TO USE AT A GIVEN TIME

The last major Aspect of the coach's work as Master is being responsive and flexible as the needs of the client change. It is as the Master that the coach coordinates the Voices, moving among them as necessary.

Here's an example from my own practice. I was coaching Jack, the executive director of a health care organization of two hundred people. Jack was dealing with a critical boss, who had made a lot of negative statements about the organization's recent performance and apparently didn't trust the data and clarifications that Jack provided.

Jack and I were talking about the boss's demands and how to best respond to them.

As I asked about the situation, the level of emotion rose in Jack's voice. My observer self noticed his reactions, my own discomfort with questioning further, and my intuition that there was a significant emotional component to his reactions. As Master I shifted gears, and took a moment with Jack for us to acknowledge the level of stress he was under. It became clear that the situation was very difficult for him, and he wasn't dealing with it well. He had gotten very angry with his boss the previous week and, it turned out, had erupted in other situations with other people as well. To me it seemed clear that his difficulty handling the boss was only a symptom of a deeper stress that was disrupting his usual steady demeanor.

We needed to look at what Jack could do to take better care of himself and dissipate some of the stress that he was carrying in his body that was emerging in unhelpful ways. This required light-footed shifting from the Investigator role to Reflector and Guide. Had I been attached to my line of questioning about a different way to work with the boss, I would have missed the opportunity presented by my intuition of an underlying pattern. Once we had dealt with how Jack could dissipate the stress, he felt more empowered over his own responses, and we could move back into a discussion of strategies for dealing with his boss.

A coach who can't be flexible in this way may develop internal friction as a result of the conflict between two of her parts—two Voices—arguing, as it were, over which way to go. Friction may also arise out of holding to one agenda for the outcome of a session while the client goes in a different direction. We can experience this friction as tension or confusion; at its root are our own attachments, which are pulling us in different directions. Staying alert and self-aware—the first Aspect of the Master—is the key to overcoming internal friction.

The Master, then, maintains a watchful eye over the coaching conversation. The Master is constantly assessing the needs of the client and making conscious choices between different roles and ways of being with a client. It is the Master who chooses which of the operational Voices is most helpful and appropriate at any given time, based on a clear view of the client. Where does a person get the flexibility and ease to do this? She gets them from the coaching process and the acceptance and mindfulness that are part and parcel of the Master's practice.

We can think of the Master as the puppeteer and the operational Voices as puppets.

THE MINDFUL MASTER

The mindful coach enters each conversation curious, present, and open to learning. It is extraordinarily helpful to keep in the background three key questions that keep us fresh and attentive: Who is this client? Who am I as coach? How can I serve?

The coach's curiosity about these questions parallels the client's openness to new possibilities. The first question requires being open to seeing the client in a fresh way each time. It counters the reassuring tendency to think of our client's personality and patterns as fixed, requiring instead that we be flexible and responsive. And it requires us to let go of the falsely reassuring notion that we know our client, or that the client is predictable and knowable, or even that who he will be while entering this conversation can be extrapolated from who he was at the end of our previous conversation. Stripped of these, we have no choice but to be curious about who he is right now.

The second question does the same with regard to the coach's inner life as a professional. It requires us to pay attention to ourselves, to what is arising, to what we can offer to the relationship, to our mood and our biases and our state of presence. The third question reminds us that we have placed ourselves in service to the client, that the ways in which we can perform this service are many, and that it's our responsibility to choose which of these is most useful at a given time.

For the coach, then, mastery requires setting aside the comfort of thinking that we know what to do and have an easy formula for providing what the client needs. It requires a willingness to be influenced in the moment, to be taught by both the client and the work that we do together. This stance serves both the coach's learning and the client's. The three questions impel us toward mastery and remind us that coaching requires us to be engaged in our own ongoing work.

I have been asked a number of times if the Master role can be overused. Unlike the six other Voices, which are situationally appropriate, the Master is omnipresent. The Master's practice is to notice the attachments and aversions that arise in the course of the coaching conversation. This means that the coach pays attention to herself, notices if she is interacting with the client in a way that isn't helpful, and possibly modifies what she's doing.

As we shall see with each of the other Voices, there are pitfalls to be aware of. At times the presence the Master cultivates can come across as intensity beyond what the client needs or desires. If this happens, the client, naturally enough, can become resistant. The coach's responsibility is to pay attention to the client and notice this resistance. If the Master is present and mindful, she will notice this dissonance and adjust her behavior to bring her level of intensity back to what the client is ready for.

As with any other Voice, there's a danger that a coach will become attached to seeing himself as masterful, or to being seen by others as present and mindful. To fish unconsciously for comments like, "You're such a good listener!" or "You're so wise and present," or "I feel so safe with you," or "You're a real inspiration to me," is to pursue your own needs, not those of the client. It's fine if such compliments come. What's not fine is to finesse the way you present yourself in order to increase the likelihood that they will.

Here are ways to guard against the pitfalls of the Master Voice:

- See the cultivation of your own mindfulness as a lifelong practice. Recognize that you will never perfect it, and be compassionate with yourself when you notice your attachments and aversions. Being forgiving and accepting of your own conditioning is a necessary step toward helping your clients pursue mindfulness.

- Remember that noticing your distractions *is* success. If you find yourself absent-mindedly looking out the window as your client tells you about the emotional trauma he experienced the other day, don't focus on your "failure"; noticing and returning to the present means you are succeeding in increasing your ability to stay mindful and aware. Accepting, not judging, your deviations from mindfulness and then moving on reduces the internal friction that can impede your practice.

- Practice deep listening and being fully present with your clients. Find ways to prepare yourself before a session, and ways to remind yourself to stay present during the conversation itself.

- Recognize that your entire life is an opportunity to practice mastery, and that as you learn and grow, you become familiar with the territory of growth. All this is background and context for the coaching you provide for others; it earns you the right to work with your clients.

- Find ways to view your clients that encourage your own respect and acceptance of them. We cultivate compassion and respect when we seek to understand the behaviors and actions of our client in context and without judgment. If you are not able to find a way of viewing a client that allows you to respect him, you probably shouldn't be working with that client.

- Practice shifting flexibly and easily between Voices. Notice your own internal friction or tension as it arises. Generally this is a sign of an attachment, which makes it less easy to be fluid in responding to changing needs.

The Master begins with self-awareness and self-cultivation. Engaging in some sort of committed mindfulness practice, such as sitting (Practice 2.1) or centering (Practice 2.2) is important to build the foundation of presence required for everything that follows.

In addition, as we all pursue our ongoing development as Masters, we consistently engage with new questions, allowing our curiosity to lead us in exploring who we are and how we can contribute in the conversations and relationships that matter most to us. Exercises 4.1 and 4.2 exemplify the two-part process of identifying a learning opportunity and designing a learning process to address it. This requires some discipline, yet is at the core of self-development.

EXERCISE 4.1.
Cultivating the Master

Take some time to respond to the following questions:

- What Aspects of the Master do you consistently embody?
- Around which Aspects do you have attachments and identity? How do you know?
- Around which Aspects do you have discomfort or sense incongruence? How do you know?

EXERCISE 4.2.
Mastering Self-Observation

Based on your answers in Exercise 4.1, choose an Aspect of the Master that illuminates a development opportunity for you. This might be a way of being in your coaching conversations where you feel less authentic or mindful than you would like, or perhaps a place in your life where you recognize that you are out of alignment with how you would prefer to be.

Design one or two small and realistic action steps for yourself that represent learning steps or experiments in relation to this Aspect. Schedule each within the next week or two. When you have completed each, celebrate.

Translating curiosity and a rigorous commitment to development into learning structures supports the Master, everything that follows in this book, and coaching itself.

Each Voice chapter contains several exercises. In the subsequent chapters on the operational Voices, one or two of these exercises will specifically invite you to apply the competencies of that Voice to your own learning process as a reader of *The Mindful Coach*. The other exercises in each chapter will be almost identical in structure to these two, asking you first to self-assess, using the Aspects of that Voice as a guide, and then to design a self-observation for yourself around the results of your self-assessment.

Working with these exercises, given a modicum of diligence, will both move you more deeply into mindfulness and awareness around your use of the Voices and provide invaluable experience in using the all-important mindful coaching tool of self-observations before you do so with your own clients; this is part and parcel of your own journey to mastery.

CHAPTER SUMMARY

The Master provides the ground on which we stand as coaches. It's as the Master that the coach observes what is going on inside herself and with the client; it's the Master (puppeteer) who chooses the appropriate Voice (puppet) for each moment in the coaching process. The Master is the element of *being* that expresses itself through the operational Voices that are *doing*.

In support of the client, the Master embodies these five Aspects:

- *Maintains self-awareness,* bringing a rigorous self-observation and awareness to the coaching conversation, noticing attachments and distractions that arise, and letting go of what doesn't serve the client
- *Listens with focus and presence,* extending presence to the client, listening deeply to what the client is expressing, and recognizing that the quality of her attention is as important as what she does or says
- *Models learning and growth* with a lifelong commitment to self-development and integrates her own life experiences and self-awareness into coaching
- *Embraces the client with compassion and respect,* based on positive regard and acceptance, in order to create a supportive coaching space
- *Chooses which of the operational Voices to use at a given time,* making decisions mindfully on how to most usefully serve the client at any given moment

The Master brings the mindfulness that animates the entire coaching process and places us in authentic relationship with our clients as coexplorers. This is where coaching begins and ends.

The Partner

If you have come to help me, you are wasting your time. But if you have come because your liberation is bound up with mine, then let us work together.

Lila Watson, as spokesperson for a group of aboriginal activists

Each friend represents a world in us, a world possibly not born until they arrive, and it is only by this meeting that a new world is born.

Anaïs Nin

LEADERSHIP—WHETHER AT THE HELM OF A SHIP, AN organization, or one's own navigation through life—can be lonely. Ultimately, we are solely responsible for the choices we make in response to what life offers us. Yet as leaders we can learn to lean into our relationships with others. We can find people who can be our sounding boards, trusting them to reveal new perspectives and support us in accessing our own wisdom and best judgment. This makes the inherently lonely process of leading much less so.

Coaching provides such a relationship. The Partner is the specific Voice through which the coach comes to stand by the side of the client and works closely together in establishing a productive relationship. Recall from Figure 3.1 that the coaching space is the center section, the intersection between the worlds of coach and client, representing where the lives of the two individuals overlap. This is the container or arena within which useful work can happen.

The coaching space is maintained in part through the state of presence, compassion, acceptance, and respect that the Master holds with and for the client. Other explicit functions and elements of conversation are also crucial to establishing and maintaining this space. These are the responsibility of the Partner.

The Partner is particularly important at the outset, for the structural elements of the coaching relationship must be established early and are critical for the client to enter fully into the coaching process. It's the Partner who speaks most often in the beginning, when the initial agreements that guide the work are formed. The framework of these agreements is the structural basis for the relationship. Some of the agreements—regarding schedules, format, and outcomes, for example—are developed within the relationship. Others—about professional ethics, for example—are brought in from the outside. In either case, it's the coach speaking as Partner who makes them explicit; this Voice also comes forward if the agreements need to be revisited. Collectively, this work is called *contracting,* although we differentiate this initial contracting work (the function of the Partner) from the content-related work of defining and building accountability for action steps between coaching conversations (the function of the Contractor.)

By consistently following through on agreements, the coach demonstrates commitment to the client. Coaching invariably involves encouraging the client to stretch and try new behaviors, and the coach's commitment is one of the ways that allows the client to feel safe enough to do so. The Partner recognizes this and consistently seeks to reinforce it.

It's the Partner Voice that the coach uses to make the coaching process explicit and share responsibility with the client for guiding the process and direction of the coaching, thus supporting the client's competence at being a client, and ultimately his ability to coach himself. The Partner Voice continues through the course of the relationship as the coach focuses on the maintenance of appropriate and helpful ways of engaging.

Thus, the Partner represents those Aspects of coaching that involve both the practicalities of the relationship and its maintenance. It's as the Partner that the coach develops outcomes that both can commit to, keeps the relationship clear and its boundaries explicit, addresses any confusion or misunderstandings that arise about fees or the involvement of third parties, and puts issues on the table with the client in order to reach a new understanding. When we are mindful as Partner, the client experiences the coaching relationship as safe, welcoming, and solid, even when she may waver or at times feel anxious or overwhelmed.

ASPECTS OF THE PARTNER

- Establishing and honoring an explicit structure for the coaching relationship
- Advocating shared commitment to competency-based coaching outcomes
- Offering choice points and making joint decisions about the coaching process

---

ESTABLISHING AND HONORING AN EXPLICIT STRUCTURE FOR THE COACHING RELATIONSHIP

Being clear about the goals of coaching and about how to work together is the first step in establishing the partnership between coach and client. These understandings may change later, by agreement of both people involved.

Some coaches feel comfortable simply discussing the details of this partnership with the client until both are clear about them and feel no need to put them down on paper. Others prefer to spell them out in a letter of understanding or formal contract. If a third party is involved, certain parts of the agreement may be dictated by that party (by company policy, for example, or the client intake protocol of a social services agency).

Generally the partnership agreement, arrived at after one or more conversations between the coach and the client, answers the following questions:

- How often and by what means (face to face, by phone, by e-mail, or by other means) will we meet?
- How long will our coaching sessions last?
- For how long are we committing to this structure?

- What assessments, intake processes, and other initial data gathering will best serve the client's goals?

- Who else, if anyone, is involved? When a third party is a stakeholder in the coaching relationship, it's important to identify how that party will be involved and discuss where the boundaries of confidentiality lie.

- What will a coaching session consist of, and what is each person committed to doing in preparation?

- For a relationship where fees are set by agreement between the client and the coach: What will the fees be, and how will they be paid? What happens if either party needs to reschedule or doesn't show up for an appointment?

- What are the outcomes for coaching, how will success be measured, and how will the coach and the client know that it's time to end their partnership?

Answering this last question is particularly important and is the function of the second Aspect of the Partner (advocating shared commitment to competency-based coaching outcomes). The outcomes or goals for coaching are what animates the entire process.

Several imagined dialogues illustrate how to establish and honor an explicit structure. Here we'll refer to the coach as the Partner, since that's the primary Voice he or she is using. In the first dialogue, a coach is talking to a prospective private client.

CLIENT: So what would this arrangement look like?

PARTNER: Well, since you're three hours away, I'd say we'd have to do most of our work by phone. But we might want to meet in person every so often, say, for a morning or an afternoon. I've always found that works better if we want to look at something in more depth, or if there's something complicated you want me to help with.

CLIENT: That makes sense. But I'm not ready to have you come into the office and meet my people. In fact, I'm not entirely sure I want to be coached at all.

PARTNER: I don't blame you. This is our first conversation. I often work with clients I've never met in person. It can work that way.

It's up to you. I just wanted to let you know what's possible. *The coach is making it clear that arrangements are flexible and responsive to the client's needs.*

CLIENT: I'm open to getting together at some point, but first I need to know more about what I'm getting into.

PARTNER: I'd want the same thing. The first thing about coaching is that you're in charge of where we go with it. Let's take a few minutes for me to tell you a little more about coaching and for you to tell me what it is you want to work on. Then if you decide to try it out, we'll talk on the phone once a week for an hour. Once you know me better and you start seeing results, you can decide if that's enough or if you want us to try other approaches. Does that work for you? *The coach is putting the client at choice.*

CLIENT: Yes, that seems fine. Let me tell you about the situation I'm facing, and then you can tell me how you'd work with me if I decide to hire you. Okay?

In this dialogue, the "client" isn't actually a client yet. She's considering trying out coaching but isn't fully convinced. The coach is beginning to establish the safety on which the relationship would rest by acknowledging her concerns and telling her that she's in charge of where it goes. The coach's aim is to give the client the room she needs to explore what coaching might look like and how it could serve her. Implied in this conversation are ongoing agreements about who is in charge.

Now let's look at a situation in which an earlier agreement needs to be revisited. Since significant trust issues are involved, it's important that she and the client (a sales director we're calling Claire) talk changes through together. In this scenario, the client's boss (we're calling him Rob) has a close and longstanding relationship with the coach. In fact, it was Rob who suggested that she work with Claire, and Rob is paying the bill.

PARTNER: I was in the office the other day, and Rob asked me how we were doing with the coaching.

CLIENT: Oh? And what did you tell him?

PARTNER: I said I was enjoying it. He wanted me to say more, but I reminded him that what you and I talk about is just between us and he'd have to judge the results for himself. But he knows that's the deal. *The coach reiterates the confidentiality commitment.*

CLIENT: I was hoping that he'd seen that things are going better with the manufacturing people. That he'd notice I've been working pretty hard at it and that not all the problems we've been having are my fault.

PARTNER: I don't know what he's noticed. I do need to say again that my relationship with Rob gives us a potential conflict of interest. That's why I wanted the three of us to talk before we began—to get us all on the same page about confidentiality and what you and I are doing. If you ever have questions or doubts about that, let's talk, okay?

CLIENT: Sure. I trust you on that.

COACH AS GUIDE: Thanks. (pauses) You know, Claire, I think it might be a good idea to get together with Rob again—the three of us. He obviously wants some reassurance about how you're doing. He can't get it from me. What if you take the lead here and ask for a meeting? I can give you some support if you want to ask him if he sees any progress in the last few weeks. *The coach, speaking in the Guide Voice, is proposing a change in the way they are coordinating the coaching, but Claire is clearly in charge.*

CLIENT: What would I tell him about the purpose of the meeting?

COACH AS GUIDE: You could say that you want to fill him in on what you've been doing.

CLIENT: What would you say if he asks you what you think about how I'm doing—with the coaching?

PARTNER: Well. Getting specific about anything you and I have been working on would mean changing our understanding about confidentiality, but it might be useful here. I can share whatever you and I agree will be helpful. I can be as vocal or as tight-lipped as you want. I can say that you've worked very hard to bridge a gap with a couple of people you don't particularly like or respect. I know it's important to you that your boss sees that. I'm willing to play whatever role you want me to, but you should take the lead. *The coach, as Partner, is placing herself in service to Claire by offering to play whatever role is most helpful.*

CLIENT: Okay. (pauses) That all makes sense. But how I can approach this without it seeming just self-serving?

PARTNER: Well, first of all, it's not all bad to be self-serving. I think you'd be showing Rob that you're addressing what he wants you to address. I think you're being proactive and accountable by letting him know what you've already done to try to solve the problems he's worried about.

CLIENT: Yeah, thanks for that. I think you're right.

COACH AS INVESTIGATOR: And what can you ask Rob to do for you? *Note the question, in the Investigator Voice.*

CLIENT: Ah! Now that you mention it, I've been wanting to ask him for his support on the supply chain project we talked about last week. Hey! I think that's the pitch in the meeting with Rob. I want to update him and ask for his support.

PARTNER: Great idea! That's perfect: progress report plus you're asking him for something. That's good because it gives him an opportunity to demonstrate his commitment to you. Now let's get clear about what you're giving me permission to talk about— or not. *The Partner wants a clear understanding before going into a possible meeting with Rob; this is part of the structure that supports the coaching space.*

Notice that in this dialogue, the client and coach are working from an existing agreement about confidentiality. The coach, speaking mainly in the Partner Voice, uses her encounter with Rob to bring potential conflict-of-interest issues to the fore in such a way that the client is alerted to an opportunity to be proactive on her own behalf. At the same time, the coach is acting ethically and maintaining the integrity of both her primary relationship with the client and her obligations to a third party to whom she has some loyalty and who is paying the bills.

Transparency and clear communication are the keys here. Both the coaching partnership and the coach's relationship with the third party are strengthened by reaffirming their agreements, by the coach's clear commitment to both of them, and by the importance placed on being explicit about priorities and expectations in a potentially sticky situation.

Note, too, that the coach occasionally uses other Voices. I will parse alternative Voices as they appear in the dialogues that follow. While each dialogue primarily illustrates one particular Voice, it's instructive to see that the process is in fact rather loose and fluid.

As the next dialogue shows, mutuality is a third key to keeping the structure of the coaching relationship in good repair. Here the Partner is taking care of the agreed-on structure for the coaching space.

CLIENT: I'm so sorry I missed our call the other day. I had an emergency meeting that came up at the last minute.

PARTNER: I understand. It happens. No problem here. You understand, of course, that I intend to bill you. *The coach maintains accountability by reiterating prior agreement.*

CLIENT: Yes, I understand. I'm sorry. I would have let you know, but it came up at the last minute.

PARTNER: Just to be clear—if you need to reschedule, as long as you let me know *before* our appointment, I'm happy to reschedule without charging you. But if I don't hear from you, it means that I'm here reviewing notes, thinking about you, and sitting at the phone waiting for your call. And not doing other things. I know you understand.

CLIENT: Yes, of course. Thanks for going over it again.

PARTNER: No problem; we're both accountable to each other. *Short pause, then switches to Investigator.* So what's important to address today?

Here the coach hasn't just gone over his cancellation policy with the client; he's also reminded the client of the mutuality of commitment in place in their relationship. Agreements must be structured to take care of both parties' needs.

ADVOCATING SHARED COMMITMENT TO COMPETENCY-BASED COACHING OUTCOMES

When I began coaching many years ago, it was a relatively new field, and a fairly standard arrangement was to charge a certain fee per month for a certain amount of contact time. There were no overall time frames for the duration of the coaching process, and no specific outcomes were defined. While many corporate coaching engagements had more accountability than this implies, that was (and still is, in some circles) a common arrangement.

This approach poses two major problems. First, not having a specified duration for coaching means that it is up to the client to essentially "fire" someone she has come to trust and rely on. This puts in place a problematic mutual dependency, where the coach is unlikely to declare the engagement complete and the client might understandably find it difficult to do so. When the coach's incentive is to keep the client and extend the work, this can subvert the coach's commitment to long-term self-generation (read: independence) in the client.

Second, the lack of clearly delineated outcomes makes it incumbent on the client to determine success. There are no objective criteria for assessing success or toward which to organize the coaching effort. Without this, it is much easier for the course of the coaching process to be shaped by the coach's expertise and standard coaching model rather than to be driven by what the client actually wants.

I now contract for a set initial period of time for coaching, usually six months to a year in duration. An early step in the process, led by the Partner Voice, is to jointly develop a concise set of outcomes to which we can both make a firm commitment. It is important that these outcomes be specific and observable, realistic to achieve in the duration of the engagement, motivating and energizing for the client, and within the coach's competency to coach toward.

The outcomes are competency based rather than performance based. This focuses the coaching more usefully on building skills and capabilities that the client will have for a lifetime rather than on specific results that are short term and subject to many influences outside the client's control.

Once agreed on, coaching outcomes serve as the end point of an emerging curriculum. While things will assuredly happen in the client's life that couldn't have been anticipated at the outset, and these things will provide raw material for the coaching conversation, the outcomes provide both directionality and accountability for the conversation. Joint commitment to explicit outcomes provides accountability as both people enter the process knowing that they need to get results within a specified period of time. I have found that this arrangement greatly energizes the coaching partnership.

Here's an imaginary dialogue in which the coach and client are working together to define an outcome in concrete terms. This may or may not be the first major discussion in the coaching relationship, but it most certainly must happen before coaching begins in earnest.

PARTNER: Jack, you said you wanted to focus on giving your people more feedback. Is this a good time to talk more about how coaching can be helpful in this? *The coach initiates clarifying conversation about an important coaching outcome.*

CLIENT: Yeah. Here's the problem. I know I need to be up-front and honest about the negatives, but I don't know how to do that without making people defensive. And their reactions make me anxious, which doesn't help.

PARTNER: Well, some people get defensive whenever they think they're being criticized, and it has nothing to do with how you say it. But you *can* learn to say what you need to in a way that makes it easier to hear.

CLIENT: Okay. So how do you help me do that?

PARTNER: Well, there are a lot of ways to work with it. It's a common situation for leaders; giving negative feedback can be difficult. Before I talk about how we'd get there, it's important to define what you want to accomplish. What would success look like? *The coach pushes toward a clear picture of success.*

CLIENT: Hmm. I guess I'd formulate clearly what I want to say and be sure that it's accurate and objective, and not just my impression. And I'd try not to get anxious. I *do* know what I'm talking about, after all. And I'd say it calmly and not worry so much about how the person reacts. So how would we do all of that?

PARTNER: Hold on. Let's begin at the beginning. I hear that if you can provide tough feedback accurately and objectively, without getting anxious, and you know that it's valid and you've done your best to state it well—that's what we're shooting for in our work together? *The coach is moving toward a behavioral description, a competency, that can drive coaching conversations.*

CLIENT: Yeah, that's it.

Here the coach is encouraging Jack to define his goals in observable terms. This serves both the coach and the client. Both should want to know when the coaching process has been successful, and precisely defined outcomes make the development of a coaching strategy relatively simple. Without defining outcomes, coaching tends to lose focus as well as accountability. This, of course, lets the coach off the hook, but it doesn't serve the client.

Notice, too, in the dialogue that two competency-based outcomes are emerging. First, there is what we might call an *inner* competency (staying calm and not anxious: observable by self). Also, there's an *outer* competency (delivering accurate, objective, difficult feedback: observable by others). Often outcomes develop along these lines. The externally directed competency is what the client perhaps was looking for when he considered getting coached. And the outer competencies depend on doing some related inner work about attitude, beliefs, habits, and triggered reactions. This is the client's own mindfulness work.

Inner competencies are most often relevant to multiple areas in a client's life. For example, in the dialogue, the anxiety that gets triggered by giving tough feedback is likely present in other conversations. The anxiety might reveal, in this case, an aversion to some level of discomfort in *any* conversation where he is concerned about someone else's reaction. If so, competency in working with this habit may become a high leverage outcome of coaching.

Mindfulness, in this case and nearly always, is required for successful client outcomes. Building this capacity to stay calm and relaxed in difficult conversations will pay huge dividends in other areas of his life. (By extension, everything that we are learning in this book about mindfulness and development applies to our clients as well. Our own learning process is holographic, meaning that what we learn in relation to pursuing our own mastery as coach will be relevant to our clients as well.) Later in the relationship, we can revisit these outcomes, asking the client for evidence of progress. Clear progress is important to affirm, and it validates that coaching is successful. If there is no evidence, it will be important to realign the process or else determine that the outcome has changed or is no longer relevant.

Here's a dialogue with Jack a couple of months later in which the coach is primarily inviting the client to assess himself against the outcome defined earlier. In a way, this verges on the Reflector Voice to be explored in a later chapter, but I'm including it here because it illustrates a way that the Partner can deal with coaching outcomes.

PARTNER: Before we get into specifics today, let's step back and touch base with your outcome about being less anxious in giving difficult feedback. You've been tracking this for a couple of months now as you've been doing mindfulness practice and working on your feedback skills. What evidence do you see that your anxiety level is different?

CLIENT: I think it's quite different. When I started doing the more formal self-observation, I noticed that my palms would get sweaty, and I'd have a lot of tightness in my throat before the conversations that I thought would be tough. I'd play out a whole scenario in my mind about how defensive my people would be.

PARTNER: And what specifically is different now? *The coach is asking for the client's own evidence.*

CLIENT: I'm noticing that it's less of a big deal. I think the main change is in my own mind. I don't create a whole story about what's going to happen. I just focus on getting clear about the information I want to convey. And I think about how much I care about the individual and my commitment to his or her success. Sometimes others still get defensive, but less so, and I don't take it personally when they do.

PARTNER: And what happens in your body?

CLIENT: No more sweaty palms and tight throat. I can still spin the story, but I don't get as invested in it, and I just tell myself that it might not be like that. I focus on the skills of giving the feedback instead of on what might go wrong when I do. *The client has specific evidence for new competencies related to the outcome.*

PARTNER: Sounds like a big shift. Congratulations!

CLIENT: Thanks! It's a lot better.

PARTNER: So what's your edge with this? What pieces still feel difficult or problematic with this outcome?

CLIENT: There's one person in particular that it's really still difficult with. She has a tough home situation, and she's really not doing a good job. And I'm not convinced that she can do a better job.

So it's really hard giving her feedback that gets her upset and that she probably doesn't have the skills to do much about. I need some help with that one.

PARTNER: That sounds hard. Let's spend some time talking about how the same principles you've been working with in other situations could support you in addressing hers. Will that be helpful? *The coach offers the client a choice about how to move forward, informed by an assessment of progress toward outcome.*

Recurring evidence-based assessment of progress toward clearly defined and observable outcomes grounds the coaching process. Sometimes this assessment can be verbal, as in the dialogue. Or the client can complete a short questionnaire, reflecting on the evidence for the outcomes. Or, for outcomes that are observable by others, feedback from other people can be invaluable and can involve others in supporting the client in change.

In all cases, this assessment builds the accountability of coach and client toward the outcomes and provides the basis for self-correction. Mindful presence means that we are not attached to proving that what we're doing is working; rather, we are both curious to see what the assessment will show and committed to serving the client's learning.

OFFERING CHOICE POINTS AND MAKING JOINT DECISIONS ABOUT THE COACHING PROCESS

The essence of this Aspect of the Partner Voice is this: the coach brings the coaching expertise, but the client is the expert on what he needs from coaching. As we saw in the previous dialogue, focusing now and then on how we're working together and how we're using our time makes the coach more accountable to the client, and it makes the client more responsible as well.

This interchange occurs on a couple of levels. On one level, we discuss with the client what he wants overall from the coaching relationship. Is he looking for a supportive listener, or someone willing to challenge his thinking, or someone to give him guidance about alternatives? On a finer level, we also ask clients what they want out of a specific session or at a particular moment. Often the client doesn't know at first, but in pausing and pondering the question, he gets more clarity about what he's seeking from the coach. (I sometimes ask clients to fill out and e-mail me a brief form with a few questions in advance of each session; one of the questions addresses what the client wants from that particular session.)

Here are some questions that can help encourage the client to take responsibility for shaping the course of a specific conversation:

- What would be the best use of our remaining time?
- What do you want to have twenty minutes from now when we are complete?
- How can I best help you with this?
- What do you need right now?

The process of shaping the coaching strategy and tactics may involve the client to a greater or lesser degree, but I've found it useful to involve the client in mapping the coaching strategy to a slightly greater extent than he asks for. In handing off more and more responsibility to the client for managing the coaching relationship, we encourage him to stretch and increase his ability to take the initiative. Part of the message here is that the client is capable of developing himself; we seek to reinforce this message by operating from the assumption that he knows how he needs to be coached if we just ask the right questions.

It's part of our commitment to our clients that we celebrate and support the development of their own competencies, even when (especially when!) the end result is that they no longer need our services.

We cannot always know what our clients need. Although we sometimes put pressure on ourselves to create an effortless pathway for our clients, being authentic and present means sometimes feeling stuck. If we are willing to acknowledge this to both ourselves and our clients, not knowing what to do next means that we share responsibility and ask the client for help, and this can open new directions. In doing so, we create choice points for the client, trusting that she will articulate most clearly what she needs at a particular point.

Let's go back to Claire and her boss, Rob. She's decided to ask for a meeting with Rob and her coach together, and she and the coach have talked about the boundaries of confidentiality.

PARTNER: Okay, sounds good. So which should we talk about first: questions for Rob or points that you want to make with him?

CLIENT: Let's start with me asking him some questions. Maybe that'll break the ice, and that's what's important right now. I need a few really good questions that'll get him to say what he's worried about. Then I can talk about what I've been doing, and if that goes well, I can ask him to give me some support on the supply chain thing.

PARTNER: Okay. Will it be more useful for you to take a crack at some questions, or for me to suggest several? What will support you in being most resourceful here? *The coach first offers a choice point and then invites the client to consider what will provide the best learning.*

CLIENT: I'll take a whack at it. And I want to hear what you think as well.

Notice who's directing the coaching here. The Partner is monitoring the course of the conversation and seeking opportunities to offer choice points to the client. The coach is placing herself at the service of the client by asking her to articulate the direction to take. When the client makes a conscious choice about what will be most helpful, she is developing the capability to look inward and discern what she needs. This is central to building independence and the capacity to be self-generative.

The previous dialogue focuses on how best to use a few minutes of a coaching session, but the Partner Voice also asks the client to make choices about the overall direction of the work. Here's what that might look like.

COACH AS INVESTIGATOR: You've been challenged to find more time for writing. It's great you've got an agent for the proposal. And you're committed to having a draft for the first four chapters and are behind. Let's go back to that. What do you think is standing in the way?

CLIENT: Well, I need more structure around it. I have a lot of projects, and it's simply difficult to find the time to write. The ideas are there; the time's not. I've got clients with demands, and the book is easy to put off.

PARTNER: We can talk about why that is. How can I be of support to you? *Opens a conversation about joint design of the coaching process.*

CLIENT: I know there must be a way to just get better organized so I can free up some time.

PARTNER: So what would be helpful with that part? I might have some suggestions, but I think you already have some ideas. *The coach puts the client at choice and references the client's own resourcefulness.*

CLIENT: I think it would be very helpful to talk about how I organize my client work. But I don't want to lose our focus on writing either. They're related. It seems like I write best when I'm feeling uncluttered and organized.

PARTNER: That doesn't surprise me. How can we address this together? *The coach is asking the client to take responsibility for articulating where the coaching can be most helpful.*

CLIENT: It's like a loop. When I feel organized and on top of things, I don't feel guilty about writing. And when I write something I feel good about, I have more energy for getting my projects done. I guess that's the key. Maybe for the next couple of weeks, you could help me talk about time. I need to address both.

PARTNER: So be it. I'll ask you each time what you've done to get organized, and we'll talk about the writing. And we'll generate ideas about how to address snags when they come up. Will that work for you? *The coach as Partner makes a commitment to accountability for following up and supporting.*

CLIENT: Great. That sounds like a good direction.

COACH AS REFLECTOR: Notice that when I asked you what you needed from our work together, you came right back with clear ideas about how I could support you. You're already getting better at asking yourself what you need and finding answers. *Coach provides a validating assessment of the client's competency.*

Out of this dialogue comes a new "contract"—a new agreement for how coach and client will direct the coaching effort over the next several weeks. As the Partner, the coach is working with the client to shape the overall direction of their relationship and pushing the client, through questioning, to become clearer about what she wants from the coach. The coach, in the final comment, also makes the cognitive connection for the client that she had in fact been shaping the coaching process herself.

Not all people will be as aware of what they need as is this client. It's easy to see that it's our job as coaches to help clients become more competent in the content areas in which they are being coached. Less obvious is our responsibility in helping them develop the skill of being clients. Taking on that responsibility is how we nurture client independence and self-generation.

It can be a useful strategy to ask the client how she would coach herself through a specific situation. Doing this periodically provides a good check for both of you about whether she's understanding and internalizing the coaching process. It also strengthens the partnership.

Sometimes the client doesn't have a clue about what she needs from the coach; if true, other Voices (most probably the Reflector and the Guide) will be helpful in making suggestions and clarifying possibilities for their work together. Discerning what is needed always takes place in the light of the outcomes that the client wants to achieve.

THE MINDFUL PARTNER

Coach and client enter the coaching space at the beginning of each conversation with their own concerns that are specific to the roles that they are in. Life predictably will have delivered unpredictable experiences since the previous conversation. So the client enters coaching with these experiences of success or perceived failure, or even both. She enters the conversation with questions, breakdowns, new data from life experiences. She will be in a certain mood and will have particular interests or outcomes that she wants from the conversation.

The Partner meets the client where she is. With the full compassion and respect of the Master, the Partner engages the client in joint decisions about how best to use the time together given the unique (and unknowable in advance) state in which the client enters the conversation.

While this chapter has often focused on tactics, it is imperative that the behaviors and actions done in the name of partnership are underpinned by the same mindful awareness, attention to holding the space, and unconditional compassion and respect for the client that I have been advocating all along. The Partner is always present in the background, looking out for the relationship, and bringing mindful attention to the coaching space. This concern for the container allows everything else to emerge.

Here are some guidelines for the effective use of the Partner Voice:

- Ensure that understandings about fees, the logistics of coaching, and expected outcomes are clear and explicit. A formal contract may not be necessary, but I recommend that these understandings be written down.

- Practice mindfulness in the arena of partnership. The mindful Partner maintains a balanced relationship (not just being the "helper"), makes the process explicit and pragmatic rather than magical, and serves the client's outcomes and self-generation rather than seeking to keep the client engaged forever.

- To maintain the coaching space, be mindful when the conversation is moving into areas in which you are not trained (whether technical or psychological), and openly discuss with your client whether a referral is appropriate.

- Invest the time and energy at the beginning to develop clear, competency-based outcomes that you can jointly commit to. Refer to them often, and use them to organize the coaching conversation toward what matters to the client. Periodically assess progress against these outcomes, asking the client (or other parties) for evidence. Then correct your course as needed.

- Meet the client where she is, recognizing that she will not be the same person she was at the end of the previous conversation. She will have changed. Be willing to be surprised!

- Seek opportunities to present choice points to the client: opportunities to follow different alternatives. Making choices puts the client in charge of the session. Stay mindful about not being attached to which alternative the client chooses.

- Challenge the client to tell you how to coach her or to define for herself what she wants from you. Doing so even when she herself may feel unready to make demands on the relationship will help her learn how to discover for herself what she needs, whereas always staying within the client's comfort zone creates little movement.

- Be explicit about when the client is taking responsibility for shaping the coaching process. The client's awareness of this subtext of the coaching relationship is key; she will be empowered by knowing she is doing this.

The following exercises invite you to explore this Voice and bring your attention into the particular Aspects that you might be able to use more skillfully.

EXERCISE 5.1.
Self-Coaching as Partner: Making a Commitment

Write out your thoughts on these reflection queries. As you do so, consider them as coming from you, the coach, using your Partner Voice:

1. List three to five intended outcomes you are holding for yourself as you read and work with *The Mindful Coach*.

2. What is your relationship to the exercises at the end of each chapter? Do you give them a quick read? Skip them completely? Write out some brief comments and move on? Engage them fully as a learner? Why is this?

3. Note two choices that you can make right now about how to engage the exercises in particular, and the content in general, differently in order to better reach the outcomes from number 1 above. Make a commitment to yourself.

EXERCISE 5.2.

Partner Areas for Attention

Take some time to respond to the following questions:

- Based on the description of the Partner, what Aspects do you engage with skillfully and mindfully?
- What Partner Aspects might you tend to overuse? When? How do you know this?
- What Aspects are you less comfortable and proficient with? When? How do you know this?

EXERCISE 5.3.

Partner Self-Observation

- Choose an Aspect that represents a development opportunity for you: a skill or behavior that you wish to bring more into your coaching, or one that you perhaps have attachments to and therefore overuse. Describe this skill or behavior as specifically as possible.
- Construct a self-observation for yourself, using the explanation and structure from Chapter Two. Do this self-observation consistently and rigorously over several weeks. Notice how your mindfulness has changed in relation to this Aspect.

CHAPTER SUMMARY

Together with the felt presence of the Master, the Partner maintains the space within which coaching can happen. The Partner is the ever-present mindful Voice that ensures that the coaching relationship is guided by clear, explicit understandings in a way that reinforces the safety of the client in that relationship. The structure of this relationship must be such that the needs of both parties are addressed; this is a prerequisite to the coach's being able to place himself in service.

The Partner function encompasses three Aspects of coaching:

- *Establishes and honors an explicit structure for the coaching relationship,* such as fees, frequency and duration of conversations, confidentiality, and assessment protocols. This conversation is initially a contracting conversation and can be revisited as needed.

- *Advocates shared commitment to competency-based coaching outcomes* in order to shape the coaching conversation and build accountability for both to specific and observable new competencies. The coach's visible and demonstrated commitment to the client and her outcomes provides a clear sense of being on the same team.
- *Offers choice points and makes joint decisions about the coaching process* so that coach and client share responsibility for the process, and the client becomes a better-informed partner, and ultimately independent and self-generative.

The Investigator

Be patient toward all that is unresolved in your heart. Try to love the questions themselves. Do not now seek the answers, which cannot be given because you would not be able to live them. . . . Live the questions now. Perhaps you will then gradually without noticing it, live along some distant day into the answers.

Rainer Maria Rilke

The answers to many questions are already with us. Often we just need some help to bring them out.

Mae Jamison, first woman of color in space

ONE TRADITIONAL MODEL OF LEADERSHIP IS THAT of a strong individual, self-reliant, unquestioning, certain, reluctant to show weakness or flaws. Yet, when unquestioned, leaders often hurtle down slippery slopes and blind alleys, driven by their own habits, assumptions, and unrecognized identity needs. A new notion of strength in leadership incorporates interdependence, inquiry, and a reliance on others as checks and balances for us as we live into our commitments while developing ourselves at the same time.

This inquiry is the core process in coaching. Questions, incisive and supportive, are by far the best way to support a client in a process of learning and discovery. A leader who recognizes the dangers of unquestioned thinking and acting can find enormous value in this process alone.

113

The mindful Investigator asks questions with an engaged curiosity. She is attentive, evocative, and curious. As she enters a new area of inquiry with a client, she asks questions that evoke a new view of the client's situation. Next, she moves toward questions that will support the client in seeing new possibilities and new choices within that situation.

"Because questions are intrinsically related to action, they spark and direct attention, perception, energy, and effort, and so are at the heart of the evolving forms that our lives assume."[1] As an action-oriented process, coaching relies on questions both to evoke new understandings and generate a movement toward action and change. But it is important to understand that the Investigator is an action-neutral role. Speaking as the Investigator will often elicit possibilities for action from the client, but the goal is simply for the client to come to see things more deeply as they truly are—first the situation and then desired outcomes and strategies.

CRITERIA FOR ARTFUL QUESTIONS

- The client doesn't know the answer to the question before the coach asks.
- The question fosters curiosity in the client.
- The question invokes new perspectives or possibilities.

What makes a question artful? What makes it more likely to advance the coaching process toward real change? Here are three criteria:

- *The client doesn't know the answer to the question before the coach asks.* This means that the client will learn something from considering it. If the only one who learns from the answer is the coach, the question might still be important, but it's not going to open any doors for the client. An artful question goes beyond a simple search for facts or descriptions. The very process of considering and answering the question causes the client to look at the situation in a new way.

- *The question fosters curiosity in the client.* Implicit in the question is that the client is engaged in a discovery process and is a researcher in the arena of his own life. Artful questions are asked in a way that assumes that something interesting can be learned here. While the coach may also be curious about the answer, the question stimulates the inherent curiosity of the client. This curiosity is usually light and fun; asking the question invites the client into a neutral observer stance, one that is somewhat detached from the content of coaching and corresponding emotions and offers a view of that content from a larger perspective. (Think mindfulness!)

- *The question invokes new perspectives or possibilities.* It is asked in such a way that finding an answer requires the client to shift perspectives or discover new possibilities. These, as we shall see, could include a new and more empowering way of viewing the situation, an optimistic goal for the future, or previously unseen options. To quote Albert Einstein, "A problem can't be solved from the same state of mind that created it." Artful questions invite clients into a shift of frame—a new and more expansive perspective in which possibilities can be seen that were previously inaccessible. Since we as coaches ask questions out of the separate world of our own experience, we are in fact often inviting the client to view his situation from the distinct perspective from which we might view it.

The three Aspects of the Investigator Voice are centered on three core lines of questioning:

- What is the situation? (Situation)
- What do you want? (Outcome)
- What are you going to do? (Action)

In their many variations, these core questions are diagnostic in that they increase the coach's understanding of the territory through which the client wishes to navigate. Far more important, when they are skillfully designed, they serve to expand and deepen the client's understanding. The coach may contribute new perspectives about that territory and use other Voices to deepen and enrich the conversation, but it is the questions themselves that drive the process of discovery.

Taken together, the three core questions establish the creative tension described by Robert Fritz, Peter Senge, and others as critical to change.[2] Situation questions clarify what Fritz would call current reality. Questioning about outcomes elicits from the client a graphic picture of a preferred future in relation to the situation. The gap or felt tension between what the client has now and what the client wants provides the motivation and direction for change. Once this tension is established, the third area of questioning, around what the client will do, provides a channel for the client to act decisively to resolve that tension.

Notice that I describe tension between the lines of questioning rather than presenting them as a sequence to follow. Admittedly there seems to be a certain progressive logic to the three: the first line of questioning clarifies the situation and the client's part in it, the second clarifies the outcomes that the client seeks, and the third surfaces possibilities for new actions and behaviors.[3] But coaching is an intuitive, relational activity. In real life, the three Aspects don't necessarily follw each other in a predetermined sequence. Continual and creative inquiry into our evolving situations, what we want, and what actions we can take are the fundamentals of a lifetime of engaged learning. A client may be primed to start in any one of the areas, and that's where we begin.

ASPECTS OF THE INVESTIGATOR

- Asking questions that shift the client's understanding of the situation
- Asking the client to articulate desired outcomes
- Asking the client to generate courses of action

ASKING QUESTIONS THAT SHIFT THE CLIENT'S UNDERSTANDING OF THE SITUATION

The situation that the client faces could represent an opportunity, a fear, a dilemma, or the need for a plan. The situation includes those involved, organizational or family goals, and constraints and resources. The situation also includes how the client himself exists within his world: the personality, beliefs, biases, and habits that are embedded in the client are critical elements to include in a new understanding of the situation. Most often the real openings in coaching occur on the level of the client's awareness of these inner elements.

Situation questions open up new ways of seeing the client's current situation and result in a new view and more freedom of possibility. The questions can speak to three levels, listed here in order of increasing depth, leverage, and learning for the client:

- *External elements: What is going on in the view of the client?* To begin, the coach asks questions that illuminate the aspects of the situation external to the client. Generally these are the questions that are the easiest for the client to answer; the answers are likely to simply describe the situation as the client sees it from within his own interpretation. At the same time, they are likely to be less provocative, and learning will generally unfold faster and deeper at the subsequent levels of questioning.

- *Client contribution: How does the client create the situation?* This has to do with how the client influences what is going on. The client is a central causal element in any situation that he is able to perceive. A clear picture of the whole requires that the client understand how he contributes to, or even creates, that which he is seeking to change. Getting at the client's contributions to the situation leads to discovering what he can do to affect its outcome.

- *Client assumptions and interpretations: How does the client see and interpret, thus giving rise to the behaviors and actions identified in the previous level? What is the client not seeing?* This potentially most powerful level of questioning has to do with the interpretations and underlying assumptions that guide the client's behavior. It gets to the root of behavior and is even more likely to help a client discover opportunities for lasting change. These questions often expose elements of the client's identity and can open the door to significant new and expanded possibilities.

The situation questions listed in Exhibit 6.1 apply to these levels. There are, of course, thousands of potential questions; these are

EXHIBIT 6.1.
Sample Situation Questions

Situation questions open up new ways of seeing the client's current situation and result in a new view and more freedom of possibility. They address three areas, listed here in order of increasing depth, leverage, and learning for the client.

External elements: What is going on in the view of the client?

- Where? What? When? Who? How?
- How is this situation different from others you've faced in the past?
- What happened? What's at risk?
- Who is involved? Who has a stake in this?
- What makes this something to address now?
- What isn't working?
- What resources are available?
- What other relevant information is important to consider?

Client contribution: How does the client create the situation, thus owning some responsibility for the situation described at the previous level?

- What actions are you taking that create difficulties for yourself or others?
- What behaviors do you seem to fall into regularly?
- What might you be doing to contribute to the situation? Not doing?
- What actions have you taken that maintain the status quo?
- What are the ways in which you are limiting yourself?
- What behaviors might you change that could change the situation?
- What could you accept or let go of that might help?

Client assumptions and interpretations: How does the client see and interpret, thus giving rise to the behaviors and actions identified in the previous level? What is the client not seeing?

- How might another person see this?
- How will you see this two years from now?
- What limiting assumptions might you be making that preclude other possibilities?
- What might happen if you change this?
- What are you attached to in this situation?
- How does the status quo benefit you? Serve your identity?
- What are you committed to in this situation?
- Working from your core values, how might you see this differently?

intended solely to be illustrative and to illuminate the distinctions among the three levels. The best questions will not be off the shelf or components of a script, but rather arise spontaneously from a mindful connection between the coach and client. They will be driven by the coach's curiosity, compassion, and respect for the client's intrinsic wisdom and potential.

Here's a condensed dialogue that incorporates questions on all three levels. We'll call our client Ella.

INVESTIGATOR: So, Ella, what is happening that is so difficult with your boss? *External element. Ella will likely report on what's happened to date.*

CLIENT: Well, Jim didn't really want to hire me. I was pretty much forced on him by his boss, who thinks I have a lot of good experience. And he's right. But Jim hasn't really wanted me here since the first day.

INVESTIGATOR: What do you notice that makes you think that? *External element.*

CLIENT: Well, he's just cold to me. Jim's mostly pretty friendly to the other people in the department but not to me. And he criticizes me publicly, he gives me only negatives when we meet, and I can't remember if he's ever said a single good thing about me or anything I've done.

INVESTIGATOR: Sounds pretty grim. Any good news about Jim? Any hints he might not be such a bear? *External element.*

CLIENT: Hmm. (pause) When he first came in, he asked me to take on a big new project. I was pleased. I was supposed to submit a plan for how I would approach it, so I did. But he sat on the plan for months and never got back to me about it until I asked him about it. And even then, he just put me off. This hasn't been an easy ride.

INVESTIGATOR: Can you think of any ways you're contributing to this bad dynamic? *Client contribution question.*

CLIENT: Well. I have gotten pretty shut down to him. I'm sure he knows I don't have much respect for him. I tried hard for a while, but I'm looking for a way out at this point. I don't need the hostility.

INVESTIGATOR: What do you think it is about Jim? What assumptions are you making about him? *Client assumptions and interpretations.*

CLIENT: Hmm. About Jim. (pauses) I suppose he's insecure. He knows I've got more experience in software than he does. Maybe that makes him nervous. And I know he's mad at Alex [Jim's boss] for making him put me on the team; I would have resented the way he handled it if I were in Jim's shoes.

In this dialogue (we'll continue it later), the coach as Investigator asks questions at all three levels. Initially they concern the boss and the circumstances. They're about the lay of the land, external to the client (though, of course, based on her subjective interpretation, which is intrinsically limited and personal). Then the Investigator's line of questioning changes to focus on Ella's response to Jim. The coach supports Ella in looking at how she contributes to the situation. In the end, the coach questions the assumptions that Ella holds about Jim. This is where the leverage is. Helping Ella see how she views Jim will help her think more clearly about the situation, what she contributes to it, and her options for resolving its difficulties.

HELPING THE CLIENT TO ARTICULATE DESIRED OUTCOMES

Outcomes are key to coaching, and animate everything that follows. Initially, competency-based outcomes provide form for the overall coaching process. Later, continually articulating what the client wants in relation to emerging situations will provide a clear vision of the outcome. The idea is to build sufficient investment to surmount both internal resistance and external obstacles. Robert Fritz defines vision as "the inner crystallization of the result that you want to create, so that the result is conceptually specific and tangible in your imagination—so tangible and so specific, in fact, that you would recognize the manifestation of the result if it occurred."[4] This Aspect focuses us on the work of coaching.

The sample outcome questions shown in Exhibit 6.2 are generic. The best questions, of course, will emerge in the conversation; however, these will show the territory.

EXHIBIT 6.2.
Sample Outcome Questions

Outcome questions establish a distinction and creative tension for the client. The distinctions between the situation and the potential, between current reality and desired future, or between habitual and new, more effective behaviors, provide the basis for self-observation and ultimately the energy for change:

- What could be different?
- What possibility opens up for you in this?
- Looking back on this from three years out, what will have happened?
- What would it mean to you to be successful in this?
- What does it feel like when it's different?
- How will you know when you've been successful?
- What energizes you in this situation?
- What are the implications of making this change?
- What are the characteristics of the best solution?

Continuing the previous dialogue, the Investigator directs Ella's attention toward what might be possible.

INVESTIGATOR: So, Ella, let's play with those assumptions. If you're right, does that say anything about how your relationship with Jim could be different? *The questioning opens the possibility of something new, of a different outcome.*

CLIENT: Well, I suppose it's conceivable that he could come to see me as a help to him and not a threat. But that's a stretch right now.

INVESTIGATOR: I'm not asking you to believe that it's realistic right away, but let's spend a little time thinking about what it would look like. What would it mean to be a help to Jim?

CLIENT: He'd feel like I was helping him to reach his own goals. Helping his department look good. Helping *him* look good. For the most part, I'm already supporting his agenda, but there's been so much tension that he doesn't get it.

INVESTIGATOR: How would you know if he thinks you're being supportive? *This question makes this outcome more visible.*

CLIENT: Well, when I do good work, he'd acknowledge it somehow. He'd give me public credit for my contributions, and he'd call on me when tough issues come up. He'd use what I have to offer.

INVESTIGATOR: And how would that make a difference for you?

CLIENT: Well. (pauses) Obviously I'd feel like we were working together instead of at odds. We'd be able to share ideas. We'd support each other. It would go both ways. I might enjoy work again! *The client's energy is increasing.*

INVESTIGATOR: Can you see that as at least a possibility sometime in the future?

CLIENT: I don't know. But I don't like to give up on things. I don't think it's likely, but I do see how imagining it could be different opens things up a bit.

INVESTIGATOR: Yes, it's important to understand what you want to be different. Knowing the outcome you want is what will shape your strategy.

Notice that in this dialogue the coach isn't asking the client to commit to the outcome yet. There's too much they don't know about what that would entail. As the Investigator, the coach is just asking the client to try on some possibilities—to be willing to consider that things could change. This in itself opens up some additional spaciousness for the client.

ASKING THE CLIENT TO GENERATE COURSES OF ACTION

As Investigator, the coach asks the client directly for ideas on courses of action or behaviors that could bring the desired outcome into being. It is important to understand, however, that the Investigator does not advocate action; he is detached. Any impetus toward action must come from the client. The Investigator is there only to support the discovery of the client's ideas about how to move forward. (Insofar as the coach does suggest ideas or provide an impetus toward action, he does so in the Voice of Guide, discussed in Chapter Nine.)

Once the shape of the desired outcome is clear, the client is often ready and eager to get to work on it. Articulating a picture of what

EXHIBIT 6.3.

Sample Action Questions

The insight and awareness from coaching ultimately express themselves in new behaviors, actions, and competencies in the world. Action questions help direct the energy of creative tension into substantive learning or behavioral actions outside coaching:

- What is the best first step toward your outcome?
- What would go on your list of action items?
- When you've been successful in similar situations, what did you do first?
- What one new action will be energizing and break new ground for you?
- What steps can you take to help you learn more about this?
- What would help make this easier?
- What actions will help you learn how to do this?

---

the client wants can release a lot of energy that was formerly bound up in confusion about alternatives. The example outcome questions offered in Exhibit 6.3 will be useful.

Let's go back to Ella, whom we left at a critical juncture. I'll repeat the last thing she said, just before the coach interrupted to discuss the importance of defining outcomes.

CLIENT: I don't know. But I don't like to give up on things. I don't think it's likely, but I do see how imagining this opens things up a bit.

INVESTIGATOR: Yes, it's important to understand what you want to be different. Knowing the outcome you want is what will shape your strategy. So what do you think *you* could do differently if you kept this new perspective? *Action question.*

CLIENT: I thought you'd put it back on me! To tell the truth, I think I know. I think the opportunity is to try to start from scratch. I need to make more of an effort to get to know Jim. To find out how *he* sees things and what his goals are.

INVESTIGATOR: And how will you do this? *Action question.*

CLIENT: I have to take the initiative. I need to figure out what Jim needs from me, I guess. And that'll help him know I'm on his side, that I'm really not out to undermine him or replace him.

It won't be easy, and I'm not too optimistic that he'll change, but it's worth a try.

INVESTIGATOR: What would be your first step? *Action question.*

CLIENT: I'll call him tomorrow and set up a time to meet. I think that if I take the initiative, he'll do lunch with me. I'll need to really think through my agenda so I'm ready when I go in, but I think I know how to get there.

A couple of things are notable here. First, Ella already has an impetus for action. As soon as a possible new outcome became clear to her, the creative tension between the current unpleasant situation and a potential resolution provided its own urge toward action. New energy arose in Ella and came out when she said, "I don't like to give up on things." The coach is simply staying present, asking artful questions. Ella is generating her own ideas and her own commitment.

Second, Ella pretty much knows what to do. By using questions to shift her perspective, the Investigator releases energy that she's been bottling up for some time. With a clearer and more expansive view of the situation and a better idea of what the outcome she wants would look like, the coaching session practically runs itself. Ella is a skilled person, and she's able to come up with specific possibilities for action on her own. Other people might need more guidance or ideas, which would require a different Voice from that of the Investigator. But the Investigator provides what Ella needs to generate a plan of her own.

The next dialogue concerns a specific job-related situation where the coach is the client's supervisor in a manufacturing environment. To keep this clear, we'll call them the supervisor and the employee, but here the supervisor is coaching in the Voice of the Investigator.

SUPERVISOR: What seems to be the problem? *Situation question.*

EMPLOYEE: My scrap is getting out of control. There's too much of it, and Eric isn't picking it up often enough.

SUPERVISOR: What do you think it should look like at this workstation? *Outcome question.*

EMPLOYEE: Better than this.

SUPERVISOR: But how. What should it look like? *Outcome question.*

EMPLOYEE: Well, the scrap should be piled up over there or in the bin.

SUPERVISOR: If you kept it piled up over there or put it in the bin, would that solve the problem? *Action question.*

EMPLOYEE: Yeah, for a while. Until the bin is full.

SUPERVISOR: If all the scrap is either in that pile or in the bin, how would that help you do your job? *Action question.*

EMPLOYEE: Well, I could walk around my press without tripping on all this stuff underfoot.

SUPERVISOR: Will that solve the problem?

EMPLOYEE: Yeah, that'll be better.

In this dialogue, the supervisor (coach) supports the employee (client) in articulating what his work area should look like. It's not a complicated problem. Both the employee and the supervisor know what the solution is and that the employee is basically whining. The supervisor could just tell the employee to do a better job of cleaning up after himself. But that would be an authority-based interaction, as opposed to a coaching interaction. The supervisor doesn't want to be adversarial, and so he chooses to ask a lighthearted series of questions—to use the Investigator Voice—to get the employee to define the desired outcome. This bypasses the need for a confrontation. In this case, defining the desired outcome is about all that's necessary; once that's done, the steps are obvious.

I include this example not because most readers of this book will be supervisors coaching hourly employees on the shop floor, but simply to illustrate that the principles here can be applied in myriad situations. We're all provided with any number of situations to help others learn, whether we call it coaching or something else. The principles outlined here aren't magic or rocket science. They work because they encompass fundamental principles, and the way in which we interact with people makes a critical difference in whether they actually learn.

The choice about when to shift from level of questioning to another, or between Investigator Aspects, isn't cut and dried. In general, there will be a significant increase in energy with a shift in the client's view of the situation. New possibilities will open up. The same is true when the client articulates a clear outcome that's distinct from what currently exists. These increased levels of energy propel the coaching process and provide motivation for change.

It's sometimes useful to dwell longer in a particular place in the conversation than is immediately apparent; sometimes new insights or possibilities can emerge from this deeper digging. Again, the key is not to be driven by a timetable or by our own urges, but rather to listen deeply to what is emerging within the client, and to be mindful, present, patient, and curious as the process unfolds.

THE MINDFUL INVESTIGATOR

While a healthy curiosity on the part of the coach animates the conversation, the coach must remain clear that the conversation isn't for the coach's benefit. This seems obvious, but when the coach is interested in the client's story (and clients are inherently fascinating), it's easy to get wrapped up in just pursuing that story, even when it leads into areas that aren't relevant to the coaching. The mindful Investigator stays present with this inquiry, designing questions that tap into the client's curiosity, so that the client begins to drive the discovery process.

A second mindfulness consideration is that a coach may be attached to his social identity as a brilliant question asker. It's fun to ask questions that resonate and provide the seeds for new client understanding, fun to watch the light bulbs go on. To the extent that we identify with that role and are attached to this image of ourselves as the artful Investigator, we may use the Voice beyond the point that it is helpful.

Another hazard is that we can become overly invested in the idea that asking questions is what a coach does. If we believe, as a philosophical stance, that the answers are always within the client, we'll be tempted to do nothing but probe until those answers are found. Sometimes, though, the answers are simply not available in the client's world, and she needs additional information or guidance in order to move forward. In this situation, the Investigator Voice will quickly seem to both parties to offer diminishing value.

Most problematic, our own identification with more directive Voices (for example, the Teacher or Guide, discussed later) or our lack of confidence as a question asker may cause us to underuse the Investigator role. When we do this, we will tend to drive or guide the process in a more directive fashion. This is sometimes necessary, but if we do this too readily, we will be depriving the client of the opportunity to think independently and may undermine his or her sense of ownership in the process. The resulting dependency is very unhelpful.

The following suggestions will help you maintain mindfulness in the Investigator role:

- Be clear in your own mind about why you are asking a particular question or following a line of questioning. The questions should relate to the larger context of your coaching, and they should move the client toward new understanding. Remember that the relationship between the questions of the three Aspects enables the experience of creative tension and the resulting energy for change.

- Stay aware of which Aspect of the Investigator you are using: situational, outcome, or course of action. Each is useful, and each has a lot of variations. It will support your mindfulness to be attentive to which line of questioning you're pursuing in a given conversation.

- Remain mindful that the Investigator Voice is just one of the possibilities. Although it is central and you will most often be leading with this Voice, hold it lightly, remembering that other Voices may be more appropriate in a given context.

- Be aware, and let go of your own need to get to resolution, ask just the right question, or follow a certain line of questioning to the end. You're engaging the client in curiosity. Ask your questions with presence and with a belief in the capacity of the client to see things in a different way.

- Asking the client to tell all the details about the situation can embed them more deeply in a limited and unhelpful view of the situation and can lead to the coach's asking lots of diagnostic questions from which the client learns little, but from which a coach attached to providing solutions can prescribe something. This is a classic trap. Notice who's doing the work in this situation. Are *you* working hard to figure out what the client should do? Or is the *client* digging to discover new insights and possibilities? The former is a good indicator that you're either joining the client in supporting her story or taking too much responsibility for solving a problem, or both.

- Pay attention to the nuances in the client's responses to your questions. Is she opening up? Is she defensive and stuck? Are light bulbs going on in her mind? As we discussed in Chapter Four on the Master, while the client's reaction—hesitation, defensiveness, excitement—shouldn't be the sole determinant of how we move forward, we need to maintain a broad awareness and emotional sensitivity to the client's body language and emotional tone.

- Make the coaching process explicit. This is the best way to hold yourself accountable to the client.

Exercises 6.1, 6.2, and 6.3 will develop your mindfulness as the Investigator. Additional Investigator-specific exercises are in the "Navigating the Model" section of Chapter Eleven.

EXERCISE 6.1.
Self-Coaching as Investigator: Three Lines of Questioning

Imagine that your inner Investigator is working with you on your learning process around this book. You will increase your understanding of the Investigator Voice by taking your time and responding mindfully to these Investigator questions in a journal or written notes:

1. *Situation: external elements:* What is emerging so far as useful and valuable in this work? What, if anything, has been disappointing for you in your learning?

2. *Situation: contribution:* What are you doing that makes this learning valuable? And what might you be doing that shortcuts the value that you could obtain (skipping the exercises or reading too quickly, for example)?

3. *Situation: assumptions and interpretations:* What judgments and interpretations about the material are you making that drive the behaviors you listed in response to the previous question?

4. *Outcome:* Given how you now see this material and your current understanding of it, what are the two most important possible outcomes for you from this book and exercises?

5. *Action:* What will you do, starting now, to build your commitment and move you toward these outcomes?

EXERCISE 6.2.
Investigator Areas for Attention

Take some time to respond to the following questions:

- Based on the description of the Investigator, what Aspects do you engage with skillfully and mindfully?
- What Investigator Aspects might you tend to overuse? When? How do you know this?
- What Aspects are you less comfortable and proficient with? When? How do you know this?

EXERCISE 6.3.
Investigator Self-Observation

- Choose an Aspect of the Investigator that represents a development opportunity for you: a skill or behavior that you wish to bring more into your coaching, or one that you perhaps have attachments to and therefore overuse. Describe this skill or behavior as specifically as possible.
- Construct a self-observation for yourself using the explanation and structure from Chapter Two. Do this self-observation consistently and rigorously over several weeks. Notice how your mindfulness has changed in relation to this Aspect.

CHAPTER SUMMARY

The Investigator Voice is central to the coaching process. It's largely through asking questions that we support clients in seeing a situation anew, formulating the outcomes they want, and developing new strategies for getting there.

The Investigator leads the way through the coach conversation with artful questions that impel the client into a learning and discovery process. These are distinct from questions that gather sufficient information so that the coach can suggest solutions. Rather, an artful question engages the client's curiosity, inviting her to discover new answers that are revealed precisely as the question is asked.

Three lines of Investigator questioning provide the backbone of the coaching process, and each is the basis for one Aspect. The Investigator:

- *Asks questions that shift the client's understanding of the situation,* such that a new view and new possibilities become available. This is done by moving down through three levels of questioning, increasing depth and leverage for learning. These explore, in turn, the external elements, client contribution (behaviors) to the current situation, and the client assumptions and interpretations that give rise to the behaviors and situation identified in the previous levels.
- *Asks the client to articulate desired outcomes,* or a possible preferred future revealed by the new view of the situation. The more clearly this is defined, the more it galvanizes action.
- *Asks the client to generate courses of action* that help the client learn, build competency, and move toward the newly articulated future.

The creative tension produced by the disparity between the situation and the outcome motivates action and change.

7

The Reflector

We don't see things as they are, we see them as we are.

Anaïs Nin

People love as self-recognition what they hate as an accusation.

Elias Canetti

A S LEADERS, WE ARE CRIPPLED IN OUR EFFECTIVENESS if we are unable to see ourselves clearly. Consider that, when going out for an important engagement, we nearly always look in the mirror to be sure we are properly put together for the occasion. Yet when it comes to our behaviors and actions and facial expressions—which arguably are much more fundamentally relevant to our effectiveness than whether our tie is straight or our hair in place—we fly blind most of the time.

Most of us, and this is often increasingly true at higher levels of power and authority, get precious little candor from others about our behaviors and thinking, how we come across, and how we affect those around us. Further, many leaders are relatively unskilled at the reflective practices that lead to self-awareness. Yet, as should be evident by now, this self-awareness is fundamental to the ability to rise above our default habits and tendencies to become ever more resourceful in leading our lives and in leading other people.

As the Reflector, the coach provides honest and timely feedback to the client and encourages him to develop his own ability to observe himself and consider the consequences of the choices that he makes. For the client, listening to the Reflector Voice is a bit like looking in a mirror.

The Reflector is often called into play to help the client refine his responses to the lines of questioning the coach pursues as the Investigator. It is the first of the three "sharpener" Voices, supporting the client in developing a different, clearer understanding of his situation (as opposed to outcome or action). Seeing ourselves accurately, including our behaviors and assumptions, is essential to an actionable view of our situation.

The Reflector Voice must be taken on mindfully. It is a privilege to share such intimate territory as our perceptions of a person. We have been invited into an inner room, within which many of the usual barriers and defenses are gone. In this room, we are allowed to speak honestly, tell the truth, support another human in seeing himself in a more accurate and expansive way. This requires of us the utmost respect and compassion.

The mindful Reflector maintains an awareness of his own judgments and agendas as they arise, coming back to a deep appreciation and acceptance of the client and how the client approaches the work that they are engaged in together. There is no hurry. The client's awareness will unfold, but only as the client is ready.

Never does the coach use this Voice to make the client feel put in the wrong or inadequate. Rather, he employs it to share perspectives and encourage the client to do the work of becoming self-aware.

The three Aspects of the Reflector Voice are interrelated and support each other; collectively they also support the rest of the coaching process.

ASPECTS OF THE REFLECTOR

- Providing direct and honest feedback
- Directing the client's attention toward his or her capabilities and potential
- Encouraging self-observation and reflection

The first Aspect ensures that the client can count on the coach to tell the truth, to be candid, and to be direct. A new perspective on himself and his involvement coming from a trusted and supportive person who is outside the politics of the immediate situation can be invaluable. The perspective of the coach, as a valued and trusted support person, carries weight and is more likely to be heard without the defensiveness that might be triggered by comments from someone with her own agenda within the situation. This means that the Reflector role requires mindfulness, considering deeply what to say and keeping her comments as free of her own biases and judgments as possible.

In the second Aspect, the Reflector encourages the client to acknowledge his own strengths, capabilities, and potential. This aspect of the Reflector is optimistic: the coach infuses energy into the process by providing evidence of the client's inherent wholeness and ability to make a difference.

In the third Aspect, the Reflector encourages the client to look in the mirror. Here the coach encourages the client to be self-reliant by helping him to develop the capacity to observe himself clearly in action. This capacity for self-observation is one of the keys to wise action. The Reflector supports the client in considering the implications of his feelings and behaviors. It is essential to be able to see clearly the choices that one is making and to understand how those choices affect others and one's own possibilities.

PROVIDING DIRECT AND HONEST FEEDBACK

As the Reflector, the coach will sometimes provide direct feedback to the client. This is appropriate when the client seems to be missing a piece of information about himself that could perhaps help him understand why he's getting the results he is. It is key to understand that this feedback is offered with the purpose that the client will be better able to be self-aware. We are not expecting the client to simply accept our feedback, but rather to question how it fits, what seems true, and what does not. The client always remains the authority on whether and how to incorporate this information.

The basic rules of feedback apply in this context: provide comments that are very specific, timely (that is, close in time to the relevant event), descriptive of behaviors that the client has control over, and embedded in the compassion and respect that help maintain the coaching space.

CLIENT: I want to spend some time here talking about an interaction that I had with George yesterday. He was way out of line after our meeting. I know my presentation was a bit rough, but he jumped all over me. There was no call for that!

REFLECTOR: You sound pretty upset about what happened. *The coach reflects an emotion.*

CLIENT: It's his job to give me feedback. But he didn't acknowledge that I'd been up until midnight working on the slides, and Jerry didn't get me what I needed. And he didn't even warn me that Ruth was dead set against the project in the first place and was going to be loaded for bear. George is supposed to be on my team here. I feel set up.

REFLECTOR: Sounds like an impossible situation. I can understand why you might feel upset.

CLIENT: Yes, that's how I feel. Except "run over" would be more accurate.

REFLECTOR: And also you sound a little defensive. I'm guessing you don't feel appreciated for all the work you put into this. *The coach reflects an assessment he has about the client's reaction.*

CLIENT: Yes, I see that I *am* feeling defensive. I really care about this project.

Here the coach is providing feedback to the client by reflecting back what he hears in the client's comments. This level of feedback is often described as a component of active listening: the coach's comments are rooted in solid attention and in staying present as the client vents his frustration. Ideally, this helps the client articulate and understand his experience.

Before this exchange, the client was wrapped up in the injustice of the situation. If we can take the client's account at face value, it *was* difficult and he *was* set up in some sense. Certainly several circumstances seem to have contributed to the fact that the meeting was not going very well from his point of view. However, as long as he's wrapped up in the anger and emotionality of it, as long as his field of view encompasses only the negativity and a perceived injustice, moving forward will be difficult. The coach as Reflector supports him in voicing his emotions in the moment, acknowledging them, and then moving on to the next stage. This increases the client's mindfulness about his own emotional state.

Sometimes it's useful for the coach to use this Voice to provide feedback about the coaching relationship itself. A coach could tell a client about an issue that affects their ability to work together, for example, being consistently late to sessions or using the session to defend a behavior or decision when the stated desire is to identify more effective alternatives. Awareness creates the possibility of new choices; feedback is a key component of awareness.

In the next dialogue, the coach is reflecting how the client's behaviors are showing up in the coaching relationship and making this relevant to the client's larger concerns.

CLIENT: I think there's a lot of resistance to my new dress code initiative—some of it not so subtle. Everyone's poking holes in it or joking about it, but nobody's talking to me about it. There's even a cartoon up in the break room that someone drew. I wish they'd just bring their concerns to me.

REFLECTOR: Jack, maybe they don't bring their concerns to you because they are intimidated by how strongly you feel about professional dress. *Coach offers a different interpretation for consideration.*

CLIENT: Well, I really am open to modifying a couple of the specifics. But (raises voice slightly) I do see this pretty strongly. Dress reflects on us and makes a statement to our customers.

REFLECTOR: Do you remember the feedback from your subordinates about shooting the messenger?

CLIENT: (rather heatedly) Yes! I disagree with it! I welcome input, and I'd never shoot the messenger! Frankly, I just want people to come forward and be straightforward. Otherwise how can we work together?

REFLECTOR: So right now, I'm a messenger. I'm offering that there might be a connection between your feedback and the dress code issue. And you're reacting to my offer with a lot of energy:

your voice is raised, and you are pointing your finger at me. If I were one of your direct reports, I would read this as time to cut my losses and get out of here. *The coach is reflecting the client's behavior in the moment.*

CLIENT: Oh. (pauses) I get it. That's an example of what they're talking about in the feedback, isn't it?

REFLECTOR: What do you think?

CLIENT: Well, I feel strongly about this. But others could find it intimidating even though I'm just expressing myself and looking for some good engagement.

REFLECTOR: Seems to me that may shed some light on the dress code issue. People who feel intimidated by you are much more likely to post cartoons in the break room than they are to come to you. *The coach connects the current behavior to the larger issue being discussed.*

CLIENT: Oh. (pauses) Yeah, you're right.

REFLECTOR: Is that what you want?

CLIENT: No, I don't want to be intimidating. I really don't. But I guess this is evidence that I am. Or at least that's how people experience me.

The light bulb goes on as the client recognizes how others see him. He's able to step back and see himself, for a moment, as others do. This gives him a more accurate perspective on his contribution to an issue that bothers him.

Particularly in coaching clients where relationships with others are part of the focus, it's often helpful to have additional data sources. A wide range of self-assessments, values and style inventories, and 360-degree feedback processes is available to help the coach support the client's self-awareness. Some will be driven by organizational competency models; others will be more developmental and universal in nature. Either way, these tools can be tremendously valuable in opening the client to how others might see him.

In addition, with the client's permission, a coach can interview others who interact with him or observe him in the workplace as he deals with others. Without these additional sources, the coach will have to rely solely on what the client brings to the table, but even if that's the case, the Reflector, as a sharpener Voice, can provide invaluable perspective.

Directing the Client's Attention Toward His or Her Capabilities and Potential

Personal or professional development often requires a leap of faith and a commitment to trying new and unaccustomed behaviors. Fundamental to a client's readiness to take this leap is his belief in his capacity to be successful. A client may hold in his mind a picture of failure, of the dire consequences of not doing something well. If this is the dominant image in his mind, then indeed failure is more likely. It's a self-fulfilling prophecy.

The Reflector is the particular Voice that supports the client in mobilizing his relevant prior experience and skills toward what comes next. In this, the field of appreciative inquiry (AI), pioneered by David Cooperrider and others, has much to offer the coach.[1] The principles of AI are central to coaching and to the Reflector Voice in particular. Sue Annis Hammond describes the basic concept of AI in this way:

> *The [clients] stir up memories of energizing moments of success creating a new energy that is positive and synergistic. [Clients] walk away with a sense of commitment, confidence and affirmation that they have been successful. They also know clearly how to make more moments of success. It is this energy that distinguishes the generative process that results from Appreciative Inquiry. There is no end, because it is a living process. Because the statements generated by the [clients] are grounded in real experience and history, people know how to repeat their success.[2]*

The coach is able to help a client identify his strengths, mirroring them back to him even as they work to further cultivate or discover the strengths within himself. This is a tremendous gift to offer to another human.

Early in my consulting career, I was preparing to teach a ten-day course in group facilitation and experience-based training to a group of high-powered Latin American business school faculty members in Costa Rica. They were highly skilled in the case method and relied heavily on a didactic, expert model of teaching. Most had Ph.D.s. It was easy for me to feel that my background was inadequate next to their impressive credentials. I had a good design for the program, but I was inwardly terrified.

My mentor and coach at the time, Rod Napier, had worked with me on the design of the course but would not be involved in its execution. When we talked for one last time before I flew to San José, he knew I was anxious. In response, he reminded me that the participants were brilliant and successful and that I thoroughly knew the material and concepts—that the essence of experiential learning was to learn from what happened and that my proven expertise lay in facilitating this process. As long as I worked with the emerging needs of the group, we would all be learners together. In short, he reminded me to trust what I knew.

Five minutes into the program, it was apparent that two of the participants spoke almost no English. No one had warned me this might be the case, and I was momentarily stunned. Then I remembered Rod's reminder that the entire premise was teaching these bright educators to use what emerged from the group and to be flexible in their own designs for future projects. I knew in a flash that this was my first opportunity to model what we were talking about and that I could seize the moment and change my plan. I switched languages, and we conducted the rest of the program in Spanish. Those ten days became one of the most enjoyable, satisfying, and successful experiences of my professional life. In part, this was because I was able to draw on my inherent capacity for flexibility, of which my coach had reminded me.

In identifying and honoring the client's strengths, the coach is supporting the client in his capacity to be successful. The coach may do this by directing the client's attention to prior successes and current skills, either through questioning or by making more direct statements. She can also encourage the client to develop a reminder system to use in a moment of anxiety. Whatever the approach, the outcome is that the client feels connected to his strengths and resources and will have more confidence in his ability to navigate the challenges ahead.

Here's a sample dialogue that addresses this point:

CLIENT: It seems like every year my team is drowning at budget time, and I get overwhelmed and stressed. There's too much to do and too little time.

REFLECTOR: We talked last time about creating a back-out schedule ahead of time so you can clear the decks for some of the activities that have to happen in the budget process. That way, you can schedule that work more proactively so it doesn't all pile up before the deadline.

CLIENT: Yeah, that's a good idea, but we always seem to get crazy.

REFLECTOR: So how could you prevent that? Let's look at the pieces. You've told me that you and your team know what's involved in putting the budget together—all the steps. *The coach reminds the client of his knowledge and resources.*

CLIENT: Yes, we certainly do. Everyone on this team has been through the process at least twice, and some more.

REFLECTOR: And you know how each of those pieces fits into the picture. You could probably map out the whole process. Right? *The coach reminds the client of his knowledge and resources.*

CLIENT: Well. (pauses) We've never done that, but it wouldn't be hard. It's a logical process; there are certain steps. They just go one after the other.

REFLECTOR: And does your group have the skills to do each of these well? Are they competent?

CLIENT: Yeah, we do a great job. The end result is perfect. *The client is owning the team's expertise.* It's just the stress level; it takes a big toll.

COACH AS INVESTIGATOR: It seems like you're about ready to change that. You don't have to do it the same way next time around. Do you really believe it can be easier than it has been? *The coach reconnects client to his stated outcome.*

CLIENT: Yes, I do. I know it can be easier. It has to be.

COACH AS GUIDE: So now's your chance to get ready for the next time, so it *will* be easier. You and your team obviously know what the pieces are, how they fit together, and how to do them. And so you're working from a strong position if you want to change this pattern. *The coach is encouraging action.*

CLIENT: Well, when you look at it that way, I guess we are. So you're saying we just need to think about the sequence and plan the activities better. *The client articulates the beginning of a strategy and action steps.*

REFLECTOR: Yes, that's the part you haven't done yet. Will it be hard to sit down with your people and map out the whole process from start to finish on a more relaxed time line? That's the piece that's missing.

CLIENT: No, that won't be hard. (pauses) We know how to do that.

REFLECTOR: You're right; it isn't too complex. You absolutely *can* do it. And if you do it now, you've got your road map ready for the next budget cycle. *Coach continues to connect the client's awareness to his own resources.*

In this dialogue, the focus of the coach as Reflector is to direct the client's attention to all the capabilities that he and his team can bring to bear on a situation that has previously been highly stressful. The client already has most of what is needed to solve the problem, and when the coach helps him see that this is the case, he ends up believing in his ability to work with his team to take care of the rest.

The client doesn't have to take it on faith or be convinced. For now, the coach is holding the confidence for the client until he can develop it for himself. In order to demonstrate to himself that he does have this potential, he has only to enter into a process; the evidence will follow. This provides the psychological space for movement on the client's part.

This Aspect of the Reflector supports the client's ability to see himself as successful—within reason, of course. It's not the coach's responsibility to get the client to feel differently. The coach accepts where the client is now, while holding out the belief that the client can move through the current situation to a successful outcome.

Encouraging Self-Observation
and Reflection

Self-awareness is critical to the client's ability to be self-correcting, and it's part of the coach's job as Reflector to provide encouragement and tools that facilitate the client's self-observation skills. Self-observation exercises, such as those offered throughout the book, can be of tremendous use to clients and can be designed for virtually any habit, behavior, or pattern of thought.

In the next dialogue, the Reflector encourages the client to develop his capacity to observe and reflect on his own behavior. This capacity is central to the client's capacity to become self-correcting. It is not that coach feedback isn't useful. However, in the ongoing journey toward independence and self-generation, it's key for the client to learn to observe himself. Thus, the coach becomes less critical to the ongoing development of self-awareness. Encouraging this independence is a responsibility of the coach.

CLIENT: My people seem to have a lot of gripes about me, and I need to do something about it. It's pretty clear from my feedback that they see me as snappy, reactive, and—what is it they put down here?—sometimes quick to anger. That's what they said in the evaluation.

REFLECTOR: Maybe you could get better at observing yourself in action. If you can notice when you're doing the things that all these people say you're doing, maybe you could begin to change it in real time, and your people wouldn't feel so put off. *The coach offers the possibility of increased self-awareness and connects it to the benefits.*

CLIENT: That makes sense. But if I could notice all this minor stuff, I wouldn't need to be talking to you about it. That's the problem; sometimes I don't even know what they mean when they say I do this or that. I do blow up once in a while, sure, but it's rare.

REFLECTOR: Well, we all have ingrained habits that make us do things we don't even know we're doing. Maybe the key here is paying attention to how you're feeling and how that leads you to behave. Maybe you don't even notice it when you're being snappy. If we become more self-aware, we can all get better at choosing what works best—for us and for other people too. *The coach normalizes the issue by using "we."*

CLIENT: I don't have a clue how to begin with this. But I guess I want to. I'm tired of being seen as some kind of ogre.

REFLECTOR: I can get you started with a self-observation exercise. It's simple. Twice a day, take five minutes and jot down specific examples from the past several hours when people could have thought you were being snappy or short. They can be really minor. I'm just asking you to look for examples of how you're reacting to things and how others might experience you. I'm not asking you to try to change anything or judge yourself, just be your normal self and pay attention. Collect as many examples as you can, however minor. That's the game. Are you willing to try it? *The coach encourages a specific practice of self-observation that will boost the client's self-awareness, and makes a game out of it.*

CLIENT: Sure, I'll give it a try for a few days.

REFLECTOR: Good. After you observe yourself in action for a while, I'm going to ask you what you see. *Builds accountability.*

Here the Reflector is issuing an invitation to self-awareness. First she offers the guidance that it's important to be able to notice what's going on inside oneself; then she suggests a pragmatic process for doing so. Again, the ability to see ourselves clearly helps us get beyond our habits, in particular, our self-defensive behaviors and routines.

Drawing from Chris Argyris's work, Peter Senge describes defensive routines as

> the entrenched habits we use to protect ourselves from the embarrassment and threat that come with exposing our thinking. Defensive routines form a sort of protective shell around our deepest assumptions, defending us against pain, but also keeping us from learning about the causes of the pain. . . . The most effective defensive routines, like that of the forceful CEO [someone Senge used as an example], are those we cannot see. Ostensibly, the CEO hoped to provoke others into expressing their thoughts. But his overbearing behavior reliably prevented them from doing so, thereby protecting his own views from challenge. If expressed as a conscious strategy, the defensiveness is

transparent: "Keep people on the defensive through intimidation, so they won't confront my thinking." If the CEO saw his strategy presented in such bald terms, he would almost certainly disavow it. The fact that it remains hidden to him keeps it operative.[3]

In this Aspect, the Reflector is an advocate for client self-observation and reflection. She represents the value of doing this and supports the client as he develops trust in both the usefulness of observing himself and his ability to do so. In most cases, it will take time for the client to cultivate this trust and to see that he really can increase his self-awareness. But this awareness is a prerequisite for replacing habits and defensive routines with something potentially more useful.

As the client goes through this developmental process, the Reflector consistently provides tools and structures while being supportive in encouraging him to keep at the self-observation.

THE MINDFUL REFLECTOR

The Reflector is a key supporter of the client's enhanced awareness of the choices he is making and of their consequences. Well played, the Reflector role can reduce a client's blind spots and shine a light on his defensive routines. The more firmly a behavior or a defensive routine is entrenched, the more likely it's protecting something deep and tightly held.

The Reflector helps the client to become more honest with himself. In this role, the coach must be mindful and sensitive, speaking with respect, acceptance, and caring.

One mindfulness challenge is that a coach may invest herself in a social identity, for example, as having the ability to lift the client out of his current emotional state into a more optimistic one. This identity is limiting. It's wonderful when a client leaves a session feeling more optimistic. It feels good to both parties. Ultimately, however, it is not up to us to fix our client's mood or perspective. We are not responsible for the emotional well-being of our clients. In fact, for all of us as human beings, feeling discouraged for a while may be part of the process of working our own way out of a dilemma; we must discover our own readiness to change things. To lose sight of this is to create another attachment for ourselves and a confusing message for the client.

Another pitfall of the Reflector role is that the coach's "belief in the client" may come across as false or too easy. It is a disservice to superficially prop someone up. As coaches, we believe in the fundamental capacity of every person to grow and change. What we do is provide space for our clients to develop their own realistic assessments of their unique capabilities, including those they may not have been aware of previously. That doesn't mean we believe that everyone can become a genius at calculus or a concert violinist. We need to be able to be honest and direct when we suspect that our clients are biting off more than they can chew, stating it both simply and kindly: "Jerry, let me suggest that your experience and skills haven't yet prepared you to run for president."

For a client to rely excessively on the coach, in any role the coach is playing, leads to a kind of dependence in which the client is always looking to the outside for a sense of self. This is counter to the notion of coaching, as it ultimately undermines the client's ability to be self-generating. The mindful Reflector must be alert for this dependency. If the coach feels the client pulling at the coach's energy and the coach feels drained at the end of a conversation by the need to reassure and carry the client, he should see it as a red flag that some form of dependency is taking place.

We can sometimes feel anxious about telling the truth. We fear the client's defensiveness. We have projections about what it might feel like to hear what we are about to say. We desire to protect the client's feelings. All of these may lead us to soft-pedal or avoid speaking the truth. Here, as always, we must be aware of our own aversions and fears, and let them go in order to be present with the client. Our feedback and reflections must always be delivered on a foundation of compassion and respect.

Finally, if serious warning signs are present in the client, such as depression or unrelenting anxiety, or if the client appears to be incapable of mustering sufficient energy or optimism to take action, therapeutic issues may be involved. Unless you are a trained clinician, referrals to other professionals with the requisite skills may well be in order.

These guidelines can help you maintain mindful reflection:

- Ask permission from the client before providing feedback. Ensure that there is a clear understanding between you about the purpose and the client's readiness to receive it.

- Own your interpretation as yours, making clear that there are other interpretations that are just as valid. You are simply sharing one person's perspective.

- Recognize that because you are the coach, the client has granted you a certain authority and presumably sees you as credible. As the Reflector, be mindful that we are ultimately seeking to build the client's capacity to self-observe; our feedback and our encouragement toward reflection ultimately serve the client's self-awareness. Our coaching and assessments should never override the client's sense of herself.

- Mean what you say. Be clear about what you see. Be a good enough observer that you have concrete and specific examples of your client's unhelpful behaviors or skills and capabilities. A fuzzy, generalized belief in someone will mean less than grounded specifics that the person can understand and relate to.

- Pay attention to your own need to be the fixer—one who needs to be needed. If you and the client cooperate to prop up your social identity as a Reflector, this may undermine his ability to provide a positive perspective for himself. This is another opportunity for mindfulness and for recognizing your own attachments and ego needs.

The following exercises provide an opportunity to bring your attention more to the nuances of using this Voice.

EXERCISE 7.1.
Self-Coaching as Reflector: Providing Feedback

Accurate self-assessment is key for good understanding. The Reflector, among other Aspects, provides feedback to the client and encourages her to self-observe. Practice this by inviting your own inner Reflector to provide you some direct and candid feedback. Of course, this is also a simultaneous opportunity to practice holding yourself with compassion and respect!

1. State two or three situations in which you have successfully applied what you've been learning in this book. This could be in your coaching or in other areas of your life.

2. Identify, if possible, two missed opportunities to apply what you've been learning. Without judgment, notice and then describe the (probably unconscious) story that you told yourself in order to justify not taking advantage of these opportunities.

3. Identify two great things that you know to be true about yourself as a learner that will shape and improve your application of this material assuming you apply them going forward from here.

EXERCISE 7.2.
Reflector Areas for Attention

Take some time to respond to the following questions:

- Based on the description of the Reflector, what Aspects do you engage with skillfully and mindfully?
- What Reflector Aspects might you tend to overuse? When? How do you know this?
- What Aspects are you less comfortable and proficient with? When? How do you know this?

EXERCISE 7.3.
Reflector Self-Observation

- Choose an Aspect that represents a development opportunity for you: a skill or behavior that you wish to bring more into your coaching or one that you perhaps have attachments to and therefore overuse. Describe this skill or behavior as specifically as possible.
- Construct a self-observation for yourself using the explanation and structure from Chapter Two. Do this self-observation consistently and rigorously over several weeks. Notice how your mindfulness has changed in relation to this Aspect.

CHAPTER SUMMARY

The Reflector Voice is central to helping the client be self-aware about her behaviors, her thoughts and assumptions, and how she is creating her situation. The Reflector does this through several Aspects. He:

- *Provides direct and honest feedback,* which allows the client to see herself as one other person sees her. These, of course, are simply the coach's own observations and interpretations, which serve the client in becoming more able to observe herself accurately.
- *Directs the client's attention toward his or her capabilities and potential,* thus encouraging the client to see herself as resourceful and as having available more choices for action.
- *Encourages self-observation and reflection* through bringing mindful attention to her actions. The Reflector invites the client, over and over, to build this capacity for self-awareness and self-correction. The Reflector may suggest that the client use self-observation exercises.

The roles that the coach plays in this Voice are both delicate and invaluable because they can lead us into the tender realm of the client's defenses and unconscious patterns of behavior. Mindfulness is key. The unshakable presence of the Reflector is invaluable as he gently helps the client open new perceptual doors.

CHAPTER 8

The Teacher

Believe those who are seeking the truth. Doubt those who find it.

André Gide

If you have knowledge, let others light their candles in it.

Margaret Fuller

*If you're not modeling what you're teaching,
then you're teaching something else.*

Roger Schwarz

THE TEACHER IS THE SECOND OF THE THREE VOICES that I describe as "sharpeners" of the client's responses to the Investigator's three areas of questioning. The very legitimacy of teaching in a coaching context is sometimes a topic of fierce debate; some schools of thought maintain that coaching is inherently and exclusively a questioning process and that teaching is not part of the a role. I disagree.

Any leader has blind spots and gaps in the information available to her. Expanding what she can observe for herself and incorporate into decision making greatly increases her resourcefulness. Because they inhabit a distinct world, coaches have access to information, understandings, and perceptions that the client is not likely to know. Withholding these seems to me to impoverish what might be offered.

The word *teacher*, of course, means many things to many people. Styles of teaching vary widely, and general definitions of teaching often incorporate elements described in this book as belonging to other Voices of the coach. The Socratic method of teaching, for example, is the archetypal exemplar of the Investigator behavior of asking questions to prompt the client to discover his or her own answers.

I am using the word *teacher* to describe a very specific set of roles and behaviors within the overall approach to coaching that we are using here. Other wisdom and perspectives on what teachers do are just as well informed and valid as this one, but they pertain to different contexts. The Teacher role as described and differentiated within the Septet Model is a specific subset of teaching behaviors. The Voice of the Teacher is my personal favorite—the one I go to most easily, the one I am most likely to hide behind or overuse. This is because I grew up with a mother and father who were educators professionally, as well as being my own first teachers. I was the product of physicist genes and a public school/liberal arts college education, in which I spent countless hours with at least seventy or so teachers (that may be an underestimate). I've also participated in innumerable workshops, trainings, and conferences, where I have placed myself in a learning mode with people who purported to teach something. The exposure to all of these people, who ranged in their teaching skills from mediocre to world class, socialized me into what it means to be a Teacher, and for me that archetype is generally a positive one. Some readers will notice the same bias.

It is important to be aware that the Teacher is prone to overuse. The more easily a particular role can make a coach look good in his own eyes or those of others, the more likely it is to become the basis for a social identity. The giver of answers, the provider of knowledge, the wise person: these are seductive social identities around which to build attachments. As always, being mindful is the way to avoid the temptations and pitfalls of this role.

Used mindfully, the Voice of the Teacher offers much to the client. Mindful teaching is an offering that the other person is truly free to accept or decline. Although the mindful Teacher may know that the information provided is likely to illuminate a pathway or a particular set of choices for the client, he has no attachment to the client's acceptance of the information, and it is not his goal to get the client to move in a particular direction. The Teacher simply provides the distinctions, language, and tools that enable a client to see the situation differently.

In the first Aspect, the Teacher provides distinctions, information, and frameworks that will help the client observe himself and his situation in new ways and that may also reveal possible new outcomes and actions. These distinctions, discussed at the beginning of Chapter Three, provide the basis for seeing anew.

The second Aspect of the Teacher is inviting the client to reflect on his own thinking process and supporting him in finding new ways to analyze a situation. This is sometimes an encouragement, sometimes a challenge. Either way, the desired outcome for the client is the possibility of a cognitive shift or new perspectives, or both, on the assumptions and values that shape his actions. I say "possibility" here because the aim is not to have the client think like the coach, but to help him see things in new ways that will be useful to him.

In the third Aspect, the Teacher makes visible the actual coaching process and models being used. By making coaching, the supporting change theories, and development tools and models explicit, we help the client internalize the process itself. This transparency encourages the coach to first become a more informed client and then to become a self-generative person who understands the pedagogy of change and increasingly can be the author of her own development process.

ASPECTS OF THE TEACHER

- Providing new distinctions, information, and knowledge
- Challenging and stimulating the client's thinking process
- Explaining the coaching process, theory, and models being used

---

PROVIDING NEW DISTINCTIONS, INFORMATION, AND KNOWLEDGE

The Teacher begins with the simple sharing of distinctions, knowledge, or information. We can think of these as resources garnered from the coach's experience; previously they were available in the coach's world but not in the client's. Sharing them expands what is available to the client. Information can be as simple as a referral to a good executive education course with a relevant emphasis, or as complex as a philosophy of human development.

This informational Aspect involves sharing distinctions that the client can use to observe herself in new ways. For example, the very distinction of the Teacher, with the descriptions of what it means in this chapter, will enable you to observe yourself in new ways that lead to greater self-awareness and competency. This is enabling, in that it supports new ways of seeing, which lead to new alternatives for action.

The Teacher also provides distinctions that support the client in understanding and interpreting his situation. Distinctions such as staying centered in a difficult conversation, storyboarding a process map, the steps involved in effective feedback, or visualizing a preferred future can reveal significant new possibilities for how the client can see herself or her situation that previously were unavailable to her. Without such ways of seeing, we often tend to be stuck in habitual ways of interpreting events. With them, the client has new means for communicating about, and interpreting, phenomena.

My client Terry had committed himself to a major diet and exercise plan. All went well until Thanksgiving dinner, when he politely declined the mashed potatoes and gravy because of the unwanted calories. Terry's wife, a wonderful cook who was proud of her Thanksgiving spread, was taken aback by this refusal. It was a reasonable decision for Terry to make; it was also reasonable for Terry's wife to have made the mashed potatoes. The resulting strain was minor, but Terry's diet and exercise plan was one of the things I was coaching him on, and he wanted to talk to me about the incident.

Right away, I thought of the concept of interests versus positions from the influential book *Getting to Yes*.[1] It took two minutes to explain, and then we applied it to the situation. Terry's position was that he didn't want to eat extra calories; his wife's position was that she wanted people to enjoy what she had worked so hard and lovingly to prepare. Beneath those different stances lay their common interests: both wanted Terry's program to succeed, both wanted a holiday dinner with their children to be special, and both wanted a sense of tradition. Focusing on these underlying interests would yield lots of possibilities for creating a win-win solution.

Terry was able to see the event in a whole new light. The information was neutral—just a way to think about any situation in a new way. The result, however, was very important for Terry. He was able to apply the distinction between interests and positions in a variety of situations at work and at home; he felt it greatly strengthened his on-the-job skills as a manager. And that year he and his family approached Christmas dinner very differently. After a discussion about what each of them wanted, they decided on a collaborative approach in which each person, including the kids, prepared something special for the meal. Terry's wife was thrilled at having more help than ever before, Terry stayed on his diet, and the entire family enjoyed the experience. Acting as the Teacher, I had simply provided a language and a way of seeing; Terry did the rest.

Here's another example.

CLIENT: I just don't see why Brad would feel so put out in that situation. I was just voicing a different perspective. I was direct, but, come *on!* He's a grown-up!

TEACHER: Jennifer, I can suggest a way of looking at what happened in a different way. It might be helpful. Is that of interest? *The coach offers a choice point and invites the client to consider another interpretation of the situation.*

CLIENT: Sure.

TEACHER: Think of the available energy in an interaction between two people. Ultimately there's only a certain amount, and it gets used in several ways. Quantity of airtime is part of it, but not all. Forcefulness of expression also uses up energy. Think about it for a minute. Can you see how, when they're interacting with others, some people tend to take more energy than others? *The coach invites Jennifer to consider another interpretation of the situation.*

CLIENT: Yeah. (pauses) Some people are pretty assertive. I guess I'm one of those. Others are more laid back. They wait for someone else to take the lead.

TEACHER: Exactly. What does Brad usually do?

CLIENT: He's usually pretty outspoken.

TEACHER: But in this case, your opinions about the database were strongly held.

CLIENT: Yeah. (laughs) You could say that!

TEACHER: So one way to look at what happened when you met the other day is that of the available 100 percent of the energy, you were taking up maybe 75 percent. If that's right, it leaves him with 25 percent. For someone who's used to being outspoken,

25 percent might feel a bit suffocating. Perhaps in your desire to press your point, you were simply a bit overwhelming. Does this make any sense to you? *The coach offers a new distinction that allows the client to see her situation differently.*

CLIENT: Yeah, it does. I do have strong feelings about the database, but Brad does too. He probably felt I didn't bother to listen to what he had to say. I want to be direct, and I want to argue my case, but maybe I need not get so carried away.

TEACHER: I think that's a good way to put it, Jennifer.

In this dialogue, the coach is providing a distinction (thinking of the available energy in an interaction and the amount that Jennifer took up) that is useful in interpreting an event.[2] Again, the distinction is neutral and does not point Jennifer toward any specific action. It does, however, enable Jennifer to step outside her view of what happened with Brad and see it from a larger perspective. Once she sees the picture through a new lens, the client often spontaneously knows what she needs to do differently.

Commenting on an example of his own, James Flaherty writes,

> *Each person's actions were fully consistent with the interpretation he brought, an interpretation that will persist across time, across events, across circumstances. Our job as coaches will be to understand the client's structure of interpretation, then in partnership alter this structure so that the actions that follow bring about the intended outcome. As coaches we do this by providing a new language that allows the client to make new observations.*[3]

Providing new distinctions allows the client to interpret events in very different ways; this can offer options for changed behaviors and actions that would have previously been inaccessible to the client.

CHALLENGING AND STIMULATING THE CLIENT'S THINKING PROCESS

It's sometimes helpful to make the assumption that each of us does the best we can given the information and choices we perceive. In theory, if we had all the necessary information, we'd always make the optimal choices in our lives. But of course other factors limit the choices we can see and are able to act on, and many of these have to do with our conditioning.

As we know from our earlier discussion about conditioning, humans tend to process information in predictable ways. We get caught in limited ways of seeing and thinking about the situations that we face, which limits the options we see for our lives. The coach, of course, is in the business of supporting the client in expanding options, and sometimes exposing limitations in the client's thinking process itself is enormously helpful. This means that the underlying mechanisms that the client uses to process information, draw inferences, and ultimately determine courses of action are made explicit during the coaching conversation.

This second Aspect of the Teacher is focused on the thinking process itself—the underlying mechanisms that the client uses to process information, draw inferences, and ultimately determine courses of action. The Teacher challenges the client in her thinking process and helps her to a deeper and more accurate level of understanding. This can involve exposing the client's leaps of abstraction as she moves from simple observations to complex generalizations that may or may not be true. Or it can mean helping the client examine her assumptions, which may or may not support what she says she wants.

In the next example, the client takes a simple situation and makes significant inferences without testing them. By challenging the inferences she has made, the coach helps her see how her mind works.

CLIENT: I think Susan [the client's immediate boss] really has it in for me. She barely says hello to me in the morning when she comes in. And she unfairly criticized my presentation in the staff meeting the other day.

COACH AS INVESTIGATOR: So what happened in the meeting?

CLIENT: I was presenting our sales projections. She said they were overly optimistic, and I should go back to the market data and be less starry-eyed. That's how she put it.

COACH AS INVESTIGATOR: Starry-eyed. Hmm. (pauses) Well, was she right? *The coach questions the client's implicit assumption that her boss was unfair.*

CLIENT: Well, maybe she was. My projections *were* a bit on the optimistic side. I didn't think it was appropriate for her to say that in the meeting, though.

COACH AS INVESTIGATOR: Maybe not. Is that typical of the way she responds to people?

CLIENT: Well, she can be pretty tough. Her expectations are high. I don't think she means to be hurtful, but she can be a bit cutting.

TEACHER: Perhaps it's not really about you. What if it's just her style? *The coach questions the client's inference that it was about her.*

CLIENT: Yeah. It is her style. She's tactless.

TEACHER: You mentioned how she acts in the morning. Does she say hello to everyone else? Is it just you she ignores?

CLIENT: Well, actually she just brushes in, grabs her in-box, and goes into her office. I do respect her. I just wish she was a nicer person.

TEACHER: You can't change her style, but you can choose how you react to it. Beyond style, though, it sounds like Susan's committed to accurate projections. So are you—you both want the same thing in the end. *The coach is distinguishing where the client has power and where not and is affirming that both have shared interests.*

CLIENT: Yeah, we do.

TEACHER: Well, from this discussion, it sounds to me as if she doesn't really have it in for you in particular. It sounds like she has high expectations and sometimes isn't as diplomatic as you'd like her to be. Is that a more accurate way to describe the situation? *The coach is confirming a new, more accurate interpretation of the situation.*

CLIENT: Yes, I guess it is. I think sometimes I blow things up out of proportion. And sometimes I take them too personally. When she called me starry-eyed, though, it really set me off.

TEACHER: So—you have a challenging boss! Let's talk about how you can work with her more effectively and not take her style personally. *The coach is inviting a new direction in the conversation based on this new interpretation.*

Here, the coach as Teacher challenges the client's thinking process. She had been making a set of inferences that led to the conclusion that her boss had it in for her, but when the coach challenges these inferences, the client comes to the conclusion that her initial reaction was probably unjustified. Untangling the royal mess that our minds sometimes make of a situation is a key part of coming to see the situation more clearly and thus being able to identify a useful course of action within it. This opens a new course of inquiry.

The Teacher helps by revealing the inferences that the client makes. This allows the client to come back to what is really observable and respond to it more directly, rather than responding from a set of inferences that go way beyond the data, are likely inaccurate, and may lead in a totally wrong direction.

People often hire coaches because they want to change the game and approach their situations with new strategies that are more likely to be effective. Coaches challenge the person faced with a setback to examine the fundamental assumptions and goals that led to the ineffective action strategy in the first place. By assessing the underlying thinking process, the client engages in a deeper level of learning, one more likely to lead to new solutions. With this "double-loop learning," as Chris Argyris and Don Schön explain in *Theory in Practice,* "individuals are . . . able to examine their values and assumptions in order to design and implement a quality of life that is not constrained by the status quo."[4]

This dialogue primarily uses the Teacher Voice but also includes a couple of others along the way.

COACH AS CONTRACTOR: So, Rich, how did your conversation with Michael go? *The coach is following up about a previous commitment; this is an example of the Contractor Voice.*

CLIENT: I guess it went pretty well. We ended up talking about other things for the most part.

COACH AS CONTRACTOR: What did he have to say about your new marketing idea?

CLIENT: Actually we didn't really talk about it much. I didn't feel ready to bring it up.

COACH AS CONTRACTOR: When we talked last time, you felt that it was an important time to get an outside perspective and that Michael was the one who could give you that.

CLIENT: Yeah, I did feel like that. But I'm just not ready to share it yet. I think I have to think it through a little more.

COACH AS REFLECTOR: Rich, you've worked on this idea a lot! Sounds like it has to be close to perfect before you're willing to share it with others.

CLIENT: Well, it reflects on me!

COACH AS REFLECTOR: Rich, it's very important to you for Michael to see you as competent, isn't it?.

CLIENT: Of course, wouldn't it be for you?

TEACHER: Yes. It would if I were in your shoes. May I share an observation? *The Teacher asks permission to share an important distinction.*

CLIENT: Of course.

TEACHER: I think there are two things you're trying to act on at the same time, but they conflict. The first is that it's a good thing to be getting another perspective on your idea. That would make you want to talk with Michael about it as soon as possible because you respect his opinion.

CLIENT: Yes, that's right. I think he could help me work on it.

TEACHER: Yes, but the other thing appears to be winning out.

CLIENT: What's that?

TEACHER: The other thing is that it's important to you to appear competent, to have worked out all the kinks before you share something. Maybe that's what holds you back when you meet with Michael.

CLIENT: Hmm. (pauses) I see your point. Yeah, it's a trade-off. I can't do both at the same time. But maybe by trying to make myself look good, I actually get in my own way.

TEACHER: Exactly. You make defending your competence more important than refining your thinking. It's not what you say you value most, but that's the way you act. *The coach has exposed a discrepancy between what the client says he values and what he actually does.*

CLIENT: Yeah, you're right! I do that a lot. I lay low until I'm very sure of myself. But maybe that holds me back sometimes. That's a big pattern! I have to think more about that.

The Teacher, in inviting the client to take a second look at what's motivating him, exposes these gaps between conflicting desires and old habits at work.[5] This must be done sensitively and mindfully because inner conflict may make all of us feel defensive. The key, of course, is to support the client in discovering that a resolution is possible and an alternative action might in fact get him what he truly wants.

Seeing these underlying habits at play in our lives is an eye-opener, especially when we discover that holding rigidly to them keeps us from achieving or experiencing what we say we want. (This should remind you of the attachments and aversions we introduced in Chapter One.)

The coach as Teacher works with the client on ways he can get what he says he wants. The coach takes the client's commitment to these goals at face value, and when the client is acting in ways that don't move him in that direction, seeks to catalyze his awareness about the discrepancy. The coach exposes his underlying thinking process, assumptions, and habits, so that he is better able to fit his actions to his goals.

EXPLAINING THE COACHING PROCESS, THEORY, AND MODELS BEING USED

In the third Aspect, the Teacher makes the coaching process itself visible, so the client can be a more informed partner and ultimately competent and self-generative in guiding her own development. This runs counter to the attachments of some coaches to providing something that is unique, magical, and transformative. This attachment serves the coach's identity needs beautifully but rarely serves the client.

Good coaching that can transform people's lives is founded on commonsense principles and practices about how humans learn and change. Revealing this truth, and thereby demystifying the process, is good practice, builds a more robust partnership between coach and client, and empowers the client around the learning process.

Revealing the techniques of the coaching process does a number of things:

- Provides a set of distinctions that the client can then use to observe the coaching process in a more informed way, and provide feedback to the coach about what he wants and needs

- Encourages the client to understand and take part in the shaping of the conversation

- Reveals choice points in the conversation and informs joint decisions about how to move forward

- Builds the client's understanding of the change process in order to become more self-generative and independent as a learner down the road

By now, the Voices and their Aspects are probably part of your coaching lexicon and are becoming embedded in how you think about what you are doing. If so, it makes sense for you to share the overall Septet Model with your client. Understanding its elements, the client becomes more able to distinguish among the Voices as you use them in the conversation and observe how you do what you do.

TEACHER: I want to continue to ask a series of questions here, Judy. We've talked in the past about how when I ask questions rather than offering my suggestions, it can strike you as a bit like a guessing game. Do you remember that conversation? *The coach puts the process on the table for discussion.*

CLIENT: Yes. And most of the time, it doesn't feel like a game. Just once or twice, I had the sneaking suspicion that you had a great idea you weren't sharing with me because you wanted me to come up with my own!

TEACHER: Well, it's my belief that the best ideas are ones that are developed and owned by the person who is closest to the situation and will be acting on the idea. Sometimes it's easier for both of us if I just lay out, in a neutral way, something I've seen work before. But doing that can also shortcut your discovery process, and the idea itself is unlikely to be the best one anyway. *The coach is providing information about the coaching process.*

CLIENT: Maybe.

TEACHER: Maybe. For sure there's a place for sharing action-neutral ideas and information. That's the role of the Teacher Voice in the model we've discussed, and I'm doing it now. Can you sense that I've changed my approach for right now, and I'm sharing information and my beliefs about coaching itself? *The coach both offers a distinction about coaching roles and invites the client to be aware, in the present moment, that he's using it.*

CLIENT: Yes, and you're reminding me of one of the assumptions that we've discussed before: that I have solutions available to me even in situations that I've not faced before. And your questioning is what helps to bring those out.

TEACHER: Yes, which is why I lead with what I've called the Investigator in my coaching. My experience has shown that this discovery process leads to better ideas, ownership, and greater self-confidence in solving your own challenges. Ultimately we are after your independence, and when you generate your own ideas, that's what you're building. *The coach names a belief she holds about coaching and states the benefits of questioning.*

CLIENT: That makes sense. At the same time, you've been involved in a lot of planning processes like the one you're coaching me through, and I don't want to have to reinvent the wheel.

TEACHER: Agreed. I'm also committed to sharing ideas that I think might be helpful and other resources that will support what you're doing. *The coach reassures the client that she's not going to miss out.* At the same time, I want to be rigorous in pointing you toward your own resourcefulness in the situation, toward your leading an initiative that is unique and appropriate for your company. Make sense?

CLIENT: Makes sense to me.

COACH AS PARTNER: I'll default toward asking questions about your ideas. And I promise that I won't withhold something that seems important to share. If you feel that I'm leaning too far toward questions and it seems "off" to you, say so, and we'll make an informed joint decision about how to proceed. Does that work for you? *The Partner offers an understanding of how they might work together and a commitment to making joint decisions.*

CLIENT: Yes. I want you to push me, and I see the power of thinking it through for myself. It's helpful to see this as a balancing act and to clarify that we each have a role in managing it.

COACH AS INVESTIGATOR: Okay. Switching gears, what actions can you take to support your department heads in working across departments as they align their balanced scorecards with the division's? *The coach switches back to the Investigator.*

In this brief meta-conversation between coach and client about how they're working together, the coach has made explicit the distinction between the Teacher and Investigator Voices. The coach and client have discussed the pros and cons of each, and they've made a joint decision about how to manage the balance between them. With this increased understanding and a newly clarified way to manage the balance between the Teacher and the Investigator, coach and client can move forward through the planning conversation with a better sense of being informed partners in the process.

THE MINDFUL TEACHER

The Teacher Voice is often overused. For some coaches, the Teacher becomes a means to validate their identity as competent and wise—attachments that invariably cloud the coach's ability to see the client clearly.

The Teacher is inherently neutral. There is no impetus from the Teacher toward action. (Encouraging a client's motivation to act, if and when this seems necessary, is the province of the action-oriented Guide, the topic of the next chapter.) The information the coach offers in this role is relevant to the client's concerns and presented to the client in the interest of fostering new perspectives and choices, either about the client's situation or about the coaching process itself. The Teacher contributes at any point of the Situation → Outcome → Action progression.

Constraining the time you spend as Teacher is necessary because our ultimate goal is to help the client develop his or her own ways to learn, not to rely on us for answers. That is the basis for the critical distinction between appropriate and inappropriate uses of the Teacher Voice: Does the imparting of this information to the client at this time, or challenging the client's thinking in this way, support his or her long-term ability to be effective and self-generating?

Here are some guidelines for staying mindful as the Teacher:

- Ensure that your teaching is serving a specific need or outcome that the client has articulated. Don't confuse means and ends. To introduce a model or a piece of information because you find it interesting doesn't really serve the client; doing so as a way of enabling the client to see differently and to illuminate new choices is a service.

- Be mindful of developing dependency. The collusion of the client and coach around dependency can be insidious. If you find yourself in the Teacher role a lot, it may be important to discuss this with the client and ensure that he or she is not leaning on you to an unhelpful extent.

- Watch for your identification with the Teacher role, as indicated by an energy charge or the feeling of being validated somehow by what or how you teach. Watch out for the feeling that it's "important" to share something or that you "should" teach it; this is a big clue to the presence of an attachment on your part. Ground yourself in your perspective of your client as resourceful and whole, and let that guide you as to what's important.

- Ask permission of the client before sharing information or models: "Is it okay if I share a model that I think you might find helpful?" generally leads to agreement. Sometimes, though, a client will say no. A mindful coach is not attached to having every offering accepted.

- Keep your teaching concise and clear. Providing information and new language is a small part of most coaching. It is a laser-like intervention, done to increase the accuracy and understanding with which the client can perceive the landscape and his or her available choices. It is not, however, the primary work of coaching, which is to create change and forward motion. If overdone, teaching can become a diversion from the real work.

As with each of the other Voices, you can engage in a little reflection and use self-observation to greatly increase the mindfulness and attention with which you use the Teacher. (See Exercises 8.1–8.3.)

EXERCISE 8.1.

Self-Coaching as Teacher: Making Pedagogy Visible

The Teacher makes new things, including the coaching process itself, explicit and therefore visible. Practice your Teacher by articulating for yourself a couple of significant elements from what you've read. Choose elements that have influenced how you learn and that you might rearticulate to those you coach in your own work. As an example, the emphasis on asking questions over providing solutions places responsibility on the coaching client to be generative and self-reliant.

1. Note two or three specific ideas and principles that have been described in this book that have catalyzed significant learning for you.

2. Articulate three pragmatic elements of what you can newly offer as a coach, as a result of these, that can accelerate your clients' learning.

EXERCISE 8.2.

Teacher Areas for Attention

Take some time to respond to the following questions:
- Based on the description of the Teacher in this chapter, what Aspects do you engage with skillfully and mindfully?
- What Teacher Aspects might you tend to overuse? When? How do you know this?
- What Aspects are you less comfortable and proficient with? When? How do you know this?

EXERCISE 8.3.

Teacher Self-Observation

- Choose an Aspect that represents a development opportunity for you: a skill or behavior that you wish to bring more into your coaching or one that you perhaps have attachments to and therefore overuse. Describe this skill or behavior as specifically as possible.
- Construct a self-observation for yourself using the explanation and structure from Chapter Two. Do this self-observation consistently and rigorously over several weeks. Notice how your mindfulness has changed in relation to this Aspect.

CHAPTER SUMMARY

The Teacher Voice is an important one and is sometimes excluded from other approaches to coaching. Providing information and insights into the client's thinking process can greatly improve her ability to perceive more accurately both external and internal landscapes and the possible choices available in navigating them. The Teacher:

- *Provides new distinctions, information, and knowledge* that the client can then use to self-observe and develop a fuller picture of his or her situation and possibilities.
- *Challenges and stimulates the client's thinking process* by inviting the client to examine her assumptions and thinking process by pointing out, for example, where she may be making faulty inferences that go way beyond the real data or by helping the client explore the underlying values and assumptions that subconsciously guide her actions.
- *Explains the coaching process, theory, and models being used* in order to educate the client in the very nature of development. In the short term, this serves mutuality in the coaching partnership. In the long term, the client becomes self-generative and increasingly able to author her own self-development for a lifetime.

The Teacher is prone to overuse: the coach's identity around providing information and knowledge can insinuate itself into the coaching work. The mindful Teacher is grounded in compassion and respect and intends his contribution to serve the client's development first and foremost.

CHAPTER

The Guide

*Advice is what we ask for when we already know the answer
but wish we didn't.*

Erica Jong

*I have found the best way to give advice to your children is to find out
what they want and then advise them to do it.*

Harry S. Truman

LEADERS, BY DEFINITION, ARE HEADED IN A DIRECTION
determined by the particular commitments they have entered into
with themselves and with others. Leadership implies change, action,
movement. Yet, as any of us moves toward a commitment, unanticipated challenges inevitably arise, either from the environment or from
within ourselves. The Guide can be of tremendous support in navigating the terrain and encouraging the client along the way.

As the Guide, the coach provides impetus toward action, suggests
possible directions for client action, or even makes recommendations
for what a client might do. The Guide Voice can be exceedingly helpful when the client is feeling reluctant to commit, unclear, or simply
at a loss. Generally this Voice comes to the fore later in the course
of a coaching conversation, after the territory of a situation has been
explored and when the coach and client both agree that the coach's

guidance and leadership might be appropriate and helpful. The Guide can be instrumental as the client confronts the Investigator's third question: "What are you going to do?"

Like the Teacher, the Guide draws directly from the coach's own experience and knowledge. Unlike the Teacher, the Guide is biased toward action. The Guide Voice is the most directive, and therefore the most prone to being used in a way that undermines the client's authority. For this reason, coaches need to pay particular attention to the balance between the client's legitimate need to see progress and the ultimate goal that he take charge of his own unfolding growth and development.

On one hand, the client is participating in a coaching program because he wants to be more effective or wants his life or a specific situation to change—or because a third party has brought him there in an effort to achieve these goals. Bringing about these outcomes nearly always involves commitment to challenging actions, and the coach's additional encouragement and impetus can further enable the client.

On the other hand, an overreliance on the coach can become a crutch, substituting for (and perhaps actively replacing) the client's ability to muster his own internal commitment. Some would argue that this doesn't matter—that the resulting action is the bottom line and that the benefits from acting make the source of the impetus moot. I hold that the ultimate goal of coaching is for the client to become self-generative, and not simply achieve particular results. He accomplishes this by developing his own motivation and commitment to action in service to his own vision. This is why we must be careful what we say and do as the Guide.

The more assertive nature of the Guide Voice carries with it a correspondingly greater chance that the coach will mistake his own agenda with the highest good for the client. Our very sense of identity as a coach may prompt us to move our clients too quickly into action. Some of us even hang out shingles saying something like "Mike: The Results Coach." And for all of us, seeing a client get stuck invokes questions about our own effectiveness. Our attachments, then, may mask our clarity about the client. A client can be usefully stuck. Sometimes we need to feel stuck for a while before we find the willingness to move on and try a new behavior. Protecting our clients from this discomfort by urging them on because of our own impatience to get movement, or because we assume that without our help they're going to be lost forever, doesn't serve to help them get in touch with their own desires and purposes.

I struggled for some time with how to structure my calendar to write this book. While it sounded great to devote several months to nothing but writing, I had coaching and consulting clients, a number of other projects in process, and a short attention span.

My own coach was patient with my struggle. This was an issue that I had to work my way through, and it wasn't her issue. It took several weeks, but ultimately I had to get to the point of either allocating sufficient time to write or giving up the idea of the book. It had to be my decision. If she had pushed me into committing the time, it would not have been fully my decision and I wouldn't have faced down my own indecisiveness. As a result, I might not have worked through the resistances that came up. Her willingness to let it be my struggle and my process while continually putting the choice in front of me was important to my making a true and wholehearted commitment.

The key to using the Guide Voice well is the ability to suggest alternatives, or even to provide a timely nudge or two, without developing an attachment to the client's doing what we think is best for him. When we offer suggestions in our capacity as the Guide, there are no strings attached; we continue to see our clients fully and accept them whether they are stuck and aimless or purposeful and committed to action.

This doesn't mean that we don't care or aren't committed to our client's success. It simply means that we don't confuse ourselves with them. It means that we seek to stay in our centered Master mind, seeing our clients clearly. It means providing impetus or direction when it's truly needed and staying out of the way when the client is developing them on his own or needs to take some time to work through his own resistance to get there.

ASPECTS OF THE GUIDE

- Encouraging the client to take some action of the client's choosing
- Offering options for action
- Recommending specific courses of action

The mindful Guide has three Aspects. The least directive Aspect is encouraging the client to take action without suggesting what that action should be: the Guide simply suggests that movement is desirable and encourages the client toward it. The client may have an idea (perhaps this emerged from the third Investigator line of questioning) about what he would like to do next. In performing this Aspect of the Guide role, the coach encourages the client to act on that idea, but the idea itself came from the client.

In the second Aspect, the Guide may tell the client about what she has seen others do—involving specific actions or approaches or strategies—that has brought them success in similar circumstances. Or, if it's appropriate, she may speak from her own experience. Here the coach is providing examples of possible pathways forward. There's no push for the client to follow a specific pathway, but an action orientation is usually implied by merely presenting these as options or alternatives.

If it seems to serve the client's needs, however, the third Aspect of the Guide Voice includes suggesting or recommending that the client follow a specific course of action. The coach is providing both impetus and directionality. The client is always at choice, of course, and the suggestion is usually framed as an invitation to try something. Still, this is perhaps the most assertive of all the Aspects in the Septet Model.

ENCOURAGING THE CLIENT TO TAKE SOME ACTION OF THE CLIENT'S CHOOSING

Here the Guide is stating a bias for action. This is encouragement for the client to take the plunge, to move from considering a possibility to committing to it. The Guide isn't suggesting or contributing ideas for the action to the client, but she is an advocate for movement in a direction of the client's choosing.

Often the impetus for movement will come from the client. This may derive from dissatisfaction with the status quo, the excitement and energy generated by having a new picture of a desired future, or a combination of both. The work has already been done. All the coach needs to do is provide encouragement and support.

But sometimes the client may resist taking action even when he's thought it through and all the pieces are in place; here, additional impetus is helpful. This impetus is not a replacement for the client's ability to choose; rather, it's a nudge that enables him to do something he has already fundamentally decided to do.

CLIENT: It's hard to think about letting Jeff go. He's been with the company a long time.

GUIDE: Yes, he has. From what you've told me, he's made a big contribution.

CLIENT: Yeah. And I like the guy a lot. It's going to be tough for him. And for his family. *The client is making an argument for not taking a painful action.*

COACH AS INVESTIGATOR: It's never an easy thing to do, even when you know it's the right thing. Have you explored every alternative, Dave? I want you to be sure that this is the right decision.

CLIENT: It is. I just don't want to. I know I have to do it, and sooner is better, but I really, really don't want to.

COACH AS REFLECTOR: You've made your decision, haven't you? *The coach focuses the client on the decision he's made.*

CLIENT: Yes, I've made it.

GUIDE: So now you have to move on it. It's time. (pauses) How do you think you'll feel after you talk to him?

CLIENT: Well, I'm sure I'll still feel sorry. But it'll also be a big relief because I'm really dreading it.

GUIDE: Dave, we've been talking about this for a couple of weeks. You have consistently been very clear about the need to let Jeff go. I know it's difficult, but it's time to take the plunge and do what you've already decided to do. *The coach is advocating that Dave now take the action he's committed to.* Putting it off doesn't help anyone—not you, not Jeff, certainly not Jeff's staff.

CLIENT: You're right. It's time. I'll talk to him tomorrow.

Dave knows what's ahead of him. The pathway is clear, the arguments back and forth have been weighed and decided on. He's made a decision. He's understandably reluctant and appears to need some encouragement to initiate a difficult discussion. This pushing must be done with care. It's critical that the client makes the decision. The coach is testing the client's commitment here and asking him to be sure about his decision. Once the client is sure, the coach can encourage

Dave to take action because Dave knows it's the right thing to do, not because the coach has an agenda about it.

In contrast, pushing a client into a decision that he's not yet ready to make would not serve him well. The client's commitment must be explicit; the nudge serves only to solidify it.

Besides the ethical and developmental arguments for ensuring that the decision is truly the client's, there are situations in which the coach could incur legal liability by steering the client toward a decision with legal ramifications. Some coaches carry errors-and-omissions insurance, a policy standard with many consulting firms, to cover such eventualities. The best pedagogical advice, however, is to keep the client in charge.

OFFERING OPTIONS FOR ACTION

In this second Aspect, the coach offers specific possibilities for action. Clearly this requires that the coach be somewhat knowledgeable about what actions might generally make sense. It has often been stated by people who are very knowledgeable about coaching that a coach does not need to be a subject matter expert, that being a good question asker will suffice. This is often true. While being a good question asker—a good Investigator—may fulfill most of a client's needs, the coach cannot credibly suggest particular business or technical actions with which he himself is completely unfamiliar.

Some clients need more direction. With them, the coach will need to know more about the territory he is working with. If the coach is unprepared, he will either be limited in the Voices available to him or will be extending his coaching beyond his expertise, which becomes an ethical issue. Knowing the territory can come from direct experience or from having coached many clients in one industry or one area of development. For example, if you have coached previous accountant clients, you'll have accumulated important knowledge about choices or resources available to your next client who happens also to be an accountant. The client certainly benefits from having a coach with broad experience across a number of related situations.

CLIENT: I'm interested in getting some process improvement teams going in our company. We encourage suggestions, but we really haven't done anything systematic.

GUIDE: If it would be helpful, I can suggest a couple of approaches that have worked in other companies and you can think about how they might fit.

CLIENT: That would be helpful.

GUIDE: Most of the programs I know about begin with some sort of pilot. The company gives a group of people training in process improvement methods and tools. Then they identify some low-hanging fruit—some clear-cut problem that has a high likelihood of being solved pretty easily. The idea is to get an early success and build some commitment to the methodology. This seems to work better than taking on some huge issue and wrestling with both it and the new process at the same time. *The Guide is describing specific actions and approaches for moving this forward, but without advocating that the client take these actions. He provides direction but no push.*

CLIENT: Makes sense. Who would be involved?

GUIDE: Depends on the issue. The people closest to the problem, I'd say. It would probably be a good idea to look at several issues. And pick a pilot team that includes people from different levels in the company—a few people you think of as leaders. Give them some training, pick an issue you think isn't too hard to solve, and get them on it. If they're successful they can bring what they've learned back to their departments.

CLIENT: That sounds very good. I want to do something like this. A pilot makes sense. Is this something that you can coach me through?

GUIDE: Yes, I could. And I could connect you with other resources that might be helpful. We will need to talk more about your goals, so you can think about what extra expertise you'd need and what decisions you'd have to make. When we flesh out a plan more, you'll have a better idea of what you'd be committing to and what contraindications might lead you to decide not to do it for now.

Here the coach is laying out a scenario for how the client can accomplish the goal he says he wants, providing subject matter expertise by drawing from the experience she's accumulated as a consultant, as someone familiar with the field, or as a coach for other clients who have gone through a similar process.

Notice that the impetus for action is coming from the client. The coach is laying out what she has seen work in other situations. She is neutral and does not recommend the approach to the client. In fact, she's slowing him down a bit and encouraging him to explore the possibilities in more depth before deciding. If there is implicit advocacy on the part of the coach here, it is for a sound decision based on good information, not for pursuing either a pilot or a full-blown process improvement program. The client is in charge, and the coach is keeping him there.

Exhibit 9.1 lists many common universal types of action steps.

EXHIBIT 9.1.
Sample Fieldwork Actions

In the iterative process of coaching, actions that a client can perform between coaching sessions will integrate learning into the rest of the client's life. This learning will in turn shape the next coaching conversation. Almost anything can serve as fieldwork, but here are some starters:

Attention training practices: Mindfulness practices increase self-awareness, concentration, and the ability to recognize and let go of unhelpful habits.

Body practices: Any of a wide range of regular practices engage the body and develop new capacities.

Challenging tasks: Doing a particular task (for example, creating a budget, leading a cross-functional team, championing an initiative) provides a natural laboratory for developing the requisite skills. Here a specific business objective drives the development of competency.

Conversations: Targeted conversations with specific individuals provide opportunities for practicing competencies, making requests, changing an unsatisfactory dynamic, or launching a new initiative.

Feedback: Use 360-degree surveys, ask someone to observe and then provide feedback, elicit feedback from a person or team, or ask for limited anonymous feedback around a specific issue.

Interviewing: Talk to others with a specific line of questioning, and gather information or learn how someone does a particular thing well.

Journaling: Practice daily or frequent writing, sometimes with guiding questions.

Music and visual art: Expressing one's own creativity or experiencing that of others, the arts can provide inspiration, touch empty places, and renew spirit.

Observing others: Observing someone who is already competent at a skill that one needs to develop is a powerful means to get a picture of the competency in action.

Reading: A book or article or a Web reference can provide insight into or perspective on the topic of coaching. Poems offer a distinctive way of seeing.

Requests: Building competency in making and responding to requests is essential in coordinating with others, delegating work, and getting our needs met.

Self-observations: Use structured focus on increasing self-awareness in relation to a particular behavior, narrative, or assumption.

Sitting with: This refers to holding a decision, insight, or possibility in consideration while deliberately suspending any rush to action.

Skill development: Learn and practice specific skills as a means to develop competencies (for example, giving difficult feedback, making requests, or listening).

Training: Classroom, online, or CD-based training or retreats provide a particular experience or foster a skill that supports the coaching outcomes.

Writing: Responding to specific questions, developing a mission statement or vision, and creative writing can be used to access deeper awareness.

RECOMMENDING SPECIFIC COURSES OF ACTION

In some cases, the client needs both the specific action ideas and the impetus to take action. This combination of impetus and direction is the most assertive of the three Guide Aspects and differentiates it from the first two, which provide either impetus or direction but not both.

The coach takes the lead to provide short-term encouragement toward a specific course of action. In effect, she's testing the client's willingness and commitment to move forward. To continue to provide this level of directiveness might create dependency. But if the client doesn't follow through, next week's conversation can look at resistance and procrastination and explore whether the client is really committed to addressing the issue.

Let's look at a simple scenario—one that involves first the Reflector and then the Guide.

CLIENT: I just can't seem to get going on this making-time-for-myself project.

COACH AS REFLECTOR: Yes, you seem to be making it harder than it really is.

CLIENT: I think it'll get easier after the budget is in.

COACH AS REFLECTOR: Probably, Josh, but I bet there will always be reasons for not finding time. We've talked about it before. That's the nature of the problem.

CLIENT: Yes, but this is a particularly challenging time.

GUIDE: That's why it's important to move on it right now. Now's the time you really need the balance. *Note the switch to the Guide Voice. This is advocating action.*

CLIENT: True enough, but how can I really get started when there's all this stuff I need to do?

GUIDE: You get started by starting. May I offer a concrete suggestion? *The coach asks permission.*

CLIENT: Sure.

GUIDE: We've actually talked about the specifics several times. I want you to make a commitment to work out two times this week for at least thirty minutes, and take your wife out to dinner once this weekend—for a nice evening, not just a burger and back to work. That's it. We're not going to look at a whole program. We're just going for an initial success. Then we'll talk again next week and plan what's next. *The coach makes a very specific recommendation with a strong impetus for action.*

CLIENT: That's an evening and another couple of hours.

COACH AS CONTRACTOR: Yes. Are you willing to commit to it or not? *The coach tests for commitment.*

CLIENT: It sounds like a lot.

GUIDE: Josh, many busy people wouldn't think that two visits to the gym and a date with their spouse over the course of a week was a lot. I know that you have this belief that it's impossible to find the time, and yet you've been talking about this for a while now. It's time to get off the dime and do something to prove to yourself that you can find the time to do the things that you say are important. I'm recommending that you do these specific three things, but obviously it's your decision. Will you do it? *The coach is advocating a specific action; this is a strongly directive Voice. And it's critical that the client be always at choice. Note the Contractor query at the end.*

CLIENT: Yes. Okay. I'm willing.

In this case, the client appears to be stuck; he's talked about the need for balance in his life for some time, but without doing any-thing about it. The Guide recommends specific actions and pushes the client to take them. Both know that the client can follow through on these particular suggestions if it's important enough to him, and getting specific makes it more difficult for him to make excuses. An initial success will change things, and the conversation next week can build on these successes and look at what's next. If the client doesn't follow through, then next week's conversation will look at resistance and procrastination and explore whether the client is really committed to addressing the balance issue or not. Either way, there will be a lot to talk about.

The coach is taking the lead to provide both short-term impe-tus and specific direction until he's able to develop his commitment beyond the talking stage. In effect, she's testing him because her assessment is that the client wouldn't move without a nudge, and at least some movement is what's necessary for the client to develop the energy to commit to what he says he wants.

Again, the coach must be careful here if the overall pattern in the relationship is for the client to want a lot of specificity. To continue to provide this level of impetus would create dependency. When the coach provides such specific recommendations, she must check to be sure that it's the client's decision and that the client makes a spe-cific statement of commitment. Sometimes it's just a check; in this example, the client is at least tentatively willing to commit. At other times it will be important to explore the client's commitment more carefully, to make sure the client isn't just going along with a specific plan without having to say, "Yes, I want to do this."

THE MINDFUL GUIDE

Those of us who like to solve problems and get satisfaction from help-ing others are in particular danger of overusing the Guide Voice. To the extent that we become attached to being a giver of advice, it becomes very easy to collude with the client by being more directive than is appropriate.

Besides overusing the Guide, we can also err by projecting on our clients. Sometimes we suggest a plan of action because we find it intriguing, or it's something we'd like to do. A test, as with the other Voices, is noticing if you experience extra energy or excitement as you move into this role.

It's easy for coaches to define their own success in terms of how the client takes action, so we must beware of overdoing it. Or we may find ourselves at times reluctant to push and challenge. When that's the case, we ask ourselves if it's our need to be com-fortable and avoid the tension of challenging that holds us back. To hold back from pushing the client toward action can collude with the client's own desires to stay comfortable. We balance the cli-ent's desire for movement with the developmental imperative to be grounded in that movement and in charge of the process. Always, the client's needs provide the guidance for the pacing and direction of that movement.

A third hazard of the Guide Voice is that we may seek to cover our lack of experience in a particular area by appearing more knowl-edgeable than we actually are. Speaking beyond our experience or invoking a level of authority that we don't in fact possess is mislead-ing. It serves the client better to steer him toward knowledgeable resources than to pretend to have solutions that aren't rooted in our own experience.

Use these guidelines to support your own mindfulness in the Guide role:

- Keep the client in charge. The coach's agenda slips quite easily into the Guide Voice. It can be difficult for both coach and client to know where the energy and direction are coming from and who is responsible. Ask the client for an explicit commitment after making any recommendation. A simple lack of disagreement isn't sufficient. The client should explicitly commit to a proposed action or develop his own.

- If you're moving into the Guide Voice, ask yourself why. The Guide role is very helpful when used judiciously, but it should never be the default role. Going to the Guide Voice too easily may indicate that you're operating out of your own needs. Legitimate reasons for using this Voice don't include making the coach feel smart, getting the client to move at the pace the coach wants, or fulfilling the coach's desire to be of service. They do include the client's feeling stuck, lacking a strategy, or needing the coach's experience or encouragement to commit to a plan.

- Stay within your experience in offering suggestions for actions. That doesn't mean that you must have personally experienced every strategy that you suggest. It does mean that you should have a reasonable basis in personal experience, knowledge of others' experiences, or simply knowledge of your field for believing that the strategy will make sense for your client. This seems obvious, but more than one coach has oversold her experience in the desire to increase her business.

- Ask permission before suggesting a strategy, especially if the suggestion is coming as a recommendation rather than as a neutral description of what might work. Do the inner work to let go of your attachment to the client's using your suggestion before offering it; instead, hold your suggestion as a gift, with no strings attached. Ensure that you are really asking, not just jumping through the hoop to get the client to agree to what you've already decided he should do.

The Guide is particularly prone to overuse, because it is so easy to build identity around our clients' successes. Use the following exercises to build your attention to using this Voice mindfully and without attachment.

EXERCISE 9.1.

Self-Coaching as Guide: Providing Impetus and/or Direction

Moving into action quickly anchors book learning in experience, allows real-time experimentation and integration, and either validates learning through success or opens up further investigation if things don't go the way we plan. So practice sensing the nuances of the Guide's bias for action as this Voice offers direction or impetus toward action:

1. I encourage you to take some immediate and specific action within the next two days that will give you an opportunity to practice what you've been learning about the Guide Voice. What will this be? (This paragraph provides impetus but not direction; I am urging you to take some action. Other than defining the action as being coaching related, it does not suggest specifics.)

2. One option is to experiment with your Guide Voice with a child, teenage, or a subordinate practice client. You might try communicating your bias for action to this person using each of the three distinctions described by the Guide Aspects. This is one possibility—are there others that come to mind? If so, please note them now. (This provides a possibility and invites you to identify others—direction but no impetus.)

3. If you have not already identified an action to commit to, then within the next two days, I recommend that you find two specific opportunities to offer action suggestions to someone, while being aware of asking permission to make the suggestion and letting go of your attachment to whether the person follows through. Note what happens within you as you offer these suggestions and what is required to let go of your attachment. (My recommendation here has both direction and impetus: I am urging you to take a specifically described action.)

EXERCISE 9.2.

Guide Areas for Attention

Take some time to respond to the following questions:

- Based on the description of the Guide in this chapter, what Aspects do you engage with skillfully and mindfully?
- What Guide Aspects might you tend to overuse? When? How do you know this?
- What Aspects are you less comfortable and proficient with? When? How do you know this?

EXERCISE 9.3.
Guide Self-Observation

- Choose an Aspect that represents a development opportunity for you: a skill or behavior that you wish to bring more into your coaching or one that you perhaps have attachments to and therefore overuse. Describe this skill or behavior as specifically as possible.
- Construct a self-observation for yourself using the explanation and structure from Chapter Two. Do this self-observation consistently and rigorously over several weeks. Notice how your awareness has changed in relation to this Aspect.

CHAPTER SUMMARY

The Guide Voice is especially useful when the client doesn't have a sense of the right direction to go, where the coach has specific knowledge and experience relevant to the client's challenges, or where a simple nudge will be helpful. The Guide has a bias toward action, providing a combination of impetus and/or direction toward action:

- *Encourages the client to take some action of the client's choosing,* providing impetus by nudging her toward some action. This can be particularly helpful when the client knows what she needs to do but hasn't quite taken the plunge.
- *Offers options for action* by sharing experience—her own and that of others—with successful approaches in related situations. This provides a possible direction, with no impetus for action.
- *Recommends specific courses of action,* thus providing direction and impetus. This is the most prescriptive of the three Aspects, and potentially the most problematic if the coach's agenda comes into it.

Because the Guide is the most action oriented of the coach Voices, this is an easy place for the coach to become overly invested in the client's actions and successes. As with any other Voice, there is potential for unhealthy overidentification. Mindfulness is required to stay attentive to the client's purpose and needs. The mindful Guide attends to supporting the client's own authority and agency, recognizing that sometimes the right action is none at all.

CHAPTER 10

The Contractor

*Whatever you can do, or dream you can, begin it. Boldness
has genius, power, and magic in it.*

Goethe

*The road to wisdom
Is simple to express:
Err and err and err again,
But less and less and less.*

Piet Hein

THE PULL OF HABIT IS STRONG. EVEN FOR PRACTICED
leaders who are self-aware and committed, it is easy for the tumult
and pressures of life to subvert our best intentions for change. Having
an accountability partner who can support us in building clear commitments and serve as a friendly but tough advocate for completing
these commitments can be enormously helpful in building traction
for real and sustainable change. The Contractor builds this psychological and behavioral accountability for the client.

Using this Voice, the coach develops, with the client, the structures of implementation, of action, of following through. These
structures help the client take the work that has been done during
the coaching conversation out into the world.

The Contractor can be thought of as a link between the client's desire to move toward change and the actions that will make that possible. When the coaching process creates new energy and new possibilities, the Contractor supports the client in anchoring these new possibilities in concrete action steps that change the situation on the ground. The Contractor is hard-nosed, supportive, and practical all at once.

The Contractor helps the client construct an external pathway that enables her to go forward with direction and commitment, and with a minimum of anxiety and confusion. Primarily this takes place as fieldwork—the actions that are designed and committed to during coaching conversations—and that then take place outside those conversations in the rest of the client's life. This iterative process of cycling between dialogue, design, and commitment, and fieldwork-driven learning is what enables coaching to build sustainable new behaviors and strategies. The Contractor plays a key role in structuring the transitions between the conversational and fieldwork phases of this iterative process.

These activities of the Contractor are distinct from the more traditional understanding of contracting as an activity that lays the foundation for a coaching relationship. In Chapter Five, I included the latter nuptial activities (as it were) in the domain of the Partner Voice. Those initial contracting conversations about structure, frequency, compensation, outcomes, and so forth are distinct from what I describe in this chapter as the Contractor's role.

Some clients are highly motivated and skilled at following through. When this happens, the Contractor part of the coach's job is easy. Sometimes, though, clients are resistant, disorganized, or tentative in their commitment, or they just plain feel powerless. They leave the coaching interaction saying the right things, but little or nothing happens. If this is the case, the role of the Contractor is even more important in following through and supporting the client in learning from what happened—or didn't happen.

The Voice of the Contractor is never adversarial: although the language of the Contractor is clear and focused on accountability, it is always in service to the client. In popular parlance, the Contractor can provide tough love, but this is always grounded in self-awareness and respect for the client.

As with any other Voice, there are ways in which the coach can overstep the Contractor's bounds. In particular, he can get in trouble by becoming attached to the client's follow-through, confusing the client's success with his own. The mindful Contractor's respect for, and stance toward, the client is not affected by whether the client follows through according to the coach's standards of success. No matter what has happened in follow-through, the coach maintains an attitude of compassion and acceptance.

Any coach is well advised to keep asking the question of whether the coach or the client is doing the work of commitment and follow-through. A well-coached client should be taking full responsibility for moving forward on what has been learned; constant nudging and motivational games are signs of dependency.

ASPECTS OF THE CONTRACTOR

- Establishing clear agreements about actions
- Exploring and resolving client doubts and hesitations
- Following up with client about agreed-on actions

Three Aspects represent the Contractor's Voice. The first is establishing clear agreements about what the client will do to ground the work and insights from the coaching conversation in practical and specific commitments. This framework provides accountability and focus for the fieldwork that the client does between sessions. Fieldwork is action learning. The client will sometimes experience success and sometimes breakdowns, in which he is unable or unwilling to follow through. As we will see, both can provide great learning.

In the second Aspect, the Contractor supports the client in understanding and working through resistances and hesitations about taking a particular course of action. While other Voices, particularly those of the Investigator and the Reflector, may come into play here, it's through the Contractor role that the coach helps the client take the risk of moving forward.

In the third, the Contractor follows up with the client in subsequent coaching conversations to check in on results. Just knowing that the coach will be asking, "So what happened when you . . . ?" reinforces the accountability the client feels to the commitments she has made to herself and increases the likelihood of follow-through.

Generally, in relation to a specific course of action, that is the sequence in which the Aspects of the Contractor will be employed: developing a specific course of action, exploring resistances and hesitations and modifying the agreement if necessary, and, in later conversations, discussing what the client has or has not done and the results of the action or inaction.

ESTABLISHING CLEAR AGREEMENTS ABOUT ACTIONS

Good agreements for follow-through depend on the client's becoming clear about what she wants to do, how, and when. Her willingness is a logical outcome of the coaching process summarized by the three basic Investigator questions: "What's the situation?" "What do you want?" and the final, practical, and concrete, "What are you going to do?" If the client has developed answers to this final question, with help from the three sharpener Voices (Reflector, Teacher, Guide), the Contractor's work on follow-through is already half done.

The Guide can sometimes be important in getting the client to that point of clear readiness to act. But however we get there, we must then, as Contractor, address what the client is prepared to do. If the client is already clear, there is little to do but summarize what has already been said or ask the client to do so. If it's still an overly broad course of action that the client is talking about, the Contractor helps narrow it down to immediate steps and practical, concrete commitments.

One of the challenges in coaching is to take soft behavioral changes and design hard measurable action steps to further them. There are extensive menus of alternatives for action resulting from a coaching conversation. Many major 360-degree review vendors have entire books of development suggestions keyed to specific competencies targeted by their assessment instruments. These resources can be valuable for the coach, whether or not the 360-degree review process is used. The danger, of course, is that these menus will be used as a cookbook for change and that the coach will substitute the ease and assurance of an expert system for the client's own judgment and the coach's knowledge of the specific client and her needs.

While such models are excellent resources and their suggestions can obviously be shaped and customized, the most powerful development activities in my experience are ones that emerge from the coaching conversation itself. The client's new understandings of self and her situation become embedded in a specific course of action that either increases awareness and understanding further or shifts the situation itself. The creative process of deep listening often results in fieldwork designed specifically with and for a particular client.

Self-observation exercises are one way to do this. At other times, a specific action might entail a meeting with a particular individual, a phone call, a training class, or an experiment with new behaviors. (Exhibit 9.1 listed some possible actions.)

The Contractor works with the client to design the steps that make action specific, concrete, and measurable. These should be described in terms that avoid ambiguity about whether the client has accomplished the action step; this clarity provides the basis for revisiting the commitment in a later conversation and learning from whatever happened.

CONTRACTOR: So it sounds like you're clear about your commitment to deal with the Rick situation.

CLIENT: Yes. I think it's important.

CONTRACTOR: Tell me again exactly what you're planning to do. *The coach asks the client to be specific about his commitment.*

CLIENT: Well, I need air cover from Anne on this one. It's too sensitive. So I'm going to meet with Anne and tell her that I'm worried about how other people might react if Rick has to leave. I'm going to ask for her support in putting him on probation, and tell her that I need her help in designing a damage control strategy if it doesn't work out.

CONTRACTOR: So when will you have this conversation? *The coach builds accountability around timing. This makes it very real and immediate.*

CLIENT: Before next Friday for sure. She's out of town until Tuesday.

CONTRACTOR: Okay. Will you be able to get on her schedule?

CLIENT: Yes. No problem.

CONTRACTOR: What about your conversation with Rick?

CLIENT: I may not do that until the following week. Anne may want me to jump through a couple more hoops first. For now, I'm going to concentrate on involving Anne and completing that step by Friday. After that, the exact timing may vary depending on how that goes. I am committed to doing this, though.

CONTRACTOR: Good. Next time, let's talk about what happened with Anne, and make sure the pathway is clear from there. *The coach is building in accountability.*

In this example, the client is already clear about what he needs to do to deal with an impending personnel crisis. This conversation summarizes others that he and the coach have been having and anchors it in a specific commitment. The client is clear that the first step needs to happen before he knows exactly what the next step will be, and the Contractor supports him in not adding further specifics at this time.

If the issue being addressed is very complex, it may be appropriate to schedule additional coaching time to work through the details. Alternatively, the client's action commitment may be simply to the creation of a plan; this planning work can take place step by step over the course of an agreed-on amount of time. After the plan is in place, the coach can provide support and accountability for its implementation.

For more complex courses of action and strategies that will unfold over weeks or months to develop specific competencies, the client or the coach may write out an individual development plan—or, better yet, the two of them will write one together—that outlines the steps that the client commits to taking.

There are many ways to structure a development plan. Exhibit 10.1 shows one simple version that links the *situation* to a desired *outcome* by specific *actions* the client will take to acquire the new competencies he needs. The plan structures the links. The initial plan is a template that can be revised and updated as the client moves forward. (You can download a blank development plan template at http://dougsilsbee .com/pdf/idp.pdf.)

EXHIBIT 10.1.

Sample Individual Development Plan

Declaration: A concise statement of the client's overarching coaching issue or commitment; this draws from a clear-eyed assessment of the current **situation** and the client's role in it.

> *Example:* "I am committed to active engagement in making staff meetings more efficient and energizing."

Outcome: A clear description of the **outcome** that the client wants, described in observable and behavioral terms.

> *Example:* "I will be more able to stay centered, observe my own frustration or impatience in meetings, articulate those feelings, and suggest a specific intervention or course of action to change it. I'll enjoy the meetings more and be an infectious force for fun and productivity."

Behavior, skill, or capacity required for a successful outcome: Specific skills or competencies to be developed through actions that serve the outcome.

> *Examples:* "Staying centered in the midst of fast-moving team dynamics." "Specific team intervention skills for when we get off track."

Fieldwork: **Action** steps, specified together, that the client will commit to as fieldwork between coaching conversations.

> Examples:

1. Item	2. By/Until When	3. Notes
Self-observation: At the end of each day, note meeting situations in which I felt tense, frustrated, or impatient. What was going on in the meeting? What emotions or body sensations did I have? What did I do or not do in the situation? How did I justify what I did or didn't do? What alternatives were there?	For next three weeks, until Friday, May 15.	Staff and operations meetings. Write notes in journal before leaving office each day.

(Continued)

EXHIBIT 10.1. (Continued)

1. Item	2. By/Until When	3. Notes
Body practice: Do tai chi exercises for twenty minutes, four times a week. Pay attention to sensations in body and settling myself, staying centered, deliberate, and unhurried.	Four times per week for two months	Use DVD
Action: Read Roger Schwarz material about intervening in meeting dynamics.	Read by May 5	Article
Action: Create a short list of interventions that seem appropriate for my staff meetings.	Create list by May 10	Review with coach
Action: Create a plan for experimenting with these interventions.	By May 31	Develop with coach
Action: Centering practice, ten times a day, and three times in each meeting. Track this.	Through June	Set up tracking system

Exploring and Resolving Client Doubts and Hesitations

Often resistance surfaces just at the point where the client is getting ready to make a commitment. Everything sounds good until it comes time to take the plunge. Sitting on the precipice of change has a way of bringing up every doubt and question that's lurking in the background.

It's part of the coach's job as Contractor to ensure that the client's commitment is robust and full. This doesn't mean that all of the client's anxieties and resistances have been banished; it simply means that the client is fully committed to moving forward. To do this means acknowledging anxieties and doubts in the first place. Pretending they don't exist would seem easier on the face of it, but that may come back to haunt us later. The Contractor supports the client in naming and working through concerns with the goal of building commitment.

The role of the Contractor includes increasing the client's awareness of resistance and blocks to action, and then helping to resolve them.

CLIENT: Well, I think it's a good idea to get my team together for this planning session. They've never done this together, but I think it would be a good exercise for us. We're spread all over the country. We never see each other.

CONTRACTOR: Great. Are you ready to make a commitment to this? *The Contractor tests for commitment.*

CLIENT: Yes, I think it's a good idea. But, I'm not sure the team is ready for it. *The question about commitment evokes the client's concerns.*

COACH AS INVESTIGATOR: Will you tell me more about that?

CLIENT: Well, a big one is that we don't actually have much practice in making joint decisions. This group has always been pretty top-down. I'll be taking a very different role from what they're used to with my predecessor. I expect them at best to be unenthusiastic, and they might not even want to participate. I'm the new kid on the block.

COACH AS INVESTIGATOR: So how will you get them on board? What can happen in advance so they have a real stake in this? *This is an Investigator question, focused on action; the need for additional conversation is surfaced by the concerns.*

CLIENT: Well, I can give them an idea about the process and what I want to accomplish. I can ask them what *they* think would be opportunities—sort of roll up their outcomes into the goals for the session. It'll take some conference calls.

COACH AS INVESTIGATOR: Okay, that makes sense. What else can you do? *This is also an Investigator question, focused on action, but the need for additional conversation is surfaced by the concerns.*

CLIENT: I can put together a draft agenda early on, and I can say why I think it's important for us all to do this together. The truth is, I think we ought to be operating more closely together all the time. This is an opportunity to get it started.

CONTRACTOR: That sounds like something you feel strongly about.

CLIENT: Yeah. I do. And in order to do my job, I need to be much more aware of what they think is important than I can be now. Mostly I get superficial acceptance, but I never really hear what they think. I do think I need to move on this.

CONTRACTOR: Good. So now that you've identified some of your concerns, what are you committing to? *The Contractor Voice is used to move toward a commitment.*

Here the Contractor is encouraging the client to explore her own concerns and hesitations. The client's overall commitment in this case is pretty clear, but the concerns brought into the forefront by the possibility of commitment are important. Unacknowledged concerns have a way of undermining a client's best intentions. The Contractor asks the client to go through her concerns and come up with ways of responding to each. The concerns are placed in the foreground; in the background lie the client's desired outcome; the end result is a fuller and more clear-sighted commitment.

The Contractor can also encourage a client to move toward commitment by trying on a decision. Like trying on a new outfit in a store, we wear it for a while, look in the mirror, see how it feels and looks before deciding to purchase or leave behind. We can do the same thing for any decision we face. We wear the decision, pretending we have made it, then notice what surfaces. Generally either the "Yes, I like it" gains ground, and we experience increasing energy and commitment, or the concerns gain ground, and we feel less and less like making that choice.

Testing for fit and commitment means checking out every action item that the client intends to commit to in order to determine whether the commitment is realistic to fit into an already busy life and whether the client is really fully committed to following through. This explicit two-part check is critical in ensuring that the client goes forward from the coaching conversation with the maximum commitment to realistic actions that she is likely, but not certain, to complete. Where this line of questioning reveals concerns, they can be addressed with additional or different actions, as in the previous dialogue. Or if the commitment is simply too big or beyond the client's resources to successfully complete, it can be renegotiated to be smaller, or to take place over a longer time frame.

Following Up with the Client About Agreed-On Actions

This third Aspect of the Contractor Voice involves following up with the client in subsequent conversations to discuss what has happened. Sometimes the client has completed an action successfully and there's not much to be done other than to celebrate and anchor what has been learned. At other times, there may have been breakdowns, in which the client didn't complete an action for external reasons or from lack of competence, commitment, or structure. If the latter is the case, the plan might need to be revisited and modified to make it more achievable in light of these circumstances, or it may need to be replaced with something different.

The bottom line? Learning happens whether the client experiences a success or a breakdown. Above all, the Contractor stands for a rigorous commitment to help the client follow through, look at whatever happened, and learn from it. It's the coach as Contractor who frames any results in terms of a larger perspective, moving beyond the apparent dualism of success and failure.

CONTRACTOR: So. How did it go with the first week of your training program? *The question is about a commitment made in the previous conversation.*

CLIENT: It went pretty well! I worked out on my treadmill in the basement every morning before work. I'm just getting up half an hour earlier—no big deal. And I lifted weights at the gym three times this week. I've got a chart up on the refrigerator to track my workouts. I'm checking it off every day.

CONTRACTOR: Nice going! How do you feel?

CLIENT: Great. I've got my benchmarks written down, and I've dropped four pounds just this week.

COACH AS REFLECTOR: You really *are* good at creating support systems. Didn't we talk about that as one of your talents? *Coach directs client's attention towards her resources and strengths.*

CLIENT: Well, I do it well at work. This is new.

CONTRACTOR: So what else have you found out from doing it this week?

CLIENT: Well, obviously, it's not really such a big deal, this exercise thing. I just need to make it a priority and be willing to drop my excuses and get out of bed. I guess that's true of a lot of things.

CONTRACTOR: That's it. Absolutely. That's important to see, and it does apply to many things.

The Contractor is celebrating the client here, not only because she's been so successful in her very first week of a new program, but also to reinforce her insight and her sense that she has power in her own life.

Now let's look at the Contractor as he coaches a client who didn't follow through. Here, I'll illuminate how this exploration, initiated by the Contractor, can often involve multiple Voices in quick succession.

CONTRACTOR: Well, how did your conversation with Jeff go? *The coach asks about a previous commitment.*

CLIENT: Not well. We met, but I didn't bring up the subject of the proposal.

COACH AS INVESTIGATOR: Did anything good happen at the meeting?

CLIENT: Well, we agreed to get together again to review progress on the payroll implementation.

COACH AS INVESTIGATOR: What kept you from bringing up the proposal? *The breakdown means that the Investigator is now the most helpful Voice as the coach inquires into the changed situation, now that the client hasn't followed through.*

CLIENT: I guess I didn't really want to hear what he had to say. I don't particularly respect his opinion. Bottom line, though, I chickened out.

COACH AS CONTRACTOR: Last time we discussed how important you thought it was, for your relationship with Jeff, to bring this up directly with him. *The Contractor reminds the client why she had made this previous commitment.*

CLIENT: I know. But I'm just sick of his disrespect. I'm tired of meeting with him and feeling lousy afterward. It's not worth it.

COACH AS INVESTIGATOR: Yeah, it would be easy to give it up. How important is it to continue to work on the relationship? *The coach asks about the client's values in the situation.*

CLIENT: Well, as long as I'm in this role, I'll have to deal with him. I need to give this another shot.

COACH AS REFLECTOR: So, Michelle, I really support your staying with this. I see that this is actually a great learning opportunity because we've discussed other relationships where you don't assert what you need either. *The Reflector provides a self-awareness reminder, establishing the relevance of this specific situation in her overall learning process.* How do you see this?

CLIENT: Yes, I can see it that way in principle. But I'd like to have fewer of these opportunities!

COACH AS TEACHER: Yeah. I understand. With Jeff, you can practice how to stay effective in difficult conversations. *The Teacher offers a new way to see this situation: as a practice opportunity.* This one has been pretty challenging so far.

CLIENT: Great. How do I learn to do this?

COACH AS TEACHER: By learning to stay centered and powerful in the face of someone like Jeff who pushes your buttons. And making requests for what you need from him. How do those sound to you? *The coach offers two new distinctions and asks the client how she sees it.*

CLIENT: Yes, those are right on target. They're relevant with Jeff, but also in other relationships. Let's get specific. I think if I have a more concrete plan, I can go in there and deal with him. *Michelle is reengaged with the commitment and equipped with fresh distinctions that illuminate new possibilities.*

In this dialogue, the coach as Contractor checks in with the client about an agreement they had made in their previous conversation and finds she didn't follow through on a key action item. The Contractor provides accountability by bringing her back to the original commitment.

Notice that Michelle's breakdown in fact opens up a whole new coaching conversation, this one involving the Investigator, the

Reflector, and the Teacher, about how she can stay centered and powerful in challenging conversations. This is an important competency in relationships other than with Jeff. The coach helps her see a larger pattern and that she can learn something of value with Jeff that will help her elsewhere.

This shifting fluidly between Voices points to the need to remain mindful to what is emerging in the client. If we narrow our view, yield ourselves to an attachment to a particular Voice, or latch onto the notion that now is when we should be doing a particular thing, we stop listening.

Notice the absence in the Contractor of any language of judgment or failure. The client is being hard on herself; the Contractor acknowledges her feelings and empathizes while continuing to hold her as resourceful and whole. He doesn't add to the sense of failure that the client is experiencing; instead, he moves on quickly to her overall commitment to address her problems in a difficult relationship directly. Rather than labeling her lack of action a failure, he helps her reframe the difficult situation as a learning opportunity— and one that she can master.

This reframing provides the motivation to go back in and replan for the same action item with a new approach: a difficult conversation with Jeff. The breakdown becomes an opportunity, and the coach supports the client in responding in new ways to the challenge. Michelle will go back out, seeking to take the same action as last time, but more cognizant of the challenge and better prepared.

THE MINDFUL CONTRACTOR

As with the Guide, one of the obvious Contractor pitfalls is to identify with the client's results. In the closing minutes of most coaching conversations, the momentum is toward action. Compensating for a client's lack of commitment by pushing for one action or another can weaken the client in the long term because the impetus is coming from the outside.

When the Contractor rightfully focuses on exploring client hesitations, there's a similar danger of pushing the client toward action before doubts and resistances have been adequately addressed. While it is certainly possible to make obstacles seem more daunting than necessary, adequate exploration often yields valuable information.

Moving through it too fast can cut short what could be important and valuable work.

Asking a client to report on breakdowns and apparent failures may prove uncomfortable for both the client and the coach. It's always more pleasant to think about the times we've been successful than the times when we feel we've failed. And of course, the coach may be invested in the client's success and, on some level, regard the client's breakdowns as his own.

The same danger exists when it comes to success. Of course, we celebrate client successes. It's important to do this, and celebrating builds positive energy and confidence, which leads to more success. Clients like to look good for their coaches, and this little boost in motivation may be a good thing, but it can sometimes lead to a kind of collusion in which both the client and coach have an emotional investment in the client's appearing to perform more effectively than she is in fact doing. The Contractor provides follow-through that is both rigorous and compassionate. This accurate, ongoing assessment keeps the coaching relationship on an even keel and informs both coach and client about what needs to happen next.

Here are some other guidelines for using the Contractor Voice well for the benefit of the client:

- Failure versus success is often a false distinction that doesn't support the client's long-term development. Frame every experience as a success and a learning opportunity. The client may tend to see the lack of follow-through as a failure; the Contractor's job is to help him see the same experience in a larger context and to support the client's learning from every attempt, no matter the results.

- Simultaneously support change and accept the client as he is. These goals may appear to be in conflict, but they are not. Both accountability and discipline can be provided in the context of a fully accepting, supporting relationship.

- It is critically important for the coach to be aware of her own need for the client to get results. Like the Guide, the Contractor must diligently support the client's capacity to commit to outcomes and action plans. Mindful awareness of our own attachments and identifications with client results, and letting them go as they arise is key to doing this. It is the coach's job to support the client, not to ensure follow-through at the cost of the client's sense of self-generation.

- Explore client resistance and concerns. Their nature is a valuable source of information, and addressing them is a key component of building commitment. At the same time, keep them in proper perspective. Resistances and concerns are areas of learning en route to the outcomes the client seeks, but they are secondary to the vision and results that the client wants, and they must be kept in proportion.

- Encourage accountability and discipline. Be diligent about writing down what the client commits to and about following up about the results of these commitments.

Use the following exercises to become more skillful at working with yourself to structure follow-up actions for your clients.

EXERCISE 10.1.

Self-Coaching as Contractor: Structuring Actions and Testing for Fit and Commitment

Consider the collection of actions that you are taking over the next one or two weeks that are related to your learning and growth as a coach. These might include reading this book, mindfulness practices, and other actions that are learning-directed in their nature. Structure your commitment to yourself as the Contractor.

1. Build a structure for yourself that includes and details these commitments, as if you were writing them out in the form of an agreement with a client about what she will do between coaching conversations. It may be useful to use the Individual Development Plan template in Exhibit 10.1 for this structure.

2. Given the structure developed in the previous item, ask yourself if this set of commitments fits into your busy life. Where are there likely to be breakdowns? Are your commitments realistic? Are they sufficient? Revise the structure so that your learning commitments seem to fit well into the larger ecology of your life.

3. Ask yourself if you are committed. See how your response feels inside yourself. Being honest with yourself, are you really committed? What part of you is holding back or giving yourself an out? What will support you in developing your commitment further if it's lacking?

EXERCISE 10.2.

Contractor Areas for Attention

Take some time to respond to the following questions:

- Based on the description of the Contractor in this chapter, what Aspects do you engage with skillfully and mindfully?
- What Contractor Aspects might you tend to overuse? When? How do you know this?
- What Aspects are you less comfortable and proficient with? When? How do you know this?

EXERCISE 10.3.

Contractor Self-Observation

- Choose an Aspect that represents a development opportunity for you: a skill or behavior that you wish to bring more into your coaching, or one that you perhaps have attachments to and therefore overuse. Describe this skill or behavior as specifically as possible.
- Construct a self-observation for yourself, using the explanation and structure from Chapter Two. Do this self-observation consistently and rigorously over several weeks. Notice how your mindfulness has changed in relation to this Aspect.

CHAPTER SUMMARY

The Contractor is the role that focuses on accountability and follow-through. In taking on this role, the coach supports the client in translating insights and possibilities that emerged during coaching into concrete, practical fieldwork that extends the learning process into the rest of the client's life. The Contractor helps make coaching action oriented and thereby effective in creating real and sustainable change.

Note that this Voice is distinct from the initial contracting and setup of the coaching relationship, which we have described as an activity of the Partner. Rather, we can think of the Contractor as managing the interface between the coaching sessions and the learning components that take place outside of the coaching conversation. The Contractor:

- *Establishes clear agreements about actions* at the end of each coaching conversation, so that the client has meaningful and relevant fieldwork.

- *Explores and resolves client doubts and hesitations* by testing for fit and commitment and negotiating specifics until the client is fully committed to actions that feel realistic and achievable, given her busy life.
- *Follows up with client about agreed-on actions* in subsequent coaching conversations, building psychological and behavioral accountability. If the client ran into difficulties, the Contractor supports the client in seeing the breakdown as an opening into a new conversation.

The Contractor is generally the final "operational" Voice used in a specific coaching interaction—the one that helps set a tone of action orientation and positive momentum. It is a Voice that conveys support, accountability, and seriousness of intent, all at the same time.

Self-Development Strategies for the Coach

What you are is what you have been, and what you will be is what you do now.

The Buddha

We are always practicing. In other words, the body is incapable of not practicing. And what we practice we become.

Richard Strozzi-Heckler

THE SERIES OF ACTIVITIES AND APPROACHES IN THIS chapter will help you develop yourself as a coach. I encourage you to try out these tools and learn to use them flexibly, experimenting with them to make them as meaningful and powerful for you as possible. Lead yourself, thinking of what is offered as games or little experiments that you're conducting to better see what you're doing as a coach and to help you navigate as you explore the model.

I cannot prescribe a sequence for doing these exercises, and, in fact, there is no curriculum around the Septet Model that will serve all readers. The bottom line is that *you* are the curriculum. To follow a rigid process set out by someone else is to miss the point. At the same time, I hope you will enter the inquiry process with a degree of faith that these exercises are at the very least interesting and worth engaging with. Keep your mind open, but trust your instincts to help you discover which are most useful to you.

The model will take you as far as you want to go. Most of the exercises end with questions or additional practice suggestions. Your spirit of inquiry is the impetus behind your learning. The more curious you are about coaching and mindfulness and the more committed you are to your own journey to mastery, the richer the results will be.

Each section of this chapter describes a development strategy and exercises to help you pursue it. The exercises show you a basic structure. You can easily create your own versions, changing the emphasis and designing them to fit into the structures of your daily time management systems.

Again, I strongly recommend being coached yourself. While a commitment to our own rigorous self-development for a lifetime is important and much can be learned, there is no substitute for the commitment of a development partner who can see us clearly and offer new distinctions and possibilities that we could not easily access on our own.

SELF-ASSESSMENT TOOLS

Whether or not you feel ready to commit yourself fully to the Septet Model, a self-assessment will give you a great deal of information about where your strengths as a coach lie and which aspects of your coaching you might want to pay more attention to.

The patterns that emerge from a thoughtfully completed self-assessment can be fascinating and informative. Any method of self-assessment assumes a reasonable level of self-awareness and honesty on the part of the person entering into it. When it comes to a self-assessment, of course, there is no one to lie to except ourselves. It does not serve us to paint an idealized picture of ourselves; only we are watching anyway.

The self-assessment in Exhibit 11.1 and the one that is available online, and referred to in the exhibit, address the reality that coaches may be unaware of whether they use a behavior as little or as much as is really appropriate to a client's needs. The self-assessments measure the coach's perception of his or her use of Aspects and Voices, subject to the limitations of his or her self-awareness. Additional assessments described in a later section include the client perspective in the process, making the comparison rich indeed. Start with the self-assessment in Exercise 11.1.

The self-assessment (the one in Exercise 11.1 or the online version) gives you an opportunity to see what your overall coaching looks like and the Voices and Aspects that tend to stand out for you,

---

EXERCISE 11.1.
A Brief Coaching Self-Assessment

This brief self-assessment measures your comfort level with the twenty-three behaviors represented by the Voices and Aspects of the Septet Model. It is not a substitute for the self-assessment available online (http://dougsilsbee.com/books/tmc/assess), which is more accurate and addresses nuances of mindfulness through completely different scales.[1] It will, however, provide you with basic information about your coaching style in relation to the seven Voices.

Complete the assessment in Exhibit 11.1, filling in each *unshaded* box in the matrix with a number from 1 to 5, according to this scale:

5   I am entirely comfortable and skillful in using this behavior.

4   I use this frequently and well.

3   I do this sometimes.

2   I occasionally do this but am somewhat awkward and new at it.

1   I rarely do this or don't really understand what it means.

Then total each of the seven columns down to the row at the bottom of the matrix. Divide by the number shown to get an average for that group of behaviors.

The scores at the bottom of Exhibit 11.1 indicate your apparent comfort level with each of the seven Voices in the Septet. The seven boxes in the totals row correspond to the seven Voices. The individual items, of course, are the twenty-three Aspects. These numbers will give you some information about your general tendencies as a coach—including which roles or coaching behaviors you may be overly identified with or may underuse. These numbers are only numbers, of course; they do not provide a complete picture, nor does any specific score, whether high or low, necessarily mean that you overuse or underuse a specific behavior. (Determining this requires the perspective of clients.) Still, they point to lines of inquiry that may help you grow as a professional.

EXHIBIT 11.1.

The Operational Voices

	M	P	I	R	T	G	C
Maintains self-awareness	☐						
Directs the client's attention toward his or her capabilities and potential			☐				
Asks the client to generate courses of action			☐				
Establishes clear agreements about actions					☐		
Provides new distinctions, information, and knowledge					☐		
Encourages the client to take some action of the client's choosing						☐	
Models learning and growth	☐						
Advocates shared commitment to competency-based coaching outcomes		☐					
Offers options for action						☐	
Provides direct and honest feedback				☐			
Establishes and honors an explicit structure for the coaching relationship		☐					
Explains the coaching process, theory, and models being used					☐		
Explores and resolves client doubts and hesitations							☐
Embraces the client with compassion and respect	☐						
Asks questions that shift the client's understanding of the situation			☐				
Challenges and stimulates the client's thinking process						☐	
Chooses which of the operational Voices to use at a given time	☐						
Offers choice points and makes joint decisions about the coaching process		☐					
Recommends specific courses of action						☐	
Encourages self-observation and reflection					☐		
Follows up with client about agreed-on actions							☐
Listens with focus and presence	☐						
Asks the client to articulate desired outcomes			☐				
Total of scores from boxes in this column							
Divide by	5	3	3	3	3	3	3
Average score for this Voice							
Category initial	M	P	I	R	T	G	C

either because they're potentially overused or underused. Use the scores to generate your own questions—for example:

- What do my responses confirm to me about my strengths?
- Which Aspects, identified by higher scores, might I tend to use in service to my own attachments and identity rather than the needs of my client?
- Which Aspects might I potentially develop and seek to use more?
- Which Aspects am I curious to learn more about?
- How can I design this learning for myself?

For each of these standout Aspects, you can cultivate the curiosity of an observer who might say, for example, "Oh, how interesting! This coach [meaning you!] tends to overuse the Aspect of offering options for action. She does it with a couple of specific clients with whom she can feel intimidated. I wonder what that's about?"

Possible lines of inquiry might center around what the coach is experiencing at the times he or she takes on a particular Voice or Aspect within the range of available possibilities. Are there attachments or aversions at play? This leads us back to self-observation, which provides a logical means to explore questions raised by a self-assessment or a particular interest in a specific Voice or Aspect.

SELF-OBSERVATION AS A COACH

Let's explore how specifically designed self-observation exercises can increase your mindfulness around specific Voices or Aspects and lead to much greater skill and fluidity in navigating the coaching conversation.

Exercise 11.2 provides a general set of questions for self-observing yourself around a particular Voice or Aspect. What you choose to pay attention to might emerge from client feedback, a self-assessment, or any other source of curiosity.

Here the coach is practicing self-observation in relation to one specific Voice or Aspect. By paying attention, the coach becomes more aware of herself as she uses that specific Voice. She learns to

EXERCISE 11.2.
Self-Observation on a Specific Voice or Aspect

Choose a Voice or Aspect that you want to pay attention to. Then for several weeks, respond to these questions following each coaching session:

- When, in the just completed conversation, did you use this Voice or Aspect?
- What emotions and sensations were present in you just before and as you used this behavior?
- If you had to describe the reason that you chose this behavior, what would you say?
- What was the effect of the use of that Voice or Aspect on the client and the course of the conversation?

At the end of each week, review your notes and answer these questions:

- What did you learn about yourself from observing how you used this Voice or Aspect?
- What are the cues and observations that tell you when you are using it mindfully and in service to the client?
- What cues and observations indicate that there may be some need in you that's being addressed?
- What do you want to change or pay closer attention to moving forward?

discern, in the moment, the source of the impetus for using the role. Sometimes this impetus may derive from her attachments and aversions arising around the use of the role. At other times, the impetus may be from an attentive deep listening to her client and what he needs. With practice, this self-observation will greatly increase her ability to know the difference.

The power of a self-observation exercise stems in part from gathering the information; more important, the simple act of nonjudgmental observation brings more light and attention into our use of the behavior in question and increases our mindfulness. Committing to self-observation is a gentle reminder to be mindful and present.

Using Stronger Voices Mindfully

As coaches, we all have Voices that we use comfortably and frequently. That's the good news. The bad news is that these same Voices, which we may think of as our strengths, can often be overused in a way that doesn't serve our clients as best we could. Your mind, following a well-worn groove, may lead you to what's easiest for you and serves your needs best, even though it's not what your client most needs at the moment.

My own most pressing habit is to move to the Teacher role rather quickly. I like concepts and models, and I enjoy providing my coaching clients with new ways of seeing and interpreting their situations. My habit of mind is to teach, and I do it well. While this is often fine, it occasionally represents a misdirection of my energy relative to what my client needs. When I use it unconsciously, it can deprive the client of the opportunity to do her own work. I'm aware of this, and I work on being conscious about using this strength sparingly and at times when it will really be useful to the client.

Self-assessments, your own self-observation, and feedback from your clients will identify similar tendencies that are habitual for you. With skillful observation, you'll also likely recognize a pull or an attachment as you step into certain roles—an increase in your energy level or a subtle emotional charge. These are signs that your emotional needs are being addressed by the choices that you're making. There's nothing wrong with that, of course. It's just that the meeting of your needs isn't the purpose of the conversation.

It also can be true that the Voice that's habitual for you is exactly the one that is needed at a particular moment. Paying attention and being mindful and attentive to your client doesn't necessarily mean that you need to change what you're doing, but it creates more awareness, and therefore choice. As always, self-observation is the key to noticing what's going on beneath the surface. Exercise 11.3 is designed to increase your awareness of how you use your stronger Voices and Aspects.

The intention here is to bring more awareness into something that was previously habitual and automatic. Keep in mind each time you notice a habit is a small awakening and a real increase in your self-awareness. This is true even if you're noticing an unhelpful habit and see it only in hindsight. Suspend any self-judgment, just another unhelpful habit of mind. Practice the neutral observation of your habits at play.

Take the time to review and summarize what you've learned from this exercise; then act on this information to devise new actions for yourself. These might include such steps as actively cultivating a different approach to use in the situations that trigger your slipping

---

EXERCISE 11.3.

Bringing Awareness into Using Stronger Voices

Identify a Voice, Aspect, or specific behavior that you tend to overuse and want to use more mindfully and less habitually. Following each coaching session, respond to these questions:

- What sensations, thoughts, and emotions were associated with the impulse to use this Voice, Aspect, or behavior?
- What attachments or aversions might have triggered your habit?
- How could you have assessed whether the Voice, Aspect, or behavior was serving your client?
- What alternative approach might there have been that would have met the client's needs better?
- What practices will help you be more mindfully present in serving your client?

---

into a certain role, a practice of checking in with the client before moving into the Voice that you overuse, or recording a coaching session and getting feedback from a mentor coach. It might also involve some personal work on your part to address any issues that trigger the habitual use of one particular role. The goal is to make conscious choices rather than operating on autopilot.

Paying attention to these small awakenings, to your exercise of choice over habit, will lead to more awakenings. It is very much a cumulative process. The more you pay attention, the more times you will replace an unconscious habit with a conscious choice.

Developing Your Weaker Voices

Self-assessments, client feedback, or your own self-reflection will likely indicate Voices or Aspects that you tend to underuse in relation to the needs of the client; for example, you may sometimes not use the Voice in situations where it would be helpful. To correct your underuse, increase your competence or your confidence in that realm.

Choose a Voice or an Aspect that you think needs attention because a client brought it up, because self-observation has led you to believe that developing it would benefit your clients, or because its underuse showed up in a formal assessment. Ask yourself some questions. For example, you might ask, Am I resistant to playing the Teacher role? Is there some aspect of the Teacher that doesn't fit with how I think of myself? What do I feel comfortable teaching about? What not? How do I know what it means to teach well?

Then, based on your answers to those questions, either use Exercise 11.4 or design a self-observation exercise around that role. For example, after each coaching session, you might note times when speaking as the Teacher would have been helpful but you didn't take that role. The point of this exercise is to increase your ability to see these opportunities as they arise.

After doing this exercise for a week or two, if you identify unhelpful aversions or an inability to see opportunities, you can design a development plan for yourself. This might include reading books, practicing specific skills, designing a more narrowly focused self-observation tool, or getting feedback from other coaches about how they do it, for example. Establish goals and time frames for yourself; then follow the structure that you've established.

Exercise 11.4 is written to encompass both times when you do and times when you don't use opportunities to practice the skill or behavior. You may find it helpful to modify the exercise to emphasize the times when you *do* rather than those when you don't. Either way, of course, the point of using the self-observation exercise (SOE) is simply to keep the role in the forefront of your attention.

EXERCISE 11.4.
Increasing the Use of an Aspect

Choose a Voice, Aspect, or specific behavior that you think you're not using often enough for the maximum benefit of your clients. Following each coaching session, respond to these questions:

- In this conversation, when did you use this Voice, Aspect, or behavior? What cues told you that this was an appropriate opportunity to use it?
- When did an opportunity to use the Voice, Aspect, or behavior that you are seeking to develop arise, but you didn't use it?
- Were you aware of the opportunity at the time? If not, what got in the way of seeing or acting on the opportunity?
- What is important for you to pay attention to in becoming more fluid in this Voice, Aspect, or behavior?

Navigating the Model

Once you have some experience with working on specific Aspects or behaviors, the next step is paying attention to which roles you're using when, and how you are navigating the Septet Model as a whole.

The Investigator's questioning is the central process in coaching. Still, declarative statements ("telling") will be part of the conversation, although they belong to other Voices. The mindful coach will move easily out of questioning and into telling easily, responding to the needs of the client and the flow of the conversation. At less mindful moments, our attachment to a different identity may take over and pull us prematurely out of questioning.

Exercises 11.5 to 11.7 in this section focus on the three core Investigator Aspects. After noticing when you're using each of these Aspects and when you depart from questioning, you'll begin to pay attention to the impetus behind these choices. Later in this section, we'll expand this approach to include the entire operational portion of the model.

Exercise 11.5 zeroes in on the central role of questioning. Remember from Chapter Six that the interplay of the three lines of

---

EXERCISE 11.5.
Questioning and Telling

In your coaching conversations, use your observer mind to pay attention to whether, at any particular point, you're primarily questioning or primarily telling. Use a physical analogue as a mindfulness tool. For example, if you are coaching over the phone, draw two small circles on a sticky note and label one Questioning and one Telling. As you coach, move a coin from one circle to the other, depending on the mode you're primarily in. If you're coaching face to face, you can use a less distracting physical analogue, like crossing fingers on your left hand for questioning and on your right for telling.

Don't worry about keeping count or making mistakes. Stay gentle and relaxed; lightly pay attention, but keep most of your focus on your client.

Do this for a few coaching conversations. After each, take a couple of minutes to respond to these questions:

- What did you notice about which was easier for you?
- How did you self-manage your choice of questioning or telling in order to serve the client?
- When you left questioning to move into telling, where did the impulse arise from?
- What did you notice about your tendencies as you coach?

EXERCISE 11.6.
Building Creative Tension

Draw four circles on a piece of paper and label them Situation, Outcome, Action, and Sharpeners. Then move a quarter or small object around on the paper to represent the Voice or Aspect that you're speaking from. If you're coaching face-to-face, you can use the four fingers of your left hand to track where you are at any given point.

This self-observation will help you pay attention to yourself as creative tension builds in the conversation and when you are departing from questioning. (You can use this same structure to become more mindful in the three levels of situation questions: external elements, client contribution, and client assumptions and interpretations. Or use any other distinctions you wish to observe in your coaching.)

Respond to these questions after each coaching conversation:

- What did you notice about working with this structure of questions?
- How could you sense when it was time to shift from one Voice or Aspect to the next?
- When, and how, did you feel an internal urge to move out of one Voice or Aspect to another?
- What did you learn about your tendencies and habits as you coach?

Investigator questioning—What's the situation? What do you want? What are you going to do?—establishes the creative tension that leads to change. This exercise, then, supports your self-observation of the core process by which this tension is established. Attend to which line of questioning you're following as the Investigator and when you switch to using a sharpener Voice. Don't seek to change the way you're coaching. Simply observe lightly what you're doing, and then reflect on it afterward.

Exercises in each Voice chapter shed light on your competencies, attachments, and aversions relative to each Voice. There is much to be explored by observing yourself using each of the Voices, and we won't develop this further in this chapter. However, as you practice with each of the Voices, and integrate them more and more into a seamless whole, it becomes useful to pay attention to the switches—the moments when you change from one Voice to another. Presumably there's some sort of impetus or intuition or urge that leads you to shift, and this exercise asks you to pay close attention to which of your own attachments and aversions might be influencing your coaching choices.

EXERCISE 11.7.
Focusing on Questioning

This exercise requires the cooperation of someone—an experienced client, a colleague, or a friend—who has agreed to support you in the experiment. Because you will be paying more attention than usual to your own attachments by artificially restricting your coaching to one Voice, you will not be providing the full range of your coaching to the "client" in this session.

In your coaching, seek to stay with the Investigator Voice, asking questions of the client around the three Aspects. It may be useful to keep the Septet Model in front of you. At each point in your coaching session where you notice an impetus to depart from your Investigator questioning, notice which Voice or Aspect you are drawn to. Stop the action long enough to check out where the impetus is coming from. Perhaps an attachment? An instinct about what the "client" needs? Ask the "client" which Voice would in fact be most helpful at that moment.

Jot notes about your self-observation during or immediately after the session. After doing this for two or three sessions, use a journal to explore these questions for yourself:

- What was the feeling you had as you experienced the impetus? Was there an attachment within you? An aversion? How did you check out whether it would have served your client's needs? What did your client say if you asked her? What patterns did you notice about what triggers your urge to switch out of the Investigator Voice into a sharpener Voice?
- How can you increase your ability to discern accurately whether your switches among Voices are serving the client?
- What practice can you take from this to use in actual coaching sessions to become more mindful in your transitions?

As your self-observation skills increase, you will become more alert as to when your own habits of mind are present and better able to separate them from the work at hand. This will help you make conscious choices about what you are doing as a coach—decisions based on a clear focus on the client rather than on unconscious influences from your own habits of mind.

In Exercise 11.7, you'll seek to stay with questioning, focusing in turn on the client's situation, clear outcomes, and action ideas. The artificial restriction to stay with questioning brings any urges to do otherwise into sharp focus. As you do this exercise, you'll most likely notice impulses to shift to one or another of the sharpener

Voices. These impulses aren't necessarily off-base; in fact, they may well be on target. The purpose here is simply to notice the impulses, stay with questioning, and practice moving flexibly among the three Investigator Aspects to evoke creative tension. Here you will experiment with how to work with artful questions to do the work of coaching and begin to discern whether the impetus to move to more directive sharpening voices comes from your own needs or from an intuitive sense of what the client needs. Again, pay attention to the attachments and aversions that influence your choices.

Doing Exercise 11.7 over the course of several conversations may be a bit cumbersome, but it will provide significant insight into what's going on in those transition moments that are usually either intuitive or unconscious.

With this in mind, let's go back to considering the entire model. Exercise 11.8 asks you to go beyond the questioning-and-telling

---

EXERCISE 11.8.
Observing Your Coaching Flow

Review each of the Voices briefly so that the distinctions are clear in your mind. (These are described in Chapter Three.)

Keep the central portion of the Septet Coaching Model in front of you. You may use Figure 11.1, sketch your own, or download a PDF of the model from my Web site (http://dougsilsbee.com/pdf/septetcentral.pdf). Coach as you usually do.

With the observer part of your mind, maintain a portion of your awareness on constantly orienting yourself relative to the model. Focus on the six operational Voices you are using, moving a game piece or a quarter to the location in the model that fits the Voice that you are currently speaking in. Don't let it be too complicated; do it lightly, with a portion of your awareness. (Be aware of your own attachment to doing this well, and then let it go. It will only get in your way!)

After each session, take a couple of minutes and respond to these questions:

- What did you notice about your use of the Voices? Where are you most comfortable? Least?
- Which Voices were you using when you experienced the most energy? What do you suspect explains this?
- What are your tendencies? What patterns do you tend to fall into?
- If you were going to continue but modify this exercise to focus more closely on something, what would be interesting to pay attention to?

FIGURE 11.1. *The Operational Voices*

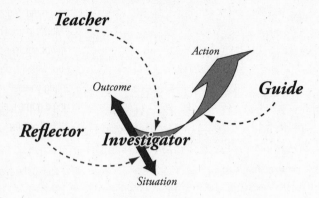

distinction to pay attention to your use of all the operational Voices of the Septet in a given coaching session. Since there are six of them, this may seem a bit daunting. As you coach, I suggest that you do your mental labeling lightly and quickly, without worrying too much about fine distinctions. Remember to keep your attention primarily on your client; self-observation is a parallel activity in which we pay constant but light attention to where we are within the model. Beware of any attachments that you might have to doing this well; think of it as a game in which you are a beginner and have something to learn.

Exercise 11.8 is complex, and getting the most out of it will take some practice. If you stay with it for a while, though, you'll find that it becomes easier and easier to keep a balance of attention between the observer mind and the coaching mind. This is important in learning to manage your use of different Voices. (I suggest that you practice this exercise for at least a couple of weeks before moving to the next one.)

Several of the previous exercises asked you to go beyond the navigation practices of simply noticing if you are questioning or telling or observing where you are on the coaching map. In Exercises 11.5–11.7, for example, you began to look at the impetus (which can include

EXERCISE 11.9.

Observing the Impetus Behind Your Coaching Flow

Review each of the Voices briefly, so that the distinctions are clear in your mind. (Again, see the overview in Chapter Three.) Keep the central portion of the Septet Model in front of you. You can use Figure 11.1, download a version from the Web site (http://dougsilsbee.com/pdf/septetcentral.pdf), or sketch your own. Coach as you usually do, but with the observer part of your mind, and maintain a portion of your awareness on orienting yourself relative to the model. Focus on the six operational Voices you are using, moving a game piece or a quarter to the location in the model that fits the Voice that you are currently using.

Following each coaching session, respond to these questions:

- Describe two or three significant shifts from one Voice to another during the coaching conversation you just completed.
- What did you notice about when you switched?
- What were the triggers or cues that told you when to switch? Was it your intuition? Some message from the client? Was the new Voice appropriate for what was needed at the time?
- As you look back, what attachments or aversions might have been influencing your choices?
- What have you learned about both the internal attachments and aversions, and the external cues from your client, that tend to trigger your shifts between Voices?

your own attachments and aversions) behind your shifts between questioning and telling and behind moving from the Investigator to any of the sharpener Voices. Exercise 11.9 applies the same discipline to the entire model. While sometimes these shifts are driven by habit or an instinctive reaction, at other times they are an appropriate response to the changing needs of the client or the discernment by the coach of an opportunity to deepen the conversation. It's important to notice what's triggering your shifts in Voice in order to become more mindful about using them.

In Exercise 11.9, you observe what is behind the choice of Voice—to make explicit and conscious that which often is subterranean or unconscious. Certainly there are intuitive choices that arise in us. But before shifting to a new approach with a client or heading down a pathway about which we have a "good feeling," it's important to inquire where the impetus comes from and to discern whether it's simply a conditioned, intuitive response to our own attachments and aversions or is truly in service to the client. (Often it will be helpful to check out our discernment verbally with the client by presenting a choice point about which way to go in the session.)

Obviously there's a lot to pay attention to here. You have sufficient tools and experience from what has been covered to this point to occupy your observer self for some time to come. I encourage you to experiment with a series of simple navigation SOEs first and then to inquire into the impetus behind your shifts and choices of Voice and Aspect. Doing so will make you a vastly more mindful helper of others.

LEARNING FROM YOUR REFLECTION

While we often seek to act as mirrors for our clients, reflecting back to them what we hear and observe about their concerns and behavior, our clients are also mirrors for ourselves. The more we see ourselves in our clients, the more compassion we are able to hold. But it is also true that the more we see ourselves in our clients, the more likely it is that we'll project our own concerns onto them or otherwise blur the boundaries between our issues and theirs. The reflection of ourselves in our clients is both a source of connection and a challenge to our mindfulness practice. The three exercises in this section will support you in getting clearer about these connections.

Remember from our discussion of projection in Chapter One that the things we resist in others tend to be things that we have not yet resolved within ourselves and that specific traits we dislike in others are often those we dislike within ourselves. Exercise 11.10 involves recognizing how we tend to project on our clients and how our clients reflect us to ourselves. I am inviting you to discover and own parts of yourself that you might rather pretend were not there. It's not easy. It will, however, open new doors to compassion for yourself and your clients.

As a coach, even though I seek to be compassionate, I can occasionally feel impatient with clients who don't seem to get it or who struggle to follow through on commitments that seem simple enough

---

EXERCISE 11.10.

Recognizing Your Projections

Choose one or two clients with whom you experience some level of resistance, irritation, or judgment. Perhaps you feel impatient with this person's defensiveness, or you just don't understand why he can't follow through. Base these choices on your observations of your own reactions to the person.

Following each coaching session with the client(s) you've chosen, respond to these questions:

- Note one or two traits in the client that you judge, resist, or struggle with. Be as specific as possible, and provide an example.
- How is the same trait manifest in you? What do you do, or how do you behave, that is similar to what you resist or judge in your client?
- What did this exercise show you about yourself and the source of your reactions to others?
- What can you do to become more compassionate toward yourself in relation to that trait?
- What is important to adjust in your coaching as a result of what you learned?

---

to me. It is key to be able to see what a client, particularly one we have some difficulty with, is showing us about ourselves.

REVIEWING AUDIO RECORDINGS

Another way to get information about what has happened in a session is to tape it and then review the tape later. This of course can be quite time-consuming: to completely review a session tape takes the same amount of time the session itself took, plus any extra time spent stopping and starting the tape, taking notes, and so forth. For busy people, this can be an obstacle. Still, it's such a powerful aid to perspective and mindfulness that I recommend Exercise 11.11 as something to do occasionally.

You can also ask another experienced coach or mentor to review the audio. With comments tied to time markers in the recording,

---

EXERCISE 11.11.

Audio Review

Create an audio- or videotape of yourself as you coach. Ask permission of your client first, letting him or her know that the tape is only for your own use and you'll keep it confidential and destroy it when you're finished. (If you intend to use such a tape for any other purpose, of course, you'll need to get permission.)

Review the recording. After observing yourself in action, answer the following questions:

- What patterns did you notice in reviewing your recording?
- What choice points were there in this session that you didn't see or name at the time?
- How did your attachments or aversions show up in the conversation?
- What elements of your self-identity as a coach were revealed?
- What opportunity for increased mindfulness is available?
- What self-observation or practice can you design for yourself to build on this awareness?

---

this person can reveal habits and tendencies that you might miss because they are so embedded in your ways of doing things. A mentor will spot openings and choice points and offer distinctions that will greatly accelerate your learning process.

OBTAINING AND LISTENING TO CLIENT FEEDBACK

Our clients are our best source of information on how we coach. They have a vested interest in our effectiveness, and they see us in action regularly. While we may find ourselves resistant to doing this, a proactive cultivation of feedback will help us make our coaching more valuable to each client and contribute to our professional development at the same time.

Your clients are also your customers, whether you're a paid coach external to an organization, a manager coaching a subordinate, or an educator coaching a teacher. Most well-run businesses provide means for their customers to give them feedback. Complaint systems, customer satisfaction surveys, partnerships with customers to enhance service delivery: these are standard practices. In coaching, however, while many coaches tell their clients that they're open to feedback, most don't systematically gather or analyze it, and most don't insist that their clients actively influence and shape how they are being coached. I believe that they should, and that you should as well. This section of the chapter will give you some tools for doing so.

Informal Feedback

Informal feedback is all that's necessary in many situations. Many coaches ask questions of their clients, especially toward the end of the session: What worked best for you in this session? What were the most important ways in which I was helpful to you? These are useful questions because they provide a preliminary check for both people about whether the process is working. They are also affirmative questions, in the spirit of appreciative inquiry, that direct the attention of both parties to the positive aspects of what they're doing together. This is a good thing to do on a regular basis, and it provides information that helps us adjust what we're doing to better fit the needs of each client.

Even more powerful is to state an observation about your coaching relationship or about how you are coaching, and ask for feedback and discussion about that specific issue. For example, I could say something like, "Jessica, I've noticed that in our last three conversations, you've asked me for my ideas on issues about which you're more informed than I am. While I appreciate that and want to be helpful, I also think I might be shortchanging you and short-circuiting your own thinking process by providing my ideas so quickly. What do you think?"

By surfacing a potential difficulty in the way we work with clients, we invite them to help us coach them more effectively. We also send a clear message that we are committed to their fullest development. While any feedback is useful, and patterns may be evident, the most valuable outcomes of obtaining feedback are the ensuing conversations with the client.

Formal Feedback and Data-Based Assessment

My Web site offers the free self-assessment described earlier (http://dougsilsbee.com/books/tmc/assess). Also available are online tools for obtaining formal feedback from a particular client and comparing that client's assessment of you against your own self-assessment. Ideally, this will be someone you have been coaching for some time and for whom more transparency in your coaching will be of benefit. It will also be helpful to go through this process when you know that you could be coaching a client more effectively and want a common language to explore what might be needed.

The client logs onto the Web site and completes the tool, which is designed to track the appropriateness of your use of each of the twenty-three Aspects in relation to her specific needs. Both you and the client receive a graphic report that compares your self-assessment with her assessment of you. This is a way to hold up the relationship and your coaching approach with that specific person, for the scrutiny of both. The data provide a good basis for a partner conversation. In order to both review the data and prepare for the conversation, these questions can be useful guides:

- What are the ways in which you work well together? Discuss this in some depth, so that both of you are clear about the effective core of the relationship.

- What discrepancies do either of you see between the coach's self-assessment and the client's assessment of the coach? To what do you ascribe these discrepancies?

- How could increased or decreased use of particular Aspects benefit the long-term development of the client?

- How can both partners share responsibility to guide the coach's use of this Aspect?

- What agreements can you establish to make your partnership as responsive as possible to these ideas as you move forward?

These questions are just suggestions; there are lots of other questions that might occur to either of you for addressing what this shared assessment brings to light. And many of the tools provided earlier in this chapter can be used by the coach to explore opportunities identified by the assessment. The power of this exercise stems from the fact that it provides data-based neutral ground for discussing the relationship; it may also uncover issues that both the client and the coach have overlooked. Involving both parties in observing and discussing the ways in which coaching unfolds can only deepen the relationship.

The Web site also offers a multiclient (180-degree) feedback tool for use with all or a significant subset of coaching clients. The minimum number of clients is three.

Planning Your Own Development

Being mindful is the antidote to functioning mechanically—the key to making conscious choices about how we coach and about how we live the short lives we are given. A cognitive approach to identifying and working with issues is very useful, but because behaviors are deeply rooted and often driven by assumptions and paradigms that we're not even aware of, real change requires mindful and consistent practice over time.

In a recent coaching workshop, the participants and I reviewed a short list of coaching competencies with the goal that each person (including me) would choose one to develop. Since listening was so key and my listening had been suffering as a result of a distracting work environment and too much to do, I chose to construct a development plan for myself around that activity. My plan, developed after some thought, included decluttering my office, creating a new system to manage client files, and designing a self-observation exercise to be completed through brief journal entries after each coaching session. And it worked, but not exactly as I had expected.

For me, the very act of constructing the SOE brought forth an increased awareness of how I was listening and when lapses occurred. I found myself listening better. My span of attention increased significantly, and I found myself listening more regularly and consciously.

Well and good, but on review of the SOE after two weeks, other patterns became clear as well. First, I tended to listen less well when the desired coaching outcomes with a specific client were unclear. And second, because of how I was scheduling clients, I often had insufficient time to complete the centering practice before each session that my development plan called for.

This review then opened the door to new practices. I went back to a couple of clients with whom I had been feeling stuck to reclarify goals for our coaching together. I started scheduling clients differently to provide more space in between sessions and dedicated a short but sacrosanct block of time for doing my own presession internal preparation. Soon some of these new practices became habits, and I no longer needed the SOE to pay attention to them.

The cognitive review and planning portions of this cycle support and guide the self-observations and the practices that make up the core of the behavioral change program. But it's the mindful practice, self-observation, and adjustments based on those observations that fuel real change. When cognitive processes and mindfulness are coupled, we greatly increase the chances for success.

In his book *Primal Leadership,* Daniel Goleman writes,

> *Improvement plans crafted around learning—rather than performance outcomes—have been found most effective. For instance, in a program to improve communication skills, a learning agenda resulted in dramatically better presentations; a performance agenda tended to make people react defensively—not wanting to "look bad"—while neglecting to give them concrete steps to improve their actual performance.*[2]

As with your clients, in planning for your own development, it makes sense to design learning practices that reduce performance anxiety and increase commitment and motivation. Designing how to learn, how to observe yourself, how to practice—these actions lead to increased competence and increased performance. This is the purpose of most of the exercises in this book.

The Individual Development Plan I introduced in Exhibit 10.1 as a tool for use with clients can also work for you as a coach. This simple tool can incorporate a range of learning activities into an integrated, practical plan to address any theme you wish to develop. This, if you have been using the exercises in the book, is likely to relate to an aspect of the Septet Model. But such a plan can address anything else that you wish to develop, from quitting smoking, to launching a business, to developing supervisory skills, to enhancing intimacy with a spouse. (You can download a template for an Individual Development Plan at http://dougsilsbee.com/pdf/idp.pdf.)

It is relatively easy to map concrete practical change strategies using this format. I use similar tools extensively with my own coaching clients; it is useful for the Contractor in supporting the client's efforts to design concrete steps for his or her development. However, the structure that it provides is also enormously helpful when dealing with elusive changes around behaviors, and especially about becoming more mindful about behaviors in the first place.

The reality of busy lives is that we often take the path of least resistance. The development plan is one way of creating a structure to support continuous learning. Self-observations and other learning activities can easily be structured into an online system that coach and client use to track learning activities and pay attention to follow-through. A development plan takes good intentions and translates them into a practical roadmap for learning and paying attention.

CHAPTER SUMMARY

The Septet Model provides a means of deconstructing your coaching, seeing it more clearly, and then integrating the seven Voices back into a more intuitive, skilled, and responsive approach to meeting the needs of your clients. The distinctions in the model provide the basis for ongoing self-development as a coach. This chapter provides specific tools and suggestions for structuring your self-development. Of course, working with a coach yourself will reveal tendencies and habits that will be hard to catch on your own.

- *Use a self-assessment tool* to identify Voices and Aspects that may provide openings for seeing your habits and opportunities for learning.
- *Build specific self-observations for yourself,* bringing mindfulness to particular Voices or Aspects that you tend to overuse or underuse. Mindfulness will lead to more conscious use of Voices that you have some attachment to and developing Voices that you are less skillful in or have active aversions to.
- *Use self-observation to pay attention to your navigation of the model.* This might be within the levels of questioning, the Aspects of the Investigator or between different Voices. You can design a self-observation simply to pay attention to where your attention and coaching energy are focused at a particular point.
- *Notice when your urges lead you to shift into a new Voice.* These shifts are appropriate when the client's needs change, when an opportunity arises for a new line of inquiry, or when it would be useful to the client to sharpen the existing line of questioning. The key is to become increasingly aware of these shifts and to be able to recognize when your own urges and attachments are driving these shifts.

- *Keep the overall model in your awareness as a backdrop for the conversation.* You might even want to keep the representation of it—Figure 3.1, Septet Coaching Model—visible to use as a reminder of the road map and the context within which you are coaching: your mastery and the client's mastery.
- *Examine how you may be projecting yourself onto your client* and what your coaching reveals about you.
- *Use audio or video recordings* of coaching sessions to observe yourself more clearly and see things you missed at the time. A mentor coach can be greatly helpful with this.
- *Obtain client feedback, formally or informally.* Your client can provide incisive feedback, and make requests. This builds the partnership and your accountability to serving the client's needs.
- *Create a development plan for your own learning as a coach.* Applying the same discipline to your own development as you offer to your clients builds your experience with change and development and makes you a more credible and authentic learning partner. Your development earns you the right to do this work.

Coaching is fundamentally a discovery process. Mastery in coaching, as in any other field, comes from rigorous experimentation and inquiry. Start now!

Epilogue: Coaching as a Journey Toward Mastery

Let us rise up and be thankful, for if we didn't learn a lot today, at least we learned a little, and if we didn't learn a little, at least we didn't get sick, and if we got sick, at least we didn't die; so, let us all be thankful.

The Buddha

There are only two ways to live your life. One is as though nothing is a miracle. The other is as though everything is a miracle.

Albert Einstein

AS COACHES, WE SUPPORT OTHERS IN BECOMING LEADERS IN THE domains most precious to them. The requirements of our corollary commitment impel us along the trajectory of our own development. Our commitment to our own learning is what earns us the right to coach others along their path.

Paying attention, the mindful coach emerges from each coaching conversation with new information about herself and about how she coaches, reflecting on it and incorporating it as one thread in the constantly surprising ongoing process of her own learning and growth. Each coaching conversation is a new experiment.

The Septet Model supports this drive for learning in the coach while placing it in proper, subsidiary relationship to the primary purpose of serving the client. The coach on the path to mastery recognizes that coaching provides a wonderful opportunity for her own learning. She learns from each session, reviewing what she has done and why. She creates structures and practices to increase her ability to observe and pay attention. Over time, by cultivating this attentiveness and acting on what is learned, she develops her professional skills and capacities.

The master coach also takes note whenever she sees herself reflected in her client. For many of us, it's striking how often this happens. Our counsel to others seems like advice we should follow ourselves. Or our clients seem to have the same struggles that we do. ("Oh, look at that. He has a hard time saying no too. Funny how I attract kindred spirits.") This isn't a metaphysical phenomenon about synchronicity and how we always meet just the right person; rather it illuminates our own tendency to see ourselves in others, to project onto others what we have experienced ourselves.

In pursuing her own mastery, the mindful coach recognizes potential projections and entanglements and sets them aside to pay attention to later, coming back for the moment to the client. After the coaching session is over, on her own time, she explores what came up for her and what to do about it. As a learner, she recognizes the value of seeing how the client and the coaching process help her work on her own concerns and values.

In committing to serve the client—to be present, flexible, and responsive—the coach herself becomes more present and alive. She enters the conversation awake and willing to discover something new about her client and herself. She is open to new answers and the discovery that she doesn't yet know the answer. Perhaps most important, she is open to exploring who she is as a coach. She holds lightly to what she thinks she knows, recognizing that every conversation provides a wonderful opportunity to coach in a way she never has before.

The client will also have learned from the coaching process itself. By recalling and reflecting on what the coach does to support him, he learns to do the same for himself. He becomes more skilled at guiding his own development.

Not only has he acquired competence in the content area in which the coaching has taken place, he has also increased his capacity for self-generation—for taking personal responsibility for enhancing his own capabilities, for becoming more proactive. The client may engage the coach for a short time or a long time as support along this path, but eventually he will outgrow what the coach can provide and move on to other arenas for learning. This is a good thing.

Of course, there will be many challenges on the way. The client will run into unexpected obstacles, internal or external. He'll get stuck. He'll discover new questions. His successes will expand his capacity to dream. All of this is grist for the mill. One of the most important things a coach can help a client learn is that every moment is a clean slate.

The promise of coaching is that the process itself accelerates the development and self-generation of both coach and client. Far beyond the specific client competencies articulated in coaching outcomes and the pedagogical competencies required by the coach, the process inherently serves our ongoing development as human beings, transcending and including who we have been in order to make more significant contributions in the world. This is the real game.

ABOUT FLUIDITY AND INTUITION

The purpose of the Septet Model is simply to keep us oriented, to provide us with a set of distinctions with which we can become more mindful about what we're doing. While distinguishing among the Voices will help you be more aware of what you're doing as a coach at a given moment, awareness of how and why you're coaching is the point, not sticking to a rigid sequence or losing focus on the client while parsing distinctions among Voices.

While the Partner takes the lead at the outset, that order is an artifact of the model-making process, and our clients will not be well served if we adhere to it slavishly. First, the Voices represent a continuum of roles and interactions within the context of a learning partnership. The distinctions are often gray and the lines sometimes blurry between, say, the Partner and the Contractor, or the Guide and the Investigator. Within the context of the overall model, we must respond flexibly to what the client needs and shift among Voices easily and smoothly.

This process ultimately will happen fluidly; the mindful coach will move easily and frequently among Voices as the client's learning process unfolds. The compartmentalization that we resort to in talking about the Septet is in a sense illusory, a construct that we use in order to see more clearly what we are doing.

After Tiger Woods's phenomenal early successes as a professional golfer, he took the time to relearn his drive, changing habits he had acquired over years. Many wondered what on earth he was doing, how he could improve on perfection, but Tiger knew that some of his habits were limiting his game, and so he painfully deconstructed the nuances of his stroke and rebuilt it. Initially his tee shots suffered, but once he had mastered these new habits, his drive became stronger than ever before.

Just as we eventually learned to operate all the controls of a car safely and smoothly in driving, our ability to use the Voices consciously and appropriately will increase and classification will be less important. In the flow of coaching, we seek to become more mindful and discerning about what will truly serve the client and what roles we are playing at a given moment as we seek to provide it. This process can seem artificial and laborious. I can hear the critical reader say, "This requires separating the mind into two parts. But doesn't being mindful really require integrating rather than separating?"

Using the Septet Model is simply holding up what you're already doing and making it more visible so you can examine it. This allows you to affirm or change how you serve your clients. The model is, like any other, artificial and limited. We are creating a language that draws distinctions and chunks behaviors into somewhat arbitrary categories. And doing so makes us more skillful observers, better able to adjust what we do to the specific needs of a client. As we become more mindful and learn to employ the whole range of the Voices and their Aspects without having to be self-conscious, we develop the concrete skills that ground our intuitions and ensure that they serve our clients rather than our own habits of mind. Ultimately this becomes fluid and intuitive rather than compartmentalized. Paradoxically, the separation of the observer in learning leads to integration in practice.

Finally, a word on intuition. Many coaches are fond of saying that they coach "intuitively." This is sometimes a way of describing a process that is highly skilled and internalized; unfortunately, it can also be a cover for lack of rigor, not having a coaching model, and so not making conscious choices about how one is working with one's clients.

While intuition is a wonderful gift, there's a fine line between intuitive wisdom and conditioned habits. Making our choices of role and behavior more explicit and conscious in our own minds fosters the self-awareness and discernment necessary to recognize the difference. It also makes it less likely that we will coach our clients out of conditioned habits while missing the essence of who they truly are and what they can actually use. I believe in intuition, but I also hold that considerable rigor and discipline of practice is required before we can authentically claim to be coaching intuitively rather than naively.

PRACTICE AS PATH

"Practice," as I use the word, implies that the path itself is the goal. There is no point at which we will arrive when we've done sufficient practice, because there is no limit to what there is to learn. As George Leonard says in his classic book *Mastery*,

> *The people we know as masters don't devote themselves to their particular skill just to get better at it. The truth is,* they love to practice—*and because of this they do get better. . . . Ultimately, practice is the path of mastery. If you stay on it long enough, you'll find it to be a vivid place, with its ups and downs, its challenges and comforts, its surprises, disappointments, and unconditional joys. You'll take your share of bumps and bruises while traveling—bruises of the ego as well as of the body, mind, and spirit—but it might well turn out to be the most reliable thing in your life. Then, too, it might eventually make you a winner in your field, if that's what you're looking for, and then people will refer to you as a master. But that's not really the point. What is mastery? At the heart of it, mastery is practice. Mastery is staying on the path.*[1]

The joys and rewards of the path are to be found along the path itself, not from arriving at a predetermined destination. Everything that we do is part of the practice. As coaches, we practice mindfulness in each coaching session, noticing what arises, seeking to stay present and serve our clients as fully and selflessly as possible. When we're not coaching (which is most of the time!) we seek to practice mindfulness and effectiveness in all the other realms of our lives. We learn to accept that we won't get it right all the time. As they say in Alcoholics Anonymous, "Seek progress, not perfection." Being hard on ourselves for our shortcomings just increases our suffering.

This stance provides tremendous freedom. When we see all of life as practice and take pleasure in the practice itself, we begin to recognize that the pressure for perfection is just another habit of mind that gets in our way. No matter the perceived stakes in an interaction or event, we can choose to view it as nothing more than yet another opportunity to practice. As Leonard says, "Practice *is* the path."

Whatever your profession, if you are reading this book, you are in it for more than a paycheck. Whether you are an executive, a therapist, or an educator, a health care professional, a social worker, or a coach, you would not have read this far without both a zest for learning and a commitment to serve those to whom you are offering development support. The book has been written in the hope and belief that the development of people is a venture that enriches both the coach and the recipient of coaching. It is a wondrous privilege to be invited to support the growth of others. In accepting the invitation, you will be most authentic, effective, and ultimately fulfilled if you enter each engagement with the same spirit of inquiry into which you invite those you are coaching.

It is the asking of questions and seeking of answers that catalyzes learning. Become more curious about your mind, your clients, your world, and how you construct it. It is through this exploration that we find meaning and purpose.

The Voices described in this book are simply a way to see, another mirror that reflects us to ourselves. Like any other, the Septet Model is a means for increasing awareness and understanding of what we're doing and why. Some readers will have a tendency to learn about the Voices and Aspects and seek to fit them into an existing cognitive framework that they hold about what coaching should be. Others may adopt the Septet Model as their approach to coaching and fit other ideas into that framework.

I invite you to use the Septet and its related ideas expansively, as a way of opening doors. As you play with and explore the material in this book, questions will arise. What does it mean to me to be mindful as I coach? How can I remind myself, in the moment, to be present? I think I overuse the Reflector Voice—why is that? How can I learn to catch myself as that urge arises? What am I trying to reassure myself of when I tell others about how effective they are? What would it mean to truly be fully dedicated to my clients' growth? What would I have to give up?

These questions are inherently interesting. Answering one raises others. Follow them where they lead you. Mastery is a quest, rooted in the practice of chasing questions, of being relentlessly curious. Try on this mind-set, this attitude toward learning, and see where it takes you.

This work is the work of the Master. The Master is part of, essential to, and bigger than the one who coaches. By engaging fully in our own journey of mastery, we earn the right to work with our clients. This is how we coach.

Committing to consciously serve others is the pathway through which we discover our own mastery.

THE TEN THOUSAND THINGS

"A person can hold seven items in the mind at once."

I think (one) to write about these seven things
my mind can hold: (two) a slice of cold Mutsu,
the quick spurt (three) of tart-sweet juice,
(four) the thought of taste budding on my tongue's
nubbly surface (five), to seek to find the certain
word for fruit dissolving in the mouth,
or something (six) not apple, like the truth,
or sunlight pouring amber (seven) through a curtain.
By the time I've come to know of these, they're gone;
but words they spawn wing through my mind, following
the leader over the edge of moment like wild geese:
one sea, its drops—one field, a million spikes of grass—
a sky of unseen stars are jumbled in the time
this poem took to write: what flocks, what birds, have flown?

—*Ann Silsbee*

Selected Reading

I recommend the following books as useful resources as you explore deeper into this work. Additional recommendations, with annotation, can be found at http://dougsilsbee.com/books/pbc/biblio.

Argyris, C., and Schön, D. *Theory in Practice: Increasing Professional Effectiveness*. San Francisco: Jossey-Bass, 1974.

Austin, J. H. *Zen and the Brain: Toward an Understanding of Meditation and Consciousness*. Cambridge, Mass.: MIT Press, 1998.

Benson, H., and Klipper, M. Z. *The Relaxation Response*. New York: Morrow/Avon, 2000.

Brown, B. *Soul Without Shame: A Guide to Liberating Yourself from the Judge Within*. Boston: Shambhala, 1999.

Chödrön, P. *When Things Fall Apart: Heart Advice for Difficult Times*. Boston: Shambhala, 1997.

Dalai Lama. *How to Practice: The Way to a Meaningful Life*. New York: Atria Books, 2002.

Das, L. S. *Awakening the Buddha Within: Tibetan Wisdom for the Western World*. New York: Broadway Books, 1997.

Davis, B. L., and others. *Successful Manager's Handbook: Development Suggestions for Today's Managers*. Boston: Personnel Decisions International, 1992.

Egan, G. *The Skilled Helper: A Problem-Management Approach to Helping.* (6th ed.) Pacific Grove, Calif.: Brooks/Cole, 1998.

Fisher, R., and Ury, W. *Getting to Yes: Negotiating Agreement Without Giving In.* New York: Penguin Books, 1981.

Flaherty, J. *Coaching: Evoking Excellence in Others.* (2nd ed.) Burlington, Mass.: Elsevier/Butterworth-Heinemann, 2005.

Fritz, R. *The Path of Least Resistance: Principles for Creating What You Want to Create.* Salem, Mass.: DMA, 1984.

Funches, D. *Three Gifts of the Organization Development Practitioner.* Seattle, Wash.: REAP Gallery Unlimited Corporation, 1989.

Goldberg, M. C. *The Art of the Question: A Guide to Short-Term Question-Centered Therapy.* Hoboken, N.J.: Wiley, 1998.

Goldsmith, M. *What Got You Here Won't Get You There: How Successful People Become Even More Successful.* New York: Hyperion, 2007.

Goleman, D., Boyatzis, R., and McKee, A. *Primal Leadership: Realizing the Power of Emotional Intelligence.* Boston: Harvard Business School Press, 2002.

Gunaratana, H. *Mindfulness in Plain English.* Somerville, Mass.: Wisdom Publications, 1994.

Hanh, T. N. *The Miracle of Mindfulness: A Manual on Meditation.* Boston: Beacon Press, 1975.

Hudson, F. M. *The Handbook of Coaching: A Comprehensive Resource Guide for Managers, Executives, Consultants, and Human Resource Professionals.* San Francisco: Jossey-Bass, 1999.

Kegan, R., and Lahey, L. L. *Immunity to Change: How to Overcome It and Unlock the Potential in Yourself and Your Organization.* Boston: Harvard Business School Press, 2009.

Langer, E. J. *Mindfulness.* Reading, Mass.: Addison-Wesley, 1989.

Leonard, G. *Mastery.* New York: Plume, 1992.

Levine, P. *Healing Trauma: A Pioneering Program for Restoring the Wisdom of Your Body.* Boulder, Colo.: Soundstrue, 2005.

Mingyur Rinpoche, Y. *The Joy of Living: Unlocking the Secret and Science of Happiness.* New York: Harmony, 2007.

O'Neill, M. B. *Executive Coaching with Backbone and Heart: A Systems Approach to Engaging Leaders with Their Challenges.* San Francisco: Jossey-Bass, 2000.

Scharmer, O. *Theory U: Leading from the Future as It Emerges.* Cambridge, Mass.: Society for Organizational Learning, 2007.

Schwartz, J. M., and Begley, S. *The Mind and the Brain: Neuroplasticity and the Power of Mental Force.* New York: HarperCollins, 2002.

Schwarz, D., and Davidson, A. *Facilitative Coaching: A Toolkit for Expanding Your Repertoire and Achieving Lasting Results.* San Francisco: Jossey-Bass/Pfeiffer, 2009.

Seligman, M. *Learned Optimism: How to Change Your Mind and Your Life.* New York: Pocket Books, 1998.

Senge, P. *The Fifth Discipline: The Art and Practice of the Learning Organization.* New York: Doubleday Currency, 1990.

Shafir, R. Z. *The Zen of Listening: Mindful Communication in the Age of Distraction.* Wheaton, Ill.: Theosophical Publishing House, 2000.

Silsbee, D. *Presence-Based Coaching: Cultivating Self-Generative Leaders Through Body, Mind, and Heart.* San Francisco: Jossey-Bass, 2008.

Spence, N. *Back to Basics: An Awareness Primer.* Bryson City, N.C.: Inner Vision, 1995.

Stone, D., Heen, S., and Patton, B. *Difficult Conversations: How to Discuss What Matters Most.* New York: Viking Penguin, 1999.

Strozzi-Heckler, R. *The Leadership Dojo: Build Your Foundation as an Exemplary Leader.* Berkeley, Calif.: Frog, 2007.

Tolle, E. *The Power of Now: A Guide to Spiritual Enlightenment.* Novato, Calif.: New World Library, 1999.

Wegela, K. K. *How to Be a Help Instead of a Nuisance: Practical Approaches to Giving Support, Service, and Encouragement to Others.* Boston: Shambhala, 1996.

Whitney, D., and Trosten-Bloom, A. *The Power of Appreciative Inquiry: A Practical Guide to Positive Change.* San Francisco: Berrett-Koehler, 2003.

Whitworth, L., Kimsey-House, H., and Sandhal, P. *Co-Active Coaching: New Skills for Coaching People Toward Success at Work and in Life.* Palo Alto, Calif.: Davies-Black Publishing, 1998.

Wilber, K. *A Brief History of Everything.* Boston: Shambhala, 2000.

Notes

Inroduction

1. "Long-term development of effectiveness and self-generation" borrows from James Flaherty's work, which has been a significant influence on my own. See his *Coaching: Evoking Excellence in Others* (Burlington, Mass.: Elsevier/Butterworth-Heinemann, 2005).
2. Flaherty, *Coaching.*
3. Flaherty, *Coaching,* pp. 65–68, provides a coherent description of the conditions that represent an opening for coaching. This is a good basis for assessing a client's readiness. Another readiness assessment can be found at http://dougsilsbee.com/pdf/readiness.pdf.

Chapter One

1. This literature encompasses everything from books on emotional intelligence and leadership—see R. Boyatzis and A. McKee, *Resonant Leadership* (Boston: Harvard Business School Press, 2005)—to studies of high-reliability organizations such as nuclear power plants and aircraft carrier flight decks—see K. Weick and K. Sutcliffe, *Managing the Unexpected: Resilient Performance in an Age of Uncertainty* (San Francisco: Jossey-Bass, 2007).
2. D. Goleman, *Primal Leadership: Realizing the Power of Emotional Intelligence* (Boston: Harvard Business School Press, 2002), p. 39.
3. This mindful eating practice is inspired by the raisin meditation described by Lama Surya Das in his book *Awakening the Buddha Within: Tibetan Wisdom for the Western World* (New York: Broadway Books, 1997), pp. 348–350.
4. P. Levine, in his combination book/CD set, has some wonderful exercises for building somatic and sensation awareness. *Healing Trauma: A Pioneering Program for Restoring the Wisdom of Your Body* (Boulder, Colo.: Soundstrue, 2005).

5. These dichotomies are drawn from the Eight Worldly Influences, or dharmas. Good explanations of these concepts can be found in L. S. Das, *Awakening the Buddha Within: Tibetan Wisdom for the Western World* (New York: Broadway, 1997), pp. 239–242, and P. Chödrön, *When Things Fall Apart* (Boston: Shambhala, 1997), pp. 46–52.

6. Das, *Awakening the Buddha Within*, p. 241.

7. This experiment is a variant of a thought experiment described in E.J. Langer, *Mindfulness* (Reading, Mass.: Addison-Wesley, 1989), p. 23.

8. Chödrön, *When Things Fall Apart*, p. 48.

9. While it is true that most people will experience the phenomena in this sequence, this is not always the case. The explanation for the sequence is that sensation is a response of the autonomic nervous system, the fastest operating and evolutionarily oldest portion of the nervous system. Emotions are an experience of our limbic system. Thoughts originate in the cerebral cortex, the most recently evolved part of the brain and the part most responsible for higher-order consciousness and self-awareness. Each level of experience generally correlates with a major portion of our nervous system that operates in different ways and at different speeds.

10. M. Goldsmith, *What Got You Here Won't Get You There: How Successful People Become Even More Successful* (New York: Hyperion, 2007), pp. 36–103.

11. J. Flaherty, *Coaching: Evoking Excellence in Others* (Boston: Elsevier/Butterworth-Heinemann, 1999), pp. 62–63.

12. Ibid., p. 62.

13. N. Spence, *Back to Basics: An Awareness Primer* (Bryson City, N.C.: Inner Vision, 1995), p. 19.

14. Langer, *Mindfulness*, p. 43.

15. S. Suzuki, *Zen Mind, Beginner's Mind* (New York: Weatherhill, 1970), p. 22.

16. My second book, *Presence-Based Coaching* (San Francisco: Jossey-Bass, 2008), explores self-generation in great depth and offers specific coaching moves for addressing every stage of the self-generative process.

CHAPTER TWO

1. L. S. Das, *Awakening the Buddha Within* (New York: Broadway, 1997), pp. 301–302.

2. *Webster's New Universal Unabridged Dictionary* (New York: Simon and Schuster, 1983).

3. Attributed to B. Roshi, quoted by J. H. Roshi, *Living Fully, Dying Well* (Boulder, Colo.: Soundstrue, 2009), p. 133.

4. In this book, we will consider the observation of self as a developmental activity, a practice for cultivating mindfulness. In learning to be self-observant, it may be useful to think of ourselves as both the observer and the subject of inquiry, but from a rigorous point of view, there is no observer when we are truly mindful. Observer and subject are artificial separations. As you try out the practices presented here, think of the distinction as a learning device designed to increase your awareness. If one is fully present—fully mindful—the distinction disappears.

5. An extensive body of emerging research documents precisely how practice with directed attention literally rewires the brain, creating new neural pathways that support the new habit. J. M. Schwartz and S. Begley, *The Mind and the Brain: Neuroplasticity and the Power of Mental Force* (New York: HarperCollins, 2002). See also D. Rock and J. Schwartz, "The Neuroscience of Leadership," *Strategy and Business,* Summer 2006, available at http://www.strategy-business.com/press/freearticle/06207.

6. G. Leonard, in his wonderful book *Mastery* (New York: Plume, 1992), explores the nature of practice. This book belongs on the shelf of anyone committed to lifelong learning.

7. Visit my Web site at http://dougsilsbee.com/subscribe to access a private section of the site with extensive practices and links to other sites with good collections of practices.

8. Books with very practical basic instruction in meditation are included in the Selected Reading section of this book. I recommend the books by the following authors: Thich Nhat Hanh, Lama Surya Das, the Dalai Lama, and Bhante Henepola Gunaratana. The reader can take or leave the Buddhist context within which the practices are presented; they stand on their own. On the other hand, exploring these resources will greatly enrich the reader's understanding of why meditation works.

9. H. Benson and M. Klipper, *The Relaxation Response,* is a good introduction to meditation from a medical perspective, with no religious trappings whatsoever. First published in 1975 and since updated and reissued (New York: Morrow/Avon, 2000), the book is a classic in the field of the mind-body connection. Benson is a Harvard-affiliated cardiologist whose extensive research clearly demonstrates the health benefits of meditation on, for example, blood pressure and heart disease. Y. Mingyur Rinpoche, *The Joy of Living: Unlocking the Secret and Science of Happiness* (New York: Harmony, 2007) is a delightful exploration of the intersection of meditation and neuroscience.

10. D. Silsbee, "Exercises and Practices," available at http://dougsilsbee.com/books/pbc/practices.

11. The classic book on the subject is W. T. Gallwey, *The Inner Game of Tennis* (New York: Random House, 1997), first published in 1972. An important contribution to the field of sports psychology, Gallwey's book draws from Zen and psychology in presenting methods for increasing self-awareness and focus. While ostensibly about tennis, these lessons are translatable to many activities.

12. J. Cameron, *The Artist's Way* (New York: Putnam, 1992), provides a wonderful road map for those seeking to discover their creative side and includes a number of practices.

13. An assessment tool that allows clients to provide detailed feedback to their coach is available at http://dougsilsbee.com/books/tmc/assess.

CHAPTER THREE

1. My book *Presence-Based Coaching* (San Francisco: Jossey-Bass, 2008), Chapters Five and Eight, discusses the quality of compassion, practices for

developing it, and ways to extend compassion into the relational field in which coaching takes place.

2. See J. M. Schwartz and S. Begley, *The Mind and the Brain: Neuroplasticity and the Power of Mental Force* (New York: HarperCollins, 2002), and D. Rock and J. Schwartz, "The Neuroscience of Leadership," *Strategy and Business,* Summer 2006, available at http://www.strategy-business .com/press/freearticle/06207.

Chapter Four

1. See my book *Presence-Based Coaching* (San Francisco: Jossey-Bass, 2008).
2. D. Funches, *Three Gifts of the Organization Development Practitioner* (Seattle: REAP Gallery Unlimited Corporation, 1989), p. 157.
3. L. Whitworth, H. Kimsey-House, and P. Sandahl, *Co-Active Coaching: New Skills for Coaching People Toward Success in Work and Life* (Palo Alto, Calif.: Davies-Black, 1998), pp. 17–18.
4. J. Flaherty, *Coaching: Evoking Excellence in Others* (Burlington, Mass.: Elsevier/Butterworth-Heinemann, 2005), p. 53.
5. Whitworth, Kimsey-House, and Sandahl, *Co-Active Coaching,* pp. 34–39.
6. Funches, *Three Gifts of the Organization Development Practitioner,* p. 157.
7. P. Chödrön, *When Things Fall Apart* (Boston: Shambhala, 1997), pp. 78–80.
8. Flaherty, *Coaching,* p. 51.

Chapter Six

1. M. Goldberg, *The Art of the Question* (Hoboken, N.J.: Wiley, 1998), p. 3. This excellent book on the use of questions in therapy has lots of value for coaches as well. Although the examples are clinical, the discussion of questions and language and the uses of questions to shape learning are powerful and applicable to the distinct process of coaching.
2. See R. Fritz, *The Path of Least Resistance: Principles for Creating What You Want to Create* (Salem, Mass.: DMA, 1984), and P. Senge, *The Fifth Discipline: The Art and Practice of the Learning Organization* (New York: Doubleday Currency, 1990) for two good descriptions of creative tension. G. Egan, in his important book, *The Skilled Helper: A Problem-Management Approach to Helping,* 6th ed. (Pacific Grove, Calif.: Brooks-Cole, 1998), elaborates a robust helping model for counselors and coaches based on the distinctions of current scenario, preferred scenario, and action strategies.
3. Egan, *The Skilled Helper,* outlines a rational and systematic approach to helping. Written primarily for therapists, the material is directly applicable to coaching. Egan presents three stages: current scenario, preferred scenario, and action strategies.
4. Fritz, *The Path of Least Resistance,* p. 66.

CHAPTER SEVEN

1. See D. Whitney and A. Trosten-Bloom, *The Power of Appreciative Inquiry: A Practical Guide to Positive Change* (San Francisco: Berrett-Koehler, 2003), which provides a good overview of the field.
2. S. A. Hammond, *The Thin Book of Appreciative Inquiry* (Plano, Tex.: CCS Publishing Company, 1996), pp. 7–8.
3. P. Senge, *The Fifth Discipline: The Art and Practice of the Learning Organization* (New York: Doubleday Currency, 1990), p. 250.

CHAPTER EIGHT

1. R. Fisher and W. Ury, *Getting to Yes: Negotiating Agreement Without Giving In* (New York: Penguin Books, 1981), p. 40.
2. This model draws from Loy Young's unpublished relationship awareness work (personal communication with the author, 1995).
3. J. Flaherty, *Coaching: Evoking Excellence in Others* (Burlington, Mass.: Elsevier/Butterworth-Heinemann, 2005), p. 9.
4. C. Argyris and D. Schön, *Theory in Practice* (San Francisco: Jossey-Bass, 1974), p. 638.
5. A. Davidson and D. Schwarz offer a number of related coaching interventions in their book, *Facilitative Coaching: A Toolkit for Expanding Your Repertoire and Achieving Lasting Results* (San Francisco: Jossey-Bass/Pfeiffer, 2009).

CHAPTER ELEVEN

1. This validated self-assessment tool can be completed online. It has more nuanced scales and asks you to assess the use of each of the Aspects relative to the needs of your clients. After taking the self-assessment, you'll receive a report about your relative use of the Septet Voices and each of the twenty-three Aspects of the model. The online process provides supporting materials to help you interpret the more detailed data you've gathered. Go to http://dougsilsbee.com/books/tmc/assess.
2. D. Goleman, R. Boyatzis, and A. McKee, *Primal Leadership: Realizing the Power of Emotional Intelligence* (Boston: Harvard Business School Press, 2002), p. 141.

EPILOGUE

1. G. Leonard, *Mastery* (New York: Plume, 1992), pp. 75–80.

Acknowledgments

No ray of sunshine is ever lost. But the green which it awakens into existence needs time to sprout, and it is not always granted for the sower to see the harvest. All work that is worth anything is done in faith.

Albert Schweitzer

IT IS TRITE BUT TRUE FOR AN AUTHOR TO SAY THAT BUT for the contributions of many people, a book would never have been born. It has been a humbling experience to contemplate the family, teachers, coaches, colleagues, and clients who have contributed directly or indirectly to the writing of this book, and the degree to which I am indebted to so many for the experiences that led to my being able to write it.

First, I'm immensely grateful to my father, Bob Silsbee, who continues to teach me by example to observe the world keenly and with curiosity, and who has an astounding ability to help me learn by asking me questions that make me think. From him, I learned how to ask artful questions, and he, more than any other, represents the Teacher for me. I'm also deeply grateful to my mother, Ann, who passed away during the writing of the original edition of this book. She showed me what following one's passion looks like and was an unbelievable fountain of creativity and inspiration. Two of her poems grace the beginning and ending of this book, shedding a special light on the subject we are addressing.

Loving thanks to my wife, Walker, for supporting me without qualification in following my aspirations to write this book, providing me with feedback and wise counsel, and believing in me when sometimes I faltered. She has given far more than she knows. A robust thank you to my wonderful children, Alisia, Megan, and Nathan, all of whom forgave innumerable absences when I know it cost them, and who continue to inspire me with their zest on their own journeys. And to Miles Amilio, my grandson, who continually opens me to love and represents the future for which this work is so deeply important.

My gratitude is also extended to those who helped in the development of the model and tools, especially Judy Futch, Anna Florey, Richard Garzarelli, Carrie Mozena, and Paul Smith. Jim Burke, Gretchen Cherington, Candia Dye, Bo Hughes, C. J. Wilson, and Terri Zwierzynski provided valuable feedback along the way. Thanks to those who read sections or the entire manuscript and who gave me their thoughtful feedback and criticisms: Alex Bolaños, Annie Caulkins, Gretchen Cherington, Judy Futch, Bo Hughes, Chris Kochansky, Chris Larson, Maggie Lichtenberg, Bev Miller, Teijo Munnich, Rod Napier, Nancy Spence, Kathe Sweeney, Alan Venable, Hannah Wilder, and Karen Wunderlin.

Seminal catalysts in this work were Scott Ziemer, who provided the original seed for the Seven Hats, which later evolved into the Septet; and Alex Bolaños, who suggested to me that the model should become a book. While it was a surprise to me at the time, he was most certainly right!

For this edition in particular, I offer my appreciation to Kathe Sweeney and the other people at Jossey-Bass, including Rob Brandt, Brian Grimm, Nina Kreiden, Adrian Morgan, Dani Scoville, Karen Warner, as well as others. Thanks to Marshall Goldsmith, for sharing his knowledge and experience so generously and for writing the eloquent Foreword.

A deep bow to my many fine coaches and teachers along the way, including Sarita Chawla, Irmansyeh Effendi, James Flaherty, Darya Funches, Henry Lederman, Mark Mooney, Rod Napier, Richard Strozzi-Heckler, Madeline Wade, Hannah Wilder, Nancy Zimmers, and many others, and to Nancy Spence, my dharma teacher, who has been a reliable and inspiring guide for me along the pathway that led to this book. Perhaps most important, I thank all my clients who over the years have honored me with their trust and willingness, and from whom I have learned far more than I have given. You appear, if not by name, in many ways throughout this book. If some of you recognize yourselves, know that it is with deep appreciation for you and your journey that I share what I've learned along the road.

The Author

DOUG SILSBEE, PCC, IS A THOUGHT LEADER IN THE field of presence-based leadership development, coaching, and resilience. His unique approach encourages his clients to enter into strong commitments and take meaningful and skillful action to produce results they care about. Along the way, his clients build leadership presence, resilience, and capacity for fulfillment.

A master teacher, Silsbee has worked with leaders on five continents. He coaches, trains coaches, and writes in Asheville, North Carolina, and has presented executive education programs for Brookings Institution, Emory University Executive Education, the Federal Executive Institute, and UCLA Anderson School. He is a Master Somatic Coach with Strozzi Institute and the author of *Presence-Based Coaching* (Jossey-Bass, 2008). He is a frequent speaker at major conferences for International Coach Federation, International Association of Facilitators, and OD Network.

Silsbee is an outdoor adventurer, grandfather, and owner of a carbon-neutral retreat center on sixty-three acres in the North Carolina mountains, where he offers a variety of courses in his groundbreaking approaches. He can be reached at http://dougsilsbee .com or ds@dougsilsbee.com.

Index

Page references followed by *fig* indicate an illustrated figure; followed by *e* indicate an exhibit.

A

Accountability: encouraging client's, 142; in service, 55–56

Action questions, 123–125, 123*e*, 125

Actions: encouraging client to choose and take, 169, 170–172; establishing agreements about, 185, 186–190*e*; following up about agreed-on, 185, 193–196; offering options for, 169, 172–174; recommending specific courses of, 169, 174–178; resolving client doubts and hesitations about, 185, 190–193; sample fieldwork, 174*e*–175*e*. *See also* Behaviors

Alcoholics Anonymous, 230

Anxiety, 144

Appreciative inquiry (AI), 137

Argyris, C., 142, 157

Artful questions. *See* Questioning/questions

Aspects. *See* Septet Model Voices

Assessment: data-based, 219–221; evidence-based coaching outcomes, 101–103; self-assessment tools for, 202–204*e*

Attachments, 25–30

Audio recordings, 217–218

Audio Review exercise, 218

Aversions, 25–30

Awakening the Buddha Within (Das), 28

B

Behaviors: attachments and aversions driving our, 25–28; coaching habits impacting, 33–41; conditioning and habits impacting, 30–33. *See also* Actions

The Bell Exercise, 40–41

A Brief Coaching Self-Assessment exercise, 203

Bringing Awareness into Using Stronger Voices exercise, 208

The Buddha, 201, 225

Building Creative Tension exercise, 211

Building Somatic/Emotional Awareness exercise, 26

C

Canetti, E., 131

Centering practice, 51–52

Chödrön, P., 43, 82

Claire, 95–97, 105–106

Client-initiated coaching, 10–11

Clients: coaching entry points of the, 71; committing to serve the, 20, 226; creating the overlapping coaching space, 66–68*fig*; defensive routines used by, 142–143; developing integral and sustainable mastery, 71–72; different worlds of coaches and, 66; embracing them with compassion and respect, 82–84;

Clients: (*continued*)
encouraging to choose and take action, 169, 170–172; establishing agreements about actions, 185, 186–190e; explaining coaching process to, 159–162; following up about agreed-on actions, 185, 193–196; obtaining and listening to feedback from, 218–221; offering options for action, 169, 172–174; Partner Voice and coaching outcomes articulation by, 98–103; providing feedback to, 132, 133–143; providing new information/ knowledge to, 151–154; questions for generating courses of action by, 116, 122–126; questions shifting understanding of situation by, 116, 116–120; recommending specific courses of action, 169, 175–178; resolving doubts and hesitations of, 185, 190–193; stimulating thinking process of, 154–159; warning signs present in, 144. *See also* Coaching relationships; Leadership competencies

Co-Active Coaching (Whitworth, Kimsey-House, and Sandhal), 78–79

Coach self-development strategies: learning from your reflection, 216–217; navigating the model for, 210–216; obtaining and listening to client feedback, 218–221; planning your own development, 221–223; reviewing audio recordings, 217–218; self-observation as a coach, 205–209; tools to use for, 202–205

Coaches: committing to serve the client, 20, 226; creating the overlapping coaching space, 66–68fig; different worlds of client and, 66; as learner, 54–55; learning from your reflection, 216–217; self-development strategies for, 201–224; Septet Model as supporting drive for learning, 226. *See also* Coaching relationships; Mindful coaches

Coaching: Evoking Excellence in Others (Flaherty), 6

Coaching: accountability in service of, 55–56; explaining the process to clients, 159–162; as journey toward mastery, 225–231; leadership competencies developed through, 1, 3, 71–72; making commitment to, 1–2; mindful service component of, 17–42; Observing the Impetus Behind Your Coaching Flow exercise, 215; Partner Voice offering joint decisions during, 103–107; performance

versus developmental, 9–10; self-development strategies for, 202–223; working definition of, 4–6, 14–15. *See also* Presence; Septet Model

Coaching activities: compared for three professional realms, 7e; distinction between noncoaching and, 8

Coaching contexts: client-initiated coaching, 10–11; supervisory relationships and differing interests, 13–14; third-party involvement and consequences, 11–12; transitioned relationships and issues of inequality, 12–13

Coaching conversations: articulating desired outcomes, 121–122; directing client's attention to their potential, 139–140; encouraging client to take action, 171; encouraging self-observation and reflection, 132, 141–142; establishing agreements about actions, 187–188; example of contracting work, 105–107; explaining the coaching process, 160–162; following up with client on agreed-on actions, 193–195; how mindfulness looks in a, 75; incorporating questions on all experience levels, 119–120; Master Voice monitoring of, 85–86, 87; offering options for action, 172–173; Partner Voice role in, 94–98; providing client with information and knowledge, 153–154; providing direct and honest feedback, 134–136; recommending specific courses of action, 174, 176–177; resolving client doubts and hesitations, 191–192; stimulating client's thinking process using, 155–159; transparency and clear communication of, 97. *See also* Communication

Coaching exercises: Audio Review, 218; The Bell Exercise, 40–41; A Brief Coaching Self-Assessment, 203; Bringing Awareness into Using Stronger Voices, 208; Building Creative Tension, 211; Building Somatic and Emotional Awareness, 26; Contractor Areas for Attention, 199; Contractor Self-Observation, 199; Cultivating the Master, 89; Defining coaching for yourself, 9; Focusing on Questioning, 212; Guide Areas for Attention, 180; Guide Self-Observation, 181; Increasing the Use of an Aspect, 209; Investigator Areas for Attention, 129; Investigator Self-Observation, 129; Mastering Self-Observation, 89;

Mindful Eating, 21–22; Observing the Impetus Behind Your Coaching Flow, 215; Observing Your Coaching Flow, 213; Partner Areas for Attention, 110; Partner Self-Observation, 110; Questioning and Telling, 210; Recognizing Your Projections, 217; Reflector Areas for Attention, 146; Reflector Self-Observation, 146; Self-Coaching as Contractor: Structuring Actions and Testing for Fit and Commitment exercise, 198; Self-Coaching as Guide: Providing Impetus and/or Direction, 180; Self-Coaching as Investigator: Three Lines of Questioning, 128–129; Self-Coaching as Partner: Making a Commitment, 109; Self-Coaching as Reflector: Providing Feedback, 145–146; Self-Coaching as Teacher: Making Pedagogy Visible, 164; Self-Observation of a Habit, 48; Self-Observation on a Specific Voice or Aspect, 206; SOE (self-observation exercise), 209, 221; Teacher Areas for Attention, 164; Teacher Self-Observation, 164. *See also* Coaching practices

Coaching habits: distractions, 39; emotional triggers, 31, 37–38; expert mind, 39–40; listed, 33–34; philosophical positions, 37; projections, 35–37; routines, 38–39; self-judgment, 34; social identity, 34–35

Coaching outcomes: competency based, 99; evidence-based assessment of, 101–103; Investigator Voice helping client to articulate, 120–122; of mindful coaching, 226–227; mindfulness required for successful, 101; Partner Voice role in advocating shared commitment to, 98–103; sample questions for clarifying, 121*e*

Coaching practices: centering, 51; sitting, 50. *See also* Coaching exercises; Mindfulness practices

Coaching relationships: distinguished from other professional relationships, 6–9; dynamics of four contexts of, 9–14; the Partner Voice establishing/honoring, 93–98; Partner Voice offering joint coaching decisions during, 103–107; working definition of, 4–6. *See also* Clients; Coaches

Coaching space: creating the overlapping, 66–68*fig*; establishing creative tension in the, 68–69*fig*; sharpening the questioning process within, 70

Communication: feedback, 132–143, 145–146, 218–221; listening component of, 78–79, 87, 218–221. *See also* Coaching conversations

Compassion: definition of, 82; embracing client with respect and, 82–84

Conditioning, 30–33

Contracting work: coaching conversation example of, 105–107; description of, 92; as the Partner Voice function, 92

Contractor Areas for Attention exercise, 199

Contractor Self-Observation exercise, 199

The Contractor Voice: aspects of, 65*e*, 185–196; description of, 61, 64, 183–185; exercises on, 198–199; guidelines for using, 197–198; iterative action learning through fieldwork using, 70–71; mindful, 196–198

The Contractor Voice aspects: establishing clear agreements about actions, 185, 186–190*e*; exploring and resolving client doubts/hesitations, 185, 190–193; following up with client on agreed-on actions, 185, 193–196; overview of, 65*e*, 185–186

Cooperrider, D., 137

Counsciousness, 24

Covey, S., 47

Creative tension, 68–69*fig*

Creativity practice, 52–53

Cultivating the Master exercise, 89

Cultivating mindfulness: accountability in service for, 55–56; coach as learner for, 54–55; practices for, 48–53; self-observation for, 44–48

D

Das, L. S., 28

Data-based assessment, 219–221

Dave, 171–172

"Deep listening," 79, 87

Defensive routines, 142–143

Depression, 144

Developing weaker Voices, 208–209

Development plans: encouraging client to choose and take actions, 169, 170–172; establishing agreements about actions, 185, 186–190*e*; following up about agreed-on actions, 185, 193–196; offering options for actions, 169, 172–174; recommending specific courses of action, 169, 174–178; resolving client doubts and hesitations about actions, 185, 190–193; sample fieldwork actions for, 175*e*–176*e*; sample of individual, 189*e*–190*e*, 222; structuring, 188

Developmental coaching: coach self-development strategies for, 202–223; description of, 9–10. *See also* Septet Model

Dialogues. *See* Coaching conversations

Distractions, 39

E

Edelman, M. W., 17

Effectiveness development: coaching for self-generation versus, 14–15; coaching to improve, 2, 4, 6

Einstein, A., 115, 225

Ella, 119–120, 121–122, 123–125

Emotion experience level, 23, 24–25

Emotional awareness building, 26

Emotional response, 31

Emotional triggers, 31, 37–38

Executive coaching, 3

Exercises. *See* Coaching exercises

Experience levels: attachments and aversions distinctions of, 25–30; emotion, 23, 24–25; incorporating questions on all, 119–120; mindfulness and, 23–25; sensation, 23, 24–25; thoughts, 23–25

Expert mind, 39–40

F

Feedback: data-based assessment and formal, 219–221; directing client's attention toward potential, 132, 137–140; encouraging self-observation and reflection, 132, 141–143; informal, 219; obtaining and listening to client, 218–221; Reflector Voice for providing client, 132, 133–137; Self-Coaching as Reflector: Providing Feedback exercise, 145–146; 360-degree review, 186–187

Flaherty, J., 6, 34, 35, 79, 83, 154

Fluidity, 227–228

Focusing on Questioning exercise, 212

Formal feedback, 219–221

Frankl, V., 47

Fritz, R., 116, 120

Fuller, M., 149

Funches, D., 78, 80

G

Galileo, 1

Getting to Yes (Fisher and Ury), 152

Gide, A., 149

Goethe, 183

Goldsmith, M., 33

Goleman, D., 20, 222

Guide Areas for Attention exercise, 180

Guide Self-Observation exercise, 181

The Guide Voice: aspects of, 65e, 169–178; description of, 61, 63, 167–169; exercises for, 180–181; guidelines for using mindful, 178–179; questioning process role of, 70; sample fieldwork actions, 174e–175e

The Guide Voice aspects: encouraging client to choose an action, 169, 170–172; offering options for action, 169, 172–175; overview of, 65e, 169–170; recommending specific courses of action, 169, 175–178

H

Habits: coaching, 33–41; conditioning and, 30–33; five elements of, 31; self-observation of a, 48; self-observing, 45–47. *See also* Resulting behavior

Hammond, S. A., 137

Health care workers coaching, 3

Hein, P., 183

Huxley, A., 73

I

Increasing the Use of an Aspect exercise, 209

Individual Development Plan: downloading template for, 222; example of a, 189e–190e

Informal feedback, 219

Information: projections and interpretation of, 35–37, 217; reviewing audio recordings to gather, 217–218; stimulating client's thinking process about, 154–159; Teacher Voice providing new, 151–154. *See also* Knowledge

Inner competencies, 101

Internal distractibility, 39

Interpretations, 28–30

Intuition, 229

Investigator Areas for Attention exercise, 129

Investigator Self-Observation exercise, 129

The Investigator Voice: aspects of, 65e, 113–126; creative tension and, 69fig; description of, 61, 62; exercises on, 128–129; guidelines for maintaining mindfulness, 127–128; mindful, 126–128; questioning function of, 113–116

The Investigator Voice aspects: asking client to generate courses of action, 116, 122–126; helping client articulate desired outcomes, 116, 120–122; listed, 116; overview of, 65e; questions shifting client's understanding, 116, 116–120

J
Jack, 84–85, 100–103
Jackson, P., 52
James, W., 38
Jamison, M., 113
Jeff, 194
Jennifer, 153–154
Jong, E., 167
Josh, 174, 176–177

K
Kaminer, W., 1
Kimsey-House, H., 78, 79
Knowledge: stimulating client's thinking process about, 154–159; Teacher Voice providing new, 151–154. See also Information; Learning

L
Langer, E., 38
Leadership competencies: coaching outcomes focused on, 99; coaching to develop, 1, 3, 71–72; coaching to improve effectiveness, 2, 4, 6; developing inner, 101; directing client's attention to potential for, 132, 137–140; self-generation of, 6, 14. See also Clients
Learners (coach as), 54–55
Learning: fieldwork for iterative action, 70–71; modeling growth and, 79–82; from your reflection, 216–217; self-observation for sustainable change and, 47–48; Septet Model as supporting coaches' drive for, 226. See also Knowledge
Leonard, G., 229, 230
Lindbergh, A. M., 17
Listening: to client feedback, 218–221; with focus and presence, 78–79; practicing "deep listening" form of, 79, 87; three levels of, 79

M
Maintaining self-awareness, 76–78
Manager coaching, 3
Marty, 54
The Master Voice: aspects of, 65e, 73–89; description of, 61–62; entry point questions asked of the, 71; exercise on, 89; mastering self-observation exercise, 89;

mindful, 86–88; tips on guard against pitfalls of, 87–88
The Master Voice aspects: choosing which Voice to use at given time, 84–86; embracing client with compassion and respect, 82–84; listening with focus and presence, 78–79; maintaining self-awareness, 76–78; modeling learning and growth, 79–82; overview of, 65e, 73–75
Mastering Self-Observation exercise, 89
Mastery (Leonard), 229
Meditation practice, 50
Megan, 35
Melville, H., 57
Mental response, 31
Michelle, 194–196
Mindful coaches: coaching outcomes of, 226–227; journey toward mastery by, 225–231; practice as path to, 229–231; practices of, 48–53, 206–209. See also Coaches; Septet Model
Mindful Contractor Voice, 196–198
Mindful Eating exercise, 21–22
Mindful Investigator Voice, 126–128
Mindful Master Voice, 86–88
Mindful Partner Voice, 107–109
Mindful Reflector Voice, 143–145
Mindful Teacher Voice, 150
Mindfulness: as aspect of service, 19–23; attachments and aversions affecting, 25–30; as choice, 74–75; coaching habits that impede our, 33–41; committing to self-development curriculum in, 20; conditioning and habits that block, 30–33; cultivating, 43–56; definition of, 19; self-observation as a coach to increase, 205–209; successful coaching outcomes requiring, 101; three levels of experience and, 23–25. See also Mindful coaches
Mindfulness practices: centering, 51–52; creativity, 52–53; cultivating mindfulness using, 48–53; developing your weaker Voices, 208–209; mediation, 50; physical activity, 52; using stronger Voices mindfully, 206–208; time outdoors, 53. See also Coaching practices
Modeling learning/growth, 79–82

N
Napier, R., 138
Nin, A., 91, 131
Nonattachment cultivation, 24

Noncoaching activities: distinction between coaching and, 8; in three different professional realms, 7*e*

O

Observing the Impetus Behind Your Coaching Flow exercise, 215
Observing Your Coaching Flow exercise, 213
The Operational Voices, 204*e*, 214*fig*
Outcome questions, 121*e*, 124
Outcomes. *See* Coaching outcomes

P

Partner Areas for Attention exercise, 110
Partner Self-Observation exercise, 110
The Partner Voice: aspects of, 65*e*, 91–107; contracting work function of, 105–107, 192; description of, 61, 62; guidelines for effective use of, 108–109; mindful, 107–109; three exercises for, 109–110
The Partner Voice aspects: advocating shared commitment to competency-based coaching outcomes, 98–103; establishing/honoring coaching relationship structure, 93–98; listed, 93; offering choice points and making joint coaching decisions, 103–107; overview of, 65*e*, 91–93
Performance coaching: description of, 9–10; supervisory relationships during, 13–14
Philosophical positions, 37
Physical activity practice, 52
Practice as path, 229–231
Presence: compassion element of, 83; cultivation of, 80; listening with focus and, 78–79; practicing "deep listening" form of, 79, 87; requirements for, 78. *See also* Coaching
Presence-Based Coaching (Silsbee), 41, 74
Primal Leadership (Goleman), 222
Projections: Recognizing Your Projections exercise, 217; understanding our own, 35–37

Q

Questioning and Telling exercise, 210
Questioning/questions: asking client to generate courses of action, 116, 122–126; asking client to generate desired outcomes, 116, 120–122; criteria for artful, 114; exercises on, 128–129; Focusing on Questioning exercise, 212; as Investigator Voice function, 113–116; Questioning and Telling exercise, 210; sample action, 123*e*, 125; sample outcome, 121*e*, 124; sample situation, 118*e*, 124; shifting client's understanding of the situation, 116, 116–120

R

Recognizing Your Projections exercise, 217
Reflection: as coach self-development strategy, 216–217; feedback encouraging client, 132, 141–143; Reflector Areas for Attention exercise, 146; Reflector Self-Observation exercise, 146
The Reflector Voice: aspects of, 65*e*, 132–143; description of, 61, 63, 131–132; exercises on, 145–146; guidelines for using, 144–145; mindful, 143–145; questioning process role of, 70
The Reflector Voice aspects: directing client's attention toward potential capabilities, 132, 137–140; encouraging self-observation and reflection, 132, 141–143; overview of, 65*e*, 132–133; providing direct and honest feedback, 132, 133–137
Remen, R. N., 43
Respect, 84
Resulting behavior, 31. *See also* Habits
Rich, 157–158
Rick, 187–188
Rilke, R. M., 113
Roach, M., 57
Rob, 95–97, 105–106
Rock, D., 47
Roshi, B., 44
Routines, 38–39

S

Sandhal, P., 78, 79
Schön, D., 157
Schwartz, J., 47
Schwarz, R., 149
Self-assessment tools: A Brief Coaching Self-Assessment exercise, 203; for coach self-development, 202–203; The Operational Voices, 204*e*; sources for online, 219–220
Self-awareness: Bringing Awareness into Using Stronger Voices exercise, 208; definition of, 76; encouraging client's development of, 132, 141–143; maintaining, 76–78

Self-Coaching as Contractor: Structuring Actions and Testing for Fit and Commitment exercise, 198

Self-Coaching as Guide: Providing Impetus and/or Direction exercise, 180

Self-Coaching as Investigator: Three Lines of Questioning exercise, 128–129

Self-Coaching as Partner: Making a Commitment exercise, 109

Self-Coaching as Reflector: Providing Feedback exercise, 145–146

Self-Coaching as Teacher: Making Pedagogy Visible exercise, 164

Self-generation: coaching for effectiveness development versus, 14–15; of leadership competencies, 6

Self-judgment, 34

Self-observation: as coach to increase mindfulness, 205–209; Contractor Self-Observation exercise, 199; cultivating, 44–48; feedback encouraging client, 132, 141–143; Guide Self-Observation exercise, 181; Observing Your Coaching Flow exercise, 213; Reflector Self-Observation exercise, 146; self-observing habits for, 45–47; SOE (self-observation exercise), 209, 221; sustainable change and, 47–48; Teacher Self-Observation exercise, 164

Self-Observation on a Specific Voice or Aspect exercise, 206

Senge, P., 116, 142–143

Sensation experience level, 23, 24–25

Septet Model: aspects of the Voices of, 64, 65e–66; creating the overlapping coaching space, 66–68; as driving coaches' drive for learning, 226; fluidity and intuition purposes of, 227–229; individual roles or Voices of, 60–64; learning the seven Voices of the, 58–60; navigating the, 210–216; overview of, 57–58; placing the Voices in context, 64, 66–72; practice as path to mastery, 229–231. *See also* Coaching; Developmental coaching; Mindful coaches

Septet Model Voices: aspects of the individual, 64, 65e; the Contractor, 64, 65e, 70–71, 183–200; developing your weaker, 208–209; the Guide, 63, 65e, 70, 167–181; individual coaching roles of the, 60–61; the Investigator, 62, 65e, 69fig, 113–130; learning the, 58–60;

listed, 61; the Master, 61–62, 65e, 73–90; mindful use of stronger, 206–208; The Operational Voices among, 214fig; the Partner, 62, 65e, 91–111; the Reflector, 63, 65e, 70, 131–147; the Teacher, 63, 65e, 70, 149–165

Service: accountability in, 55–56; attachments and aversions aspects of, 25–30; coaching habits that impede our, 33–41; committing to, 20, 226; conditioning and habits blocking mindfulness of, 30–33; mindfulness and self-awareness aspects of, 19–23; mindfulness and three levels of experience, 23–25; placing oneself in, 18–19

Seven Voices coaching model. *See also* Septet Model

Sitting practice, 50

Situation questions, 118e, 124

Social identity, 34–35

SOE (self-observation exercise), 209, 221

Somatic awareness building, 26

Somatic response, 31

"Spaciousness" promotion, 78–79

Stronger Voices: bringing awareness into using, 208; using mindfully, 206–208

Strozzi-Heckler, R., 201

Supervisory relationships: description of, 13; four conditions of successful, 13–14

Susan, 155–156

Sustainable change, 47–48

Suzuki, S., 39

T

Teacher Areas for Attention exercise, 164

Teacher coaching, 3

Teacher Self-Observation exercise, 164

The Teacher Voice: aspects of, 65e, 151–162; description of, 61, 63, 149–150; exercises for, 164; guidelines for using, 163; mindful, 150, 162–163; questioning process role of, 70

The Teacher Voice aspects: explaining coaching process, theory, and models, 151, 159–162; overview of, 65e, 151; providing new distinctions, information, and knowledge, 151–154; stimulating client's thinking process, 151, 154–159

Teresa, Mother, 73

Terry, 152–153

Theory in Practice (Argyris and Schön), 157

Third-party involvement: consequences of, 12; description of different types of, 11–12

Thoughts experience level, 23–25

360-degree review, 186–187

Time outdoors practice, 53

Transitioned relationships: description of, 12–13; issues of inequality in, 13

Triggers, 31, 37–38

Truman, H. S., 167

V

Vision: definition of, 120; helping client articulate desired outcomes, 120–122

W

Weaker Voices development, 208–209

Whitworth, L., 78, 79

Woods, T., 228